THE GRENADIER GUARDS
IN THE GREAT WAR OF
1914–1918

MACMILLAN AND CO., Limited
LONDON · BOMBAY · CALCUTTA · MADRAS
MELBOURNE

THE MACMILLAN COMPANY
NEW YORK · BOSTON · CHICAGO
DALLAS · SAN FRANCISCO

THE MACMILLAN CO. OF CANADA, Ltd.
TORONTO

The King
Colonel-in-Chief

THE GRENADIER GUARDS IN THE GREAT WAR OF 1914-1918

BY

LIEUT.-COLONEL
THE RIGHT HON. SIR FREDERICK PONSONBY
(LATE GRENADIER GUARDS)

WITH AN INTRODUCTION BY
LIEUT.-GENERAL THE EARL OF CAVAN

MAPS BY MR. EMERY WALKER

IN THREE VOLUMES
VOL. I

MACMILLAN AND CO., LIMITED
ST. MARTIN'S STREET, LONDON
1920

COPYRIGHT

Printed and bound by Antony Rowe Ltd, Eastbourne

Dedicated

(BY PERMISSION)

TO

HIS MAJESTY THE KING

COLONEL-IN-CHIEF OF THE GRENADIER GUARDS

INTRODUCTION

I REGARD it as a high privilege to be associated with this book, which has been written by an old officer of the Regiment. I can fully appreciate the magnitude of the task which confronted him when he undertook to examine innumerable documents relating to hundreds of thousands of men and covering a period of several years, and select therefrom all that particularly concerned the Regiment.

I often think that an officer who finds himself in command of a battalion of Grenadiers on active service must be nicely poised between the weight of responsibility and the upholding power of tradition. At first the former seems to be overwhelming, but in time the feeling of confidence and trust in all ranks of the Regiment is so great that the idea of failure can be eliminated.

I think this history will make my meaning clear. As Time marches on with its many inventions, it does not become easier to uphold the traditions so nobly set by our forbears. Gas and high explosives take heavier toll of brave men than the weapons of old, and yet it is still the solid determination of the man that wins the fight, whether offensive or defensive. Although the tale of our great Dead is a long one, and thousands have been maimed in the struggle, the Regiment has borne its part in a manner worthy of it, and in accordance with the parting words of trust of our Sovereign and Colonel-in-Chief.

CAVAN,
Lieut.-General.

PREFACE

THIS account of the part taken by the Grenadier Guards in the European War is, substantially, the work of the officers of the Regiment themselves. Letters and diaries full of interesting detail have been sent to me, and a vast amount of information collected by Colonel Sir H. Streatfeild at the Regimental Orderly Room has been placed at my disposal.

The military historian who writes of past centuries has in some ways an easier task than one who attempts to put contemporary events into their historical perspective. In the first place, with every desire to be accurate, the latter finds that the accounts of eye-witnesses differ so much that he is forced to form his own conclusions, and to adopt what, according to his judgment, is the most probable version. In the second place, after reading a private letter giving a graphic account of a particular part of a battle, he may easily derive a totally false impression of the whole. Moreover, he writes in the constant presence of the criticism of eye-witnesses.

A special difficulty also arises from the unequal quality of the material placed at his disposal. There is sometimes a wealth of information on unimportant incidents and no material for the history of important or dramatic events, in which the principal actors were almost invariably killed. Even the Battalion diaries, which were kept with meticulous accuracy during the early days of the war, contain less and less material as the fighting became more and more serious.

With a war of such astounding magnitude, when millions of men are fighting on a front of hundreds of miles, any attempt to give an intelligible picture of what is going on in a modern battle becomes practically impossible. Even if such a course were desirable in a regimental history, the material supplied, which consists for the most part of letters and diaries of regimental officers, would be totally inadequate, since regimental officers know little of what is going on except in their immediate neighbourhood. A tactical study was out of the question, since a battalion plays such a small part in modern battles, and to describe the movements of corps and armies appeared to be beyond the scope of a regimental history.

I therefore decided to depart from tradition, and to write a narrative giving, as far as I was able, details about companies, and even platoons. It seemed to me that this was what the officers themselves would prefer.

The absence of information concerning the German Army necessarily takes some of the life and colour out of such a record as this. In all military histories the account of the enemy's movements adds enormously to the interest of the narrative; but at present, beyond a few accounts from neutral journalists inspired by the Germans,

PREFACE

there is no authentic information as to the movements of the German Army, and the motives which actuated the German General Staff can only be inferred.

Time will of course rectify this, and after the war detailed accounts of the German Army will be available, though it will inevitably be some years before anything worth reading about the enemy can be published. It has therefore been suggested that it might be best to defer the publication of this history for some years. But it is doubtful whether with the lapse of time any valuable additions could be made to a regimental history, though for a national history some knowledge of the enemy's plans will be essential.

The long periods of monotonous trench life, in which practically the same incidents recur daily, have been particularly difficult to deal with; and, although the greatest care has been taken to chronicle every event of importance, I am conscious that many acts of bravery and devotion to duty which have been omitted in the letters and diaries must go unrecorded.

The terrible list of casualties has made it impossible to do more than simply record the deaths of the officers of the Regiment who fell during the war. Had more space been available, fuller accounts of the circumstances under which they met their deaths and some personal appreciation of each officer would have been possible, but in a history which has necessarily to be restricted to three volumes, all this was out of the question.

The Regiment is indebted to Colonel Sir H.

Streatfeild, not only for the scrupulous care with which he gathered together information from every possible source, but also for his foresight in realising in the early stages of the war the importance of all documents connected with the movements of the different battalions.

The maps are the work of Mr. Emery Walker, who has succeeded in producing not only artistic pictures in the style that was prevalent among cartographers of the seventeenth century, but also perfectly clear and accurate maps. To Sergeant West I am indebted for the military detail.

To many officers I am indebted for suggestions, especially to Lieut.-General the Earl of Cavan and Major-General Jeffreys, who found time, during their few days' leave, to make many interesting additions to this history; and to Major H. L. Aubrey-Fletcher, whose knowledge and experience both as a staff and regimental officer have been invaluable.

In conclusion, I wish to take this opportunity of thanking Captain G. R. Westmacott, Lieutenant M. H. Macmillan, Lieutenant B. Samuelson, Lieutenant L. R. Abel-Smith, and Lieutenant A. C. Knollys for the excellent work they did in preparing accurate diaries for each battalion, with extracts from the officers' letters. Without their aid I should never have had the time or the energy to complete this book.

F. E. G. PONSONBY.

CONTENTS

CHAPTER I
THE SITUATION BEFORE THE WAR . . . . PAGE 1

CHAPTER II
ARRIVAL OF THE 2ND BATTALION IN FRANCE . . 9

CHAPTER III
THE RETREAT FROM MONS (2ND BATTALION) . . 23

CHAPTER IV
THE BATTLE OF THE MARNE (2ND BATTALION) . . 42

CHAPTER V
THE PASSAGE OF THE AISNE (2ND BATTALION) . . 54

CHAPTER VI
THE FIRST BATTLE OF YPRES (1ST BATTALION) . . 83

CHAPTER VII

THE FIRST BATTLE OF YPRES (2ND BATTALION) . . 143

CHAPTER VIII

NOVEMBER 1914 TO MARCH 1915 (1ST BATTALION) . 187

CHAPTER IX

NOVEMBER 1914 TO MARCH 1915 (2ND BATTALION) . 201

CHAPTER X

THE BATTLE OF NEUVE CHAPELLE (1ST BATTALION) . 224

CHAPTER XI

THE BATTLE OF FESTUBERT (1ST AND 2ND BATTALIONS) . 247

CHAPTER XII

MAY TO SEPTEMBER 1915 (1ST BATTALION) . . 264

CHAPTER XIII

MAY TO SEPTEMBER 1915 (2ND BATTALION) . . 272

CHAPTER XIV

FORMATION OF THE GUARDS DIVISION . . . 283

CHAPTER XV

THE BATTLE OF LOOS (1ST, 2ND, 3RD, AND 4TH BATTALIONS)   290

CHAPTER XVI

OCTOBER TO DECEMBER 1915 (1ST, 2ND, 3RD, AND 4TH BATTALIONS) 322

CHAPTER XVII

JANUARY 1 TO SEPTEMBER 1, 1916 (1ST AND 2ND BATTS.) . 352

ILLUSTRATIONS

The King, Colonel-in-Chief	*Frontispiece*
	FACING PAGE
Lieutenant-Colonel W. R. A. Smith, C.M.G., Commanding 2nd Battalion	144
Lieutenant-Colonel L. R. Fisher-Rowe, Commanding 1st Battalion	198
Officers of the Second Battalion Grenadier Guards	276
Colonel Sir Henry Streatfeild, K.C.V.O., Commanding the Regiment	288

MAPS

Route of the Second Battalion, 1914, and the Mons Area, 1914	16
Route taken by the Second Battalion Grenadier Guards during the Retreat from Mons, and subsequent advance to the Marne and the Aisne, 1914	24
Sketch plan of Landrecies, August 25, 1914	28
Engagement at Villers-Cotterêts, September 1, 1914	34
Battle of the Marne—Position of the British Army on September 8, 1914	46
The Passage of the Aisne, September 14, 1914	58
Ypres and the neighbouring country where the First Battle of Ypres was fought, October and November 1914	84

	FACING PAGE
Route taken by the First Battalion Grenadier Guards through Belgium in October 1914	90
The Grenadier Guards at Ypres	142
Battle of Neuve Chapelle, March 11, 1915	226
Neuve Chapelle, March 12, 1915	*Page* 235
Neuve Chapelle, March 13, 1915	,, 241
Festubert—Position on the evening of May 17, 1915	248
Battle of Loos, September 26, 1915	298

CHAPTER I

THE SITUATION BEFORE THE WAR

WHEN the Archduke Francis Ferdinand of Austria was assassinated at Sarajevo in Serbia on June 28, 1914, it never for a moment occurred to any one in this country that the crime could in any way affect the destinies of the First or Grenadier Regiment of Footguards. No one dreamed that, before another year had passed, not only would the three Battalions be fighting in a European war, but there would even be a 4th Battalion at the front, in addition to a 5th Reserve Battalion of almost unwieldy proportions.

Even when Austria began to show her teeth, it still seemed an "incident" quite beyond our horizon. If Austria and Serbia did come to blows, Great Britain was not even indirectly involved, and the British Army, therefore, remained unmoved. The Balkan peoples were constantly in a state of warlike commotion, but their troubles hardly affected the great British Empire. The war clouds, that from time to time darkened the European sky, had hitherto always been dispersed. More than once of late years the German Emperor had rattled his sword in the scabbard, and talked or telegraphed to the very limits of indiscretion, but nothing had ever come of it, nor did it seem at all probable that the assassination of an Austrian Archduke could be made the pretext for a European conflagration.

There were, however, certain elements of danger in the European situation at this particular juncture. The creation of the Triple Alliance—Germany, Austria-Hungary, and Italy—had made necessary some counter-move by the other European Powers. And the *entente* between England and France, initiated by King Edward, and originally intended merely for the settlement of outstanding differences between the two countries, became eventually the basis of a second grouping of nations. This *entente* was followed by one between England and Russia; and although in neither was there anything in the nature of a defensive alliance, it was well known that there was in existence—though the exact terms of it had never been made public—a far stronger agreement between France and Russia.

Meanwhile it was generally known that, all the time these several *ententes* were being formed, Germany had been steadily preparing for war. For forty years, with characteristic thoroughness of method, the Germans had been diligently organising their forces to this end. Not only had the Army been perfected into a first-class fighting machine, but the civil population had all been assigned the parts they were to play in the coming campaign. Trade problems had been handled, not so much with a view to commercial prosperity pure and simple, as to ensure to Germany a sufficient supply of the commodities which would be needed in a great war. Gigantic preparations had been made for a limitless output of shells and ammunition, and plans carefully elaborated for the conversion of factories of all kinds into workshops for war material. The whole State Railway system was controlled in such a way that, on the declaration of war, troops could be instantly concentrated at any selected spot with the utmost speed.

While many civilians saw and deprecated the arrogance and madness of such a policy, the military element, supported by the Emperor, was anxiously pressing for an opportunity of proving to the world the efficiency of the organisation it had created. It was only to be expected that the generals, who knew how vastly superior the German Army was to any other continental army, should hanker for an opportunity of showing off their perfect war-machine.

The attitude of the bankers and merchants towards the war was not clear. Originally, without doubt, they had favoured the insinuating methods of peaceful penetration, which had been so successful in the past, and by which they intended to dominate Europe, but just before the war they appear to have been allured by the prospect of large indemnities from France and Russia and to have withdrawn their opposition. They were persuaded by the military party that by war, and by war alone, could the domination of the world by Germany be achieved, and that now was the time to realise their dream. Young officers of both services made no secret of their wish for war, and constantly drank " to the Day " when they met at mess. The more intelligent portion of the German population quieted what conscience they had with the comfortable reflection that all military and naval preparations were merely ordinary precautions for defence. Indeed this theory, cunningly instilled into the German people by the military party, was so generally accepted that even after the war was declared the majority was under the delusion that it was fighting only for the defence of the Fatherland.

Although the attitude of Germany towards England did not play any prominent part in the events which led up to the war, there undoubtedly existed in Germany a deep hatred of this country. Commercial rivalry and the desire of the Germans to found a Colonial Empire on the same lines as ours would hardly account for this feeling, which permeated every class, and it is to the *Flotte Verein* or Navy League that we must look if we wish to find the reason. Originally instituted to instil into the youth of Germany a desire for sea power, this organisation, by means of propaganda, speeches, and pamphlets, succeeded in convincing the rising generation that we were their natural enemies. The arguments were invariably pointed by reference to the British Fleet, which, it was said, could dominate Germany's world policy, and so young Germans grew up with a feeling of terror for the British Fleet and hatred for the British nation.

CHAPTER I.

In spite of everything, England slumbered on, hypnotised by politicians who had convinced themselves by a process of mental gymnastics that war was an impossibility. The contingency of a British Army being sent to France was never even discussed by the House of Commons, and the logical outcome of our European policy appears never to have occurred to either House of Parliament.

While Germany was studiously preparing for war, we were engaged in academic discussions on disarmament, and although members of the Imperial Defence Committee and a limited number of Cabinet Ministers may have known of the possibility of our having to send an expeditionary force to France, the man in the street, and even the majority of members of Parliament, were completely in the dark as to the true significance of the position of affairs in Europe.

The whole situation was singularly favourable to the Germans. Never before had they been so strong, and probably never again would they have such a powerful Fleet and Army. For some years it had been growing clear to them that if ever they were to strike, they must strike soon. The Socialists were becoming stronger every day, and there were constant grumblings, which ever-increasing prosperity failed to stifle, at the enormous expenditure on armaments. The nation might weaken as the years went on, and there was every probability that the Government would find it impossible to maintain indefinitely a huge Army and a huge Fleet. If they failed to take advantage of this opportunity they might never again be in a position to dominate Europe.

Though Austria had long been tied to the wheels of the German chariot, there was always the danger of the Hungarians and Bohemians refusing to support Germany, should the quarrel be purely German. It was therefore necessary to make the *casus belli* essentially Austrian. What better opportunity could ever offer itself than the assassination of the heir to the Austrian throne? Moreover, the new heir, perhaps soon to be the new Emperor, might not be willing to endorse all his predecessor's pledges, and Austria might conceivably drift apart from her ally. Clearly, therefore, if Germany, with Austria's help, was to strike a blow at Russia and France, she must do so forthwith.

The war party held that together Germany and Austria were more than a match for France and Russia. Italy was a member of the Triple Alliance, and would either come in on their side or remain neutral. Great Britain, it imagined, would be unable to take any part owing to her internal troubles. It appears to have taken it for granted that the Dominions and Colonies would in any case seize the occasion for declaring their independence, and that there would certainly be a second mutiny in India. There was therefore no need to consider the British Empire in calculating the chances of success. A parade march to Paris would settle France in a short time, and then the whole forces of the two Empires would be turned on Russia. A glorious and victorious peace would be signed before the end of the year.

THE SITUATION BEFORE THE WAR

With such calculations as these, it is hardly to be wondered at that the rulers of Germany decided on war at once. To their dismay, however, Serbia submitted to the terms dictated by Austria, and it seemed at one moment that the whole incident would be closed. Acting on Russia's advice, Serbia agreed to all the points in the Austrian memorandum but two. These practically threatened her independence, but there was nothing that could not be satisfactorily settled by an impartial tribunal. But, as despatches and telegrams were exchanged between the European Powers, it gradually became clear that the original dispute between Austria and Serbia had now nothing to do with the matter. Sir Edward Grey made a final attempt to avert war by proposing a conference, but this proposal came to naught, and the determination on the part of Germany to force a war appeared to be stronger than ever. However sincere the Emperor's wish for peace may have been, he was powerless in the hands of a military autocracy which he himself had created. Ever since he had ascended the throne, he had set the military over the civilian element, and now, finding himself powerless to resist the demands of the war party, he determined to place himself at their head.

On July 31 Germany despatched an ultimatum to Russia demanding immediate demobilisation. This was tantamount to a declaration of war, but war was not actually declared till the next day. The declaration of war with France followed as a natural sequence.

Such was the situation at the beginning of

CHAPTER I.

August. With disinterested detachment the British Empire watched the preliminary negotiations, and even when war was declared between the two groups of Powers, public opinion was divided as to which course we should adopt. When, however, Germany violated the neutrality of Belgium, all doubt was removed, and we declared war on August 4. The whole Empire was stirred to the depths, and in London huge crowds paraded the streets and assembled outside Buckingham Palace to cheer the King and the Queen. The wildest rumours were circulated and believed. Fantastic tales were told to every one in confidence by well-informed men in the street, and eagerly swallowed by excited dupes.

Then the curtain was pulled down, and the British public was allowed to know nothing. What troops were going, where they were going, when they were going, all became matters of conjecture.

Meanwhile, silently and surely, the British Expeditionary Force found its way over to France.

CHAPTER II

ARRIVAL OF THE 2ND BATTALION IN FRANCE

To any neutral not completely blinded by German sympathies it must have been only too palpable that the last thing we were prepared for was a European war, for not only had we no men to speak of, but there appeared to be no competent organisation for dealing with a *levée en masse*. Relying on the warlike instinct of our race, we had clung tenaciously to the voluntary system, under the impression that it was best suited to our needs. Even if conscription had been politically possible, it was out of the question, since we had neither rifles, clothing, nor barrack accommodation. The Territorial Associations, which were expected to cope with the masses of men who at once began to flock to the colours, were found so inadequate that Lord Kitchener decided to improvise an entirely new organisation.

In the inevitable confusion which occurred after the declaration of war, there were, however, two factors which stood the test successfully, and which may be said to have saved the country from disaster in the initial stages of the war. The first was the equipment and despatch of

Chapter II.

2nd Batt. Aug. 1914.

Chapter II.
2nd Batt.
Aug. 1914.

the Expeditionary Force, which was perfect in every detail, and the second was the assembly of the Territorial Forces, originally designed to repel invasion, but now utilised to garrison India and the Colonies.

When war was declared, the 2nd Battalion Grenadier Guards was at Wellington Barracks, the rest of the Expeditionary Force being mostly at Aldershot. The speed with which the Battalion was mobilised reflected the greatest credit on all concerned. Its equipment was all ready; reservists arrived from all parts of the country with a promptitude that was truly remarkable. It was on August 4 that mobilisation orders were received, and the Battalion was soon ready to start on active service.

Meantime, while the preparations were still in progress, there occurred an unrehearsed little incident, typical in its way of the unspectacular, practical side of modern war. As the 2nd Battalion was returning to Wellington Barracks from a route march, the King and Queen came down to the gates of Buckingham Palace, quite informally, to see the troops pass by. There was neither pageantry nor gorgeous uniforms, but those who were privileged to be present on the occasion will not easily forget the businesslike body of men of splendid physique, clad in dull khaki, who marched past in fours, and saluted the King, their Colonel-in-Chief, as they returned to barracks.

Aug. 12. The start for France was made on August 12. The First Army Corps, under the command of General Sir Douglas Haig, consisted of:

SECOND BATTALION IN FRANCE

FIRST DIVISION. MAJOR-GENERAL LOMAX

1st Brigade. Brigadier-General MAXSE.
  The 1st Batt. Coldstream Guards.
  The 1st Batt. Scots Guards.
  The 1st Batt. Black Watch.
  The 2nd Batt. Munster Fusiliers.

2nd Brigade. Brigadier-General BULFIN.
  The 2nd Batt. Royal Sussex Regiment.
  The 1st Batt. North Lancashire Regiment.
  The 1st Batt. Northamptonshire Regiment.
  The 2nd Batt. King's Royal Rifles.

3rd Brigade. Brigadier-General LANDON.
  The 1st Batt. West Surrey Regiment.
  The 1st Batt. South Wales Borderers.
  The 1st Batt. Gloucestershire Regiment.
  The 2nd Batt. Welsh Regiment.

SECOND DIVISION. MAJOR-GENERAL MONRO

4th Brigade. Brigadier-General SCOTT-KERR.
  The 2nd Batt. Grenadier Guards.
  The 2nd Batt. Coldstream Guards.
  The 3rd Batt. Coldstream Guards.
  The 1st Batt. Irish Guards.

5th Brigade. Brigadier-General HAKING.
  The 2nd Batt. Worcestershire Regiment.
  The 2nd Batt. Oxfordshire Light Infantry.
  The 2nd Batt. Highland Light Infantry.
  The 2nd Batt. Connaught Rangers.

6th Brigade. Brigadier-General DAVIES.
  The 1st Batt. Liverpool Regiment.
  The 2nd Batt. South Staffordshire Regiment.
  The 1st Batt. Berkshire Regiment.
  The 1st Batt. King's Royal Rifles.

CHAPTER II.

2nd Batt.
Aug.
1914.

The Second Army Corps, under General Sir Horace Smith-Dorrien, consisted of the Third

Division, under Major-General Hamilton, and the Fifth Division under Major-General Sir Charles Fergusson, Bart. (an old Grenadier).

THE ROLL OF OFFICERS, 2ND BATTALION GRENADIER GUARDS, EMBARKED FOR ACTIVE SERVICE ON THE 12TH OF AUGUST

Headquarters—
    Lieut.-Colonel N. A. L. Corry, D.S.O., Commanding.
    Brevet-Lieut.-Colonel Lord Loch, M.V.O., D.S.O., Senior Major.
    Lieut. and Adjutant I. McDougall (Adjutant).
    Lieut. Hon. W. A. Cecil (Machine-Gun Officer).
    Hon. Lieut. and Quartermaster J. H. Skidmore (Quartermaster).

Company Commanders—
No. 2 Company.	Major Lord B. C. Gordon-Lennox.
No. 1 Company.	Major G. C. Hamilton.
No. 4 Company.	Captain the Hon. E. M. Colston, M.V.O.
No. 3 Company.	Captain D. C. L. Stephen.

Captains—
No. 2 Company.	Captain E. G. H. Powell.
No. 4 Company.	Captain E. J. L. Pike.
No. 3 Company.	Captain A. B. R. R. Gosselin.
No. 1 Company.	Captain C. Symes-Thompson.

Lieutenants—
    Lieut. Hon. F. E. Needham.
    Lieut. C. F. A. Walker.
    Lieut. A. K. Mackenzie.
    Lieut. R. W. G. Welby.
    Lieut. F. W. Des Vœux.
    Lieut. R. Wolrige Gordon.
    Lieut. H.H. Prince Alexander of Battenberg, G.C.V.O.
    Lieut. Hon. J. N. Manners.
    Lieut. M. G. Stocks.

2nd Lieutenants—
    2nd Lieut. F. W. J. M. Miller.
    2nd Lieut. G. C. Fitz H. Harcourt Vernon.

SECOND BATTALION IN FRANCE 13

2nd Lieut. G. G. B. Nugent.
2nd Lieut. J. R. Pickersgill Cunliffe.
2nd Lieut. R. H. M. Vereker.
2nd Lieut. A. K. S. Cunninghame.
2nd Lieut. G. E. Cecil.

CHAPTER
II.

2nd Batt.
Aug.
1914.

Lord Loch was appointed to the Staff after the Battalion landed in France, and Major Jeffreys took his place as senior Major on August 18.

Queen Alexandra came to see the Battalion off and wish it God-speed when it paraded at Chelsea Barracks that afternoon. With Her Majesty, to whom all the officers were presented, were Princess Victoria and Princess Beatrice. Headed by the band of the regiment, the Battalion then marched to Nine Elms and entrained for Southampton Docks, where it embarked on the *Cawdor Castle*, and finally sailed at 8 o'clock for France.

Strictest secrecy had been observed about its destination, and the captain of the ship himself did not know where he was bound for until she was actually under way. It was lucky that it was a lovely night and the sea quite calm, for the vessel was crowded to its utmost capacity. The following message from Lord Kitchener had been handed to each man when the Battalion embarked :

You are ordered abroad as a soldier of the King to help our French comrades against the invasion of a common enemy. You have to perform a task which will need your courage, your energy, your patience.

Remember that the conduct of the British Army depends on your individual conduct. It will be your duty, not only to set an example of discipline and perfect steadiness under fire, but also to maintain the most friendly relations with those whom you are helping in the struggle. The operations in which you are engaged will, for the most part, take place in a friendly country, and you can do your own country no better service than in showing yourself in France and Belgium in the true character of a British soldier.

Be invariably courteous, considerate, and kind. Never do anything likely to injure or destroy property, and always look upon looting as a disgraceful act. You are sure to meet with a welcome and to be trusted; your conduct must justify that welcome and that trust. Your duty cannot be done unless your health is sound. So keep constantly on your guard against any excesses. In this new experience you may find temptations in wine and women. You must entirely resist both temptations, and while treating women with perfect courtesy you should avoid any intimacy.

Do your duty bravely.
Fear God.
Honour the King.

KITCHENER, *Field-Marshal*.

Next morning the ship was found to be nearing Havre, and the men were full of curiosity to see what manner of land France was. Meanwhile, from French fishing-boats and trawlers came loud cheers at the welcome sight of the arrival of the forces of Great Britain. A still more enthusiastic greeting awaited the Battalion when it landed, and marched through the numerous docks on the outskirts of the town to a camp about five miles away. The inhabitants crowded round the men, and threw flowers at them as they marched by, while from all sides came welcoming shouts of " Vive les Anglais," " Vive l'Angleterre," and " Eep-eep-ooray."

SECOND BATTALION IN FRANCE 15

When the 2nd Battalion arrived in France, the German Army had already overrun Belgium. For nearly ten days the Belgian Army had held up the Germans, but Liége had fallen, and there was nothing now to prevent the enemy from pouring into France. The French Army, as soon as it was mobilised, had begun a general offensive towards Alsace and Lorraine, but after some small successes had been checked at Morhange. A complete alteration in the French plan of campaign was rendered necessary by the advance of the German Army through Belgium, and troops were now being hurried up towards the North from every part of France.

Chapter II.

2nd Batt. Aug. 1914.

The original disposition of the British Expeditionary Force was as follows : The Headquarters of the First Corps (the First and Second Divisions) under Sir Douglas Haig, at Wassigny; the Headquarters of the Second Corps (the Third and Fifth Divisions), under Sir Horace Smith-Dorrien, at Nouvion; while the Cavalry Division, under General Allenby, was sent to Maubeuge.

It was a scorching, airless day, and the march to camp was a very trying one. But after a good sleep and a bathe in the sea the men were thoroughly refreshed and fit. Then, after the usual inspections, they were formed up on parade, and the King's message was read out to them :

Aug. 14.

MESSAGE FROM THE KING TO THE TROOPS OF THE
EXPEDITIONARY FORCE

You are leaving home to fight for the safety and honour of my empire.

Belgium, whose Country we are pledged to defend,

has been attacked and France is about to be invaded by the same powerful foe.

I have implicit confidence in you, my soldiers. Duty is your watchword, and I know your duty will be nobly done.

I shall follow your every movement with deepest interest and mark with eager satisfaction your daily progress, indeed your welfare will never be absent from my thoughts.

I pray God to bless you and guard you and bring you back victorious.

GEORGE R.I.

The whole population of Havre seemed to have come out to see the Battalion when it marched the same evening to the entraining point. The crowd cheered and shouted, and the men responded with "The Marseillaise." When they reached the siding the disappointing news met them that the train would not start for another four hours. It began to rain heavily, but fortunately there were large hangars available, into which the men crowded for shelter.

Eventually when the train arrived at 2 A.M., the men were packed into it, and very crowded they were. Sleep was difficult, as the horse-wagons attached to the train were loosely coupled, and there was a succession of bumps whenever the train stopped or slowed down. The first real stop was at Rouen, where provisions were obtained for the men, and then the train bumped on to Amiens.

Fervent scenes of welcome went on all along the line. Each little wayside station, every bridge and level-crossing held a cheering throng. At Arras the Mayor turned out in state with a

SECOND BATTALION IN FRANCE 17

number of local magnates, and presented three large bouquets, for which Colonel Corry returned thanks on behalf of the officers, in his best French.

A touch of humour was not wanting at the little ceremony—if any one had been in the mood to seize hold of it. For, caught unawares, Colonel Corry, Lord Loch, and Lord Bernard Gordon-Lennox were anything but arrayed for a function, in fact, in a state of decided deshabille. But such was the enthusiasm of the inhabitants that a trifle like this passed unnoticed or unconsidered.

The stationmaster here said he was passing trains through at the rate of one every ten or fifteen minutes, which gives some idea of the great concentration of troops that was going on.

Slowly the train went on through Cambrai, Busigny, and Vaux Andigny to Flavigny, where, in pouring rain, the Battalion detrained and went into billets—surprisingly well arranged; but then Flavigny had plenty of experience in that way, and only a few days before had lodged the French troops.

Next morning parade was at 7 o'clock for the march to Grougis, about seven and a half miles off, where four days were spent in billets, and Colonel Corry took advantage of the breathing space to have his officers and men inoculated against typhoid.

The concentration of the British Force in the Busigny area was now completed, and the advance towards Mons was to begin the next day.

Off again on the 20th, the Battalion marched to Oisy (where it was again billeted), and on

VOL. I   C

the following days to Maroilles and La Longueville. Here for the first time it heard the guns, and realised that very soon it would be getting to work.

On the 21st, following the plan concerted with General Joffre, Sir John French took up a defensive position from Condé on the west to Binche to the east—a front of about twenty-five miles. The British Army was thus on the extreme left of the French lines. To the First Corps was assigned the easterly position from Mons to Binche, while the Second Corps lined the canal from Mons to Condé, the whole front being covered by the 5th Cavalry Brigade.

Originally the scheme appears to have been to await the enemy's onslaught on the Charleroi—Mons line, and then to assume the offensive and advance into Belgium.

How far-reaching the German preparations had been was at that time hardly recognised, and neither the French nor the British Commander-in-Chief seems to have had any conception of the overwhelming force which the Germans had been able to concentrate against them.

From La Longueville the 2nd Battalion Grenadiers marched on August 23, during the last stages of its journey, across the field of Malplaquet, where more than 200 years before the regiment had fought with distinction, through Blaregnies and Genly to the outskirts of Mons, where it bivouacked. There it received orders to advance, which were countermanded before they could be carried out, and the Battalion was told to remain where it was. There was nothing to do but have breakfast and an hour's sleep by the roadside, with showers falling at intervals. All the time heavy firing could be heard from the direction of Mons, and shells bursting could be observed in the distance.

Chapter II.

2nd Batt. Aug. 1914.

Orders then came for the Battalion to march back to Quevy le Petit, about five miles off, where the men fondly imagined they would again be comfortably billeted. But hardly had they arrived there when they were sent forward again. As they were marching down a dusty track General Scott-Kerr rode up, and directed the 2nd Battalion Grenadiers and the Irish Guards to move up close behind the ridge east of Spiennes in support of the Irish Rifles. At the same time the two Coldstream battalions were ordered to entrench themselves just east of Harveng, presumably as a precaution in case the Brigade should have to retire. Heavy firing was now going on all round, and the ridge which overlooked St. Symphorien to the north was being vigorously shelled by the Germans, who had got the range to a nicety, and were bursting their shells over it with accuracy. It was about 6 p.m. when the Battalion, advancing through Harveng, proceeded in artillery formation for about one and a half miles to the hill near Spiennes. The men huddled close together under the banks on the reverse slope of the hill just over the railway line, while bullets and shells whistled over their heads. As they were lying there they were amused to see the signalman walk slowly down the line as if nothing in particular was happening. He had to light the lamps, and saw no reason why the ordinary routine which he had carried out probably for many years should be interfered with. One of the officers called out to him in French, and explained that the Germans were advancing, but he merely murmured " ça m'est égal," and continued his work, apparently unconscious of the bullets that were striking the line.

Meanwhile, Colonel Corry and Major Jeffreys went up to the position occupied by the Irish Rifles, who were holding their own well under a heavy rifle fire.

When they returned to their men it was getting dark, and at 10.30 a message came from the O.C. Irish Rifles, that his battalion was retiring. It appeared therefore to Colonel Corry that the position was becoming untenable, since the Irish Rifles on his left had already retired, and both flanks of the Battalion were exposed. He consulted Colonel Morris of the Irish Guards, and they both came to the conclusion that the best course would be to retire to Harveng.

The difficulty was to communicate with the Brigadier. The telephone to Brigade Headquarters had been cut by shell-fire, and so Colonel Corry rode back to find General Scott-Kerr. He could not be discovered, and was reported to have gone to Divisional Headquarters. There seemed no prospect whatever of finding him, and it was now past midnight. Thereupon Colonel Corry determined to take upon himself the responsibility of ordering the retirement of the two battalions. His impression was that in a case like this, when local conditions could not be known to the Divisional Staff, it was for the man on the spot to make his own decision.

Superior authority, however, afterwards held that while under exceptional circumstances such powers might well be delegated to the man *in mediis rebus*, in a case like this it could not be admitted that an officer in actual touch with the enemy was the best judge of how long a position should be held. It was felt that there were many considerations in a decision of this sort, of which the officer in the front line could know very little. Colonel Corry was therefore severely blamed for his action, and was a fortnight later relieved of his command.

At 1 o'clock in the morning the 2nd Battalion Grenadiers and the Irish Guards retired, but they had only gone a couple of miles towards Harveng when they were ordered to go back and occupy the ridge they had just left. Back they went, and got as far as the foot of the hill, only to receive another order to retire to Harveng. By this time the men were absolutely tired out. They had started at 3.30 the previous morning, and had been on the move for twenty-four hours, with only occasional halts by the roadside.

It was just at this point in the engagement that Sir John French received what he described in his despatch as a most unexpected message. It came from General Joffre, who informed him that the French Forces had been compelled, by superior numbers, to retire, and that consequently the Fifth French Army, which was immediately on our right, had vacated its line. Two German corps were advancing on the British position, while a third corps was engaged in a turning movement in the direction of Tournai. Divisions of French Territorials had been promised in support of the left flank, but, except for a Brigade at Tournai, no French troops arrived from the west. There was therefore no alternative for Sir John French but to retire.

CHAPTER III

THE RETREAT FROM MONS (2ND BATTALION)

THUS began that historic, terrible, splendid retreat from Mons. Long weary marches were to be the lot of the British Army for many a day, but fortunately no one realised what lay ahead, or the stoutest hearts might well have quailed.

Chapter III.
2nd Batt. Aug. 1914.

Long before it was over, the men's boots—not Crimean ones of brown paper, but good, sound English leather—had been worn into shreds by those interminable, pitiless paving-stones, that had withstood centuries of traffic. Even the men with the toughest skins suffered badly from their feet. Clouds of dust and the heavy atmosphere arising from men in close formation added to the trials of marching. Constant cries of " Feel your right " (to let cavalry or wagons pass by), the wearisome burden of the pack on the shoulders, which drove many men to throw away their most prized possessions, the frequent futile digging of trenches, abandoned as soon as they were dug, the orders and counter-orders—all made the days that followed a positive nightmare to the Army.

Such continuous retirement had never been practised. It was against all tradition, and the

CHAPTER III.
2nd Batt.
Aug. 1914.

Aug. 24.

men grumbled constantly at the seemingly never-ending retreat. But what other course could the "contemptible little army" have followed in the face of the enemy's overwhelming force?

On the 24th Sir H. Smith-Dorrien started off with the Second Corps, while a demonstration was made by the First Corps in the direction of Binche, and dug a line four miles south of Mons to enable the First Corps to retire. It was evident that the Germans were straining every effort to surround the British Army, and therefore to hold on too long to any line was extremely dangerous. The Fifth French Army was still in full retirement, and the First French Cavalry Corps was so exhausted that General Sordet could promise no assistance. The greater part of the British Cavalry Division, with the exception of the regiments covering the retreat of the two British Corps, was guarding the left flank. The arrival of the Fourth Division at Le Cateau had been a welcome addition, but as it was only too probable that the Germans would make every effort to envelop the left of the whole line of the Allies, it was important to have strong reinforcements on that flank.

Two hours' sleep was all the 2nd Battalion Grenadiers was allowed on that fateful 24th of August, weary as it was after its twenty-four hours on end of marching and fighting. At daybreak it marched to Quevy le Grand, where the men were ordered to dig themselves in. They were quite in the dark about what was going on round them. What force was opposed to them or why they were retiring, no one knew. The

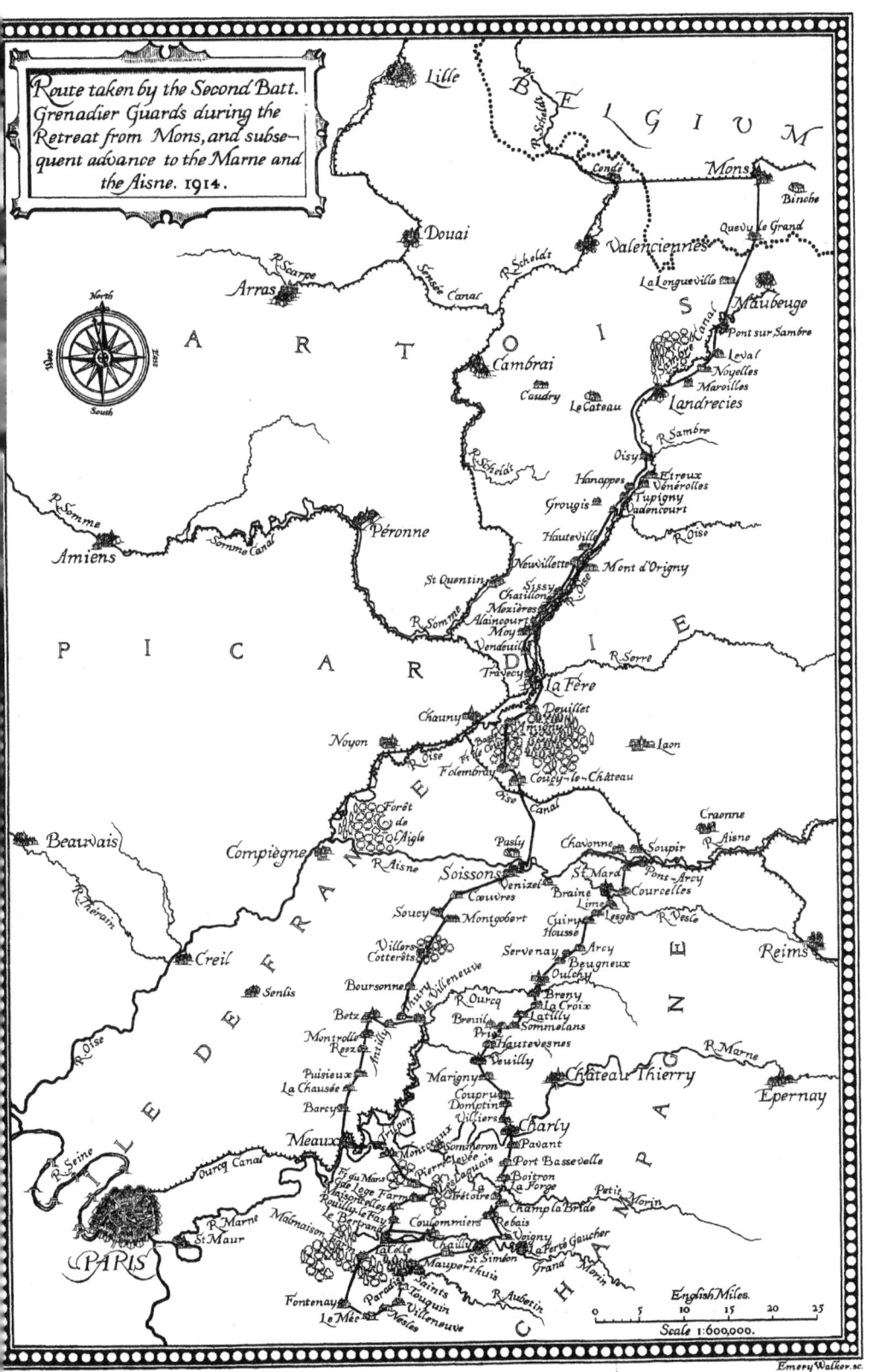

greatest secrecy prevailed. Although it was cold and foggy early, it soon became scorching hot and the men were tired, but when the word went round that this was not a rearguard action, but a determined stand, the digging became a serious matter, and they set to with a will. The Germans advanced very slowly and cautiously, gradually pushing back our Cavalry Patrols, who could be seen retiring. They shelled the Mons—Maubeuge Road and also Quevy le Grand, but as the line of the road was not held, our position being some hundreds of yards in rear of it, little damage was done, although a few men were hit in the village.

But at 2 P.M. another order came to evacuate the trenches and concentrate on the left. "Concentration" proved to be a euphemism for further retirement, and after a long and dusty march the Battalion bivouacked south of La Longueville.

Next morning at 5 o'clock it started on another hot and lengthy march through Pont sur Sambre, Leval, and Noyelles to Landrecies, which was reached at 4 P.M. It went into billets and settled down to rest. But soon afterwards a trooper from the cavalry patrols rode into the town with the news that the Germans were coming; the alarm was given, and the men stood to arms. Nothing further happened, however, and they returned to their billets. The 3rd Battalion Coldstream provided the outposts, and the rest of the brigade were just settling down once more in the hope of a restful night when a second alarm

CHAPTER III.

2nd Batt. Aug. 1914.

Aug. 25. Landrecies.

CHAPTER III.
2nd Batt.
Aug. 1914.

sounded. This time it was a real one. The Germans were advancing in force on Maroilles and Landrecies.

Though the night was very dark there was no confusion, as the men poured hurriedly out from their billets to fall in. Some were at once detailed to build emergency barricades in the streets, and as the tool limbers were taken for this purpose the Battalion never had any heavy tools for the rest of the retreat. The houses on the front of the town were rapidly put in a state of defence; loopholes were made, and the furniture, or anything handy, was pushed up to make the walls bullet-proof.

As it turned out, the enterprise of a small patrol of Uhlans, who rode unopposed into the town during the afternoon, had proved a very fortunate thing for the defenders. For it seems to have been assumed at first that the town was covered by troops from other brigades, and when the 3rd Battalion Coldstream was ordered to furnish outposts it had been considered a quite unnecessary precaution. After the Uhlan incursion, even the most optimistic could hardly have needed convincing.

When all the dispositions had been made the 2nd Battalion Grenadiers was distributed as follows: Nos. 2 and 3 Companies, under the command of Major Lord Bernard Lennox and Captain Stephen, held the level-crossing over the railway, and watched the right and left flanks of the road leading over the Sambre. No. 1 Company, under Major Hamilton, held the two sides on the left, while No. 4 Company,

THE RETREAT FROM MONS 27

under Captain Colston, in reserve, was posted on the bridge over the Sambre.

The first warning that the enemy was at hand was given at 8 P.M. by the firing of the picquets. When the alarm went there was still sufficient light for the men to get into their positions, but soon after it became pitch dark, and the rain began to fall. Suddenly shadowy forms were observed by the outposts moving in the darkness. Evidently they realised that they had been seen, for a voice was heard calling out, " Don't shoot. We are the French." The trick at that time was new to us. Our men naturally hesitated at first to fire, and this gave the Germans their opportunity for a forward rush.

Very critical moments followed. The two forces were only a short distance apart, and in the darkness a retreat would have been fatal, but the splendid discipline of the Guards saved the situation. Everywhere the attacking Germans found themselves beating up against a wall of stubborn resistance. They brought up a couple of guns and poured shells into the town at almost point-blank range; they even fired case-shot down the road. Again and again they charged, only to be met and mowed down by a withering fire. The machine-guns of the Grenadiers were moved up to help the Coldstream, and came into action at a very critical moment. They were largely instrumental in repelling the enemy's attack, and were well handled by Lieutenant the Hon. W. Cecil, who was slightly wounded. Private Rule particularly distinguished himself by sticking to his gun and continuing to fight it, although he had been blown off his feet by the blast of a H.E. shell. The brunt of the attack was borne at the start by the 3rd Battalion Coldstream, which lost heavily in this fight; but in the Grenadiers the casualties were not great.

Soon burning houses were lighting up the battlefield, and it began to be possible to distinguish friend from foe. During one of the bursts of firing Lieutenant Vereker was hit, and fell shot through the head. After the first heavy attacks had been repulsed, the enemy tried to get round the left of the Coldstream in the direction of the railway-station, but there was met by a steady fire from No. 2 Company, under Major Lord Bernard Lennox, and could make no headway. Splendid work was done by a field howitzer, which had been manhandled up to the level-crossing, and which succeeded in silencing the enemy's guns.

Finally, about midnight, the enemy evidently realised the futility of going on with the attack, and retreated once more into the darkness. But spasmodic firing continued for some time, and it was not until nearly 2 A.M. that the night became still, and the men were able to strengthen their position. It was afterwards learnt that the Germans who took part in the attack had been pushed up to Landrecies in two hundred motor lorries. How severely they had been handled may be surmised from the fact that they allowed the Grenadiers and 3rd Battalion Coldstream to retire unmolested over a single bridge across the Sambre. Writing of this engagement

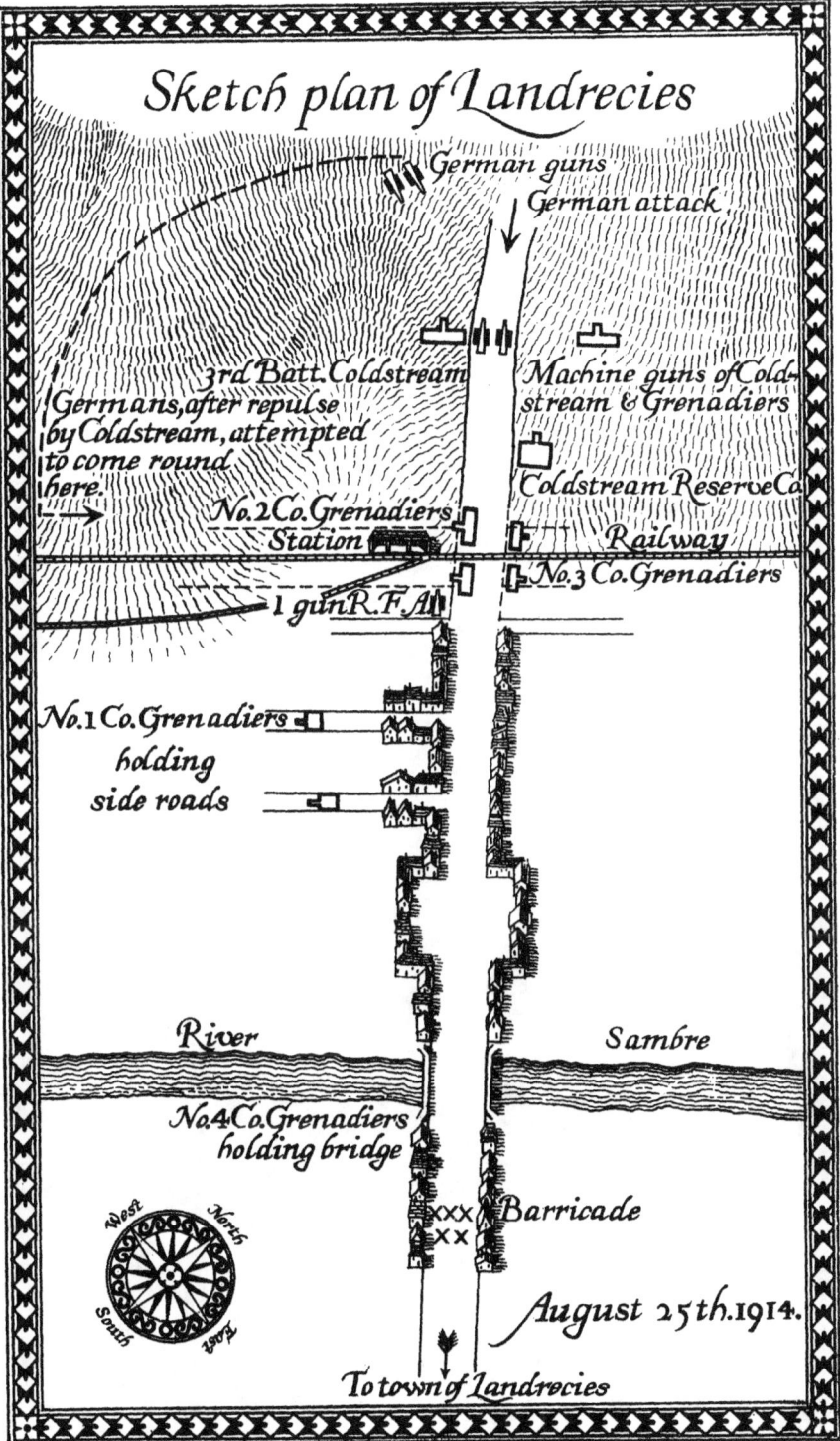

THE RETREAT FROM MONS 29

in his despatch of September 7, Sir John French said :

The 4th Guards Brigade in Landrecies was heavily attacked by troops of the Ninth German Army Corps, who were coming through the forest on the north of the town. This brigade fought most gallantly and caused the enemy to suffer tremendous loss in issuing from the forest into the narrow streets of the town. This loss has been estimated from reliable sources at from 700 to 1000.

In the meantime the Second Corps was between Le Cateau and Caudry with the 19th Brigade, which had been brought up from the lines of communication on the left and the Fourth Division south of Cambrai. The German First Army launched a serious attack along the whole of this line, and Sir H. Smith-Dorrien, finding himself outnumbered and out-gunned, had the greatest difficulty in breaking off the engagement and continuing the retirement.

At daybreak the 4th Brigade again got orders to retire, and marched unmolested to Etreux. Unfortunately many of the men had no time to retrieve their kits, which they had left at their billets, and all these were left behind. The troops were dead beat, having again had practically no sleep after a long day's marching and fighting. Every time a halt was made the whole Battalion fell fast asleep, and when the march had to be resumed it was very hard to rouse the men. It might seem hardly worth while to sleep during a brief halt of only a few minutes, with the prospect of a painful re-awakening to the realities of the situation as the

CHAPTER III.
2nd Batt.
Aug. 1914.

inevitable sequel. But most of the men were so thoroughly worn out that they eagerly welcomed even the doubtful blessing of such a respite. In the distance heavy firing could be heard in the direction of Le Cateau, and at one time it seemed probable the 4th Brigade might be sent off to support the hard-pressed Second Corps.

Etreux was reached at last, and the Battalion proceeded to dig itself in. During the afternoon a German aeroplane flew very low over the bivouac, and dropped a bomb, which, however, did no damage. Every one who had a rifle handy had a shot at the unwelcome visitor; eventually it was forced down a mile away, where it was picked up by the cavalry. In it were found three officers, two dead and one wounded.

Aug. 27. Another long dusty march lay before the Brigade on the following day. Continuing the retirement, it passed through Vénérolles, Tupigny, Vadencourt, and Hauteville to Mont d'Origny. A report was brought in that a large force of the enemy had been seen near St. Quentin, but this proved to be inaccurate. That night the First Corps was in a most critical position. The Germans had nearly surrounded them, and urgent orders to entrench the high ground north and east of Mont d'Origny were received; but although the weary troops dug on till midnight, nothing occurred, and at 3.30 A.M. the Battalion started off again.

Aug. 28. It reached Deuillet near La Fère, where it had the only day's halt during the retreat. On the way the Scots Greys and 12th Lancers

THE RETREAT FROM MONS 31

charged a large force of German cavalry and utterly routed them, making many prisoners, but otherwise nothing was seen of the enemy.

On arrival at Deuillet, the usual procedure was gone through, and a position in defence was entrenched, the men working at it all day.

In the evening an electrifying report, which cheered every one up, went round that there was to be a general advance. But when the order came it was the usual one to retire, and another hot march of twenty-eight miles followed. The weary, wearing ordeal of long day marches and but little sleep had commenced again. As soon as it was decided to continue the retreat, and the whole British Force had crossed over the Oise, the bridges were blown up. The heat was intense. There was practically no wind, and the dust was stifling; a very large number of men were suffering from sore feet, and there was a good deal of grumbling in the ranks at the endless marching in the wrong direction. But there was no prospect of a long rest, and those battalions which were unlucky enough to leave men behind never saw them again. Not a man from the 2nd Grenadiers, however, fell out.

The two corps which had been dangerously separated were now once more united, but the pursuing Germans were very near, and the situation still gave rise to much anxiety. Information was received to the effect that five or six German corps were pursuing the Fifth French Army, while at least two corps were advancing on the British Army. The situation on the left of the

British Army was obscure, but it was reported that the enemy had three or four more corps endeavouring to creep round that flank. In response to Sir John French's representations, General Joffre ordered the Fifth French Army to attack the enemy on the Somme with the object of relieving the pressure on the British Army.

<small>Chapter III.
2nd Batt.
Aug. 1914.</small>

<small>Aug. 30–31.</small>
The Battalion reached Soissons about midday on the 30th, and was ordered to occupy the ridge near Pasly, about two miles north of the town. Next day it tramped on to Soucy, a very hard march in great heat, finishing up with a steep climb. Here it bivouacked as usual, and snatched what rest it could. But a full night's sleep was always out of the question, and soon after midnight the whole Brigade was directed to form a rearguard, to cover the retirement of the Second Division.

<small>Sept. 1.
Villers-Cotterêts.</small>
Accordingly trenches were dug in the high ground above Soucy, No. 4 Company Grenadiers being detached to guard the right flank in a position leading across a deep ravine to the high ground above Montgobert. It was to rejoin the Battalion when it retired to the forest of Villers-Cotterêts. Soon after the Germans came in sight, and retirement from the first position was successfully effected. The 2nd Battalion Grenadiers and 3rd Battalion Coldstream made their way into the wood, the edges of which were held by the Irish Guards and 2nd Battalion Coldstream, and took up a fresh position along the line of the main road running east and west through Rond de la Reine.

Thick mist hung over the country, and the dense undergrowth made the passage of the wood difficult. The Germans, it was assumed, would not attempt to penetrate the wood, but would be content to use the roads and drives. The assumption proved to be wrong—fortunately for us. As it happened, they came through the very thickest part, and in so doing lost cohesion and direction. Probably, in fact, it was their doing this, and the confusion into which they were consequently thrown, that enabled the 4th Brigade to break off the action later in the evening and retire unmolested.

The 2nd Battalion Grenadiers held the right of the line. From a strategic point of view, the position it occupied could not well have been worse. But in a rearguard action there is often no choice. It was absolutely necessary to retard the advance of the enemy through the wood, so that the rest of the Division should get away.

During the time of waiting for the oncoming Germans, the Scots Greys and 12th Lancers suddenly appeared, coming down the ride on the right. They had been attracted by the firing, and came to see what was going on. They dismounted, and, finding many friends among the Grenadiers, started "coffee-housing" for a while. But the firing in the outskirts of the wood began to sound serious, and they rode off along the road to the left, with the idea of operating against the enemy's right.

A few minutes later the Germans appeared, and a fight at close quarters began. The firing became very hot, as in some places the opposing forces were hardly seventy yards apart. Good work was done by the machine-guns of the Grenadiers and Irish Guards, which accounted for a large number of Germans, while the men charged repeatedly with the bayonet and drove the enemy back. Gallantly, stolidly, the 4th Brigade held on until the order came to retire.

Even with highly-disciplined troops, a rear-guard action in a wood is one of the most difficult manœuvres to carry out well. It is quite impossible for the commanding officer to keep a firm grip of his battalion when it is scattered about in different rides; orders passed along often do not reach all the platoons, and men of different companies, and even regiments, are wont to get hopelessly mixed. Fortunately in the Brigade of Guards the men are all trained on the same system, and, except for some small characteristic differences, a man belonging to one regiment will be quite at home in any of the others.

At Villers-Cotterêts the men of the 4th Brigade became very much mixed, and officers took command of the men who happened to be near them. The wood, too, was so thick that at fifty yards' distance parties were practically out of sight of each other. One result of this difficulty of keeping in touch was that two platoons of No. 4 Company never got the order to retire.

These two platoons, under the command of Lieutenant the Hon. F. E. Needham and Lieutenant the Hon. J. N. Manners, were at the Cross Roads at Rond de la Reine. As the Germans

THE RETREAT FROM MONS 35

came on, Brigadier-General Scott-Kerr, finding that they were creeping round his left flank, ordered these two platoons down a ride to the left, to enfilade them. Making the best dispositions they could, these two officers continued to fight, when they suddenly realised that they were cut off and the Germans were on all sides of them. True to the traditions of the Regiment, they stuck to their posts, and fought on till all were killed or wounded.

Lieutenant the Hon. J. N. Manners was killed while directing the fire of his platoon, and Lieutenant the Hon. F. Needham, badly wounded, was taken prisoner. Lieutenant G. E. Cecil, another officer belonging to these platoons, seeing the Germans streaming across a ride to his left, dashed off with some men to stop them. He had not gone far before he was shot through the hand; stumbling forward, he recovered his feet, and, drawing his sword, he called on the men to charge when a bullet struck him in the head. And there were other casualties among the officers. Earlier in the day the Adjutant of the Battalion, Lieutenant I. MacDougall, was shot dead while carrying orders to the firing-line. His place was taken by Captain E. J. L. Pike. The Brigadier-General, Scott-Kerr, who rode up to give some orders, was badly wounded in the thigh, and the command of the Brigade passed to Colonel Corry, while Major Jeffreys took over the 2nd Battalion Grenadiers. Field-Marshal Sir John French, on hearing of this, sent the following telegram to Brigadier-General Scott-Kerr, care of Communications:

My warm congratulations on gallantry of your Brigade A A A am deeply grieved to hear you are wounded A A A I shall miss your valuable help very much A A A my best wishes for your recovery. FRENCH.

Captain W. T. Payne-Gallwey, M.V.O., who was in charge of the machine-guns in the First Brigade, was reported missing.

Orders were given to retire, and the Battalion quietly withdrew in single file of half-platoons, covered by a rear party from No. 2 Company. The enemy, as already stated, had been thrown into hopeless confusion in the wood, and, in spite of a prodigious amount of shouting and blowing of horns, could not get forward. Some three hours later a second engagement was fought on the other side of Villers-Cotterêts. The 4th Brigade retired through the 6th Brigade, which with the field artillery had taken up a position at the edge of another wood. The enemy's first shells came over as the 4th Brigade moved into the wood. The British guns succeeded in keeping the Germans at bay, but were only got away with the utmost difficulty and some loss.

Having borne the brunt of the fighting, the 4th Brigade had necessarily suffered heavy casualties.

The 2nd Battalion Grenadiers lost 4 officers and 160 men, while the Irish Guards lost 4 officers and the Coldstream 7, as well as a large number of men. Two exceptionally good officers in the Irish Guards were killed—Colonel the Hon. G. Morris and Major H. F. Crichton. The latter served in the Grenadiers for some years before exchanging into the Irish Guards.[1]

[1] In November 1914, when the Allies regained possession of Villers-

THE RETREAT FROM MONS 37

On emerging once more into open country, the 2nd Battalion Grenadiers was sent off to march to Boursonne, which it reached about 4 P.M. Two companies of the 2nd Battalion Coldstream were ordered back to support the 6th Brigade, which was now protecting the retreat of the guns; but they were not wanted after all, and were sent back to Boursonne after a fruitless journey. Then General Monro rode up, and ordered the 2nd Battalion Grenadiers to take up a rear-guard position about Boursonne, to cover the retirement of the 6th Brigade. Meanwhile, the Brigade Headquarters, the Irish Guards, and the 3rd Battalion Coldstream went on to Betz.

When the 6th Brigade had passed through, the 2nd Battalion Grenadiers and 2nd Battalion Coldstream retired to Thury. Unfortunately no orders had been given them to go to Betz, and through following the 6th Brigade these two battalions missed the guide whom Battalion Headquarters had sent to meet them. Once more the men were absolutely dead beat. They had had nothing to eat since tea the day before, but when the matter of food was inquired into

CHAPTER III.
2nd Batt. Sept. 1914.

Cotterêts, the bodies of those who had fallen there were reverently buried. Lieut.-Colonel the Hon. G. Morris, Captain Tisdall of the Irish Guards, Lieut. Geoffrey Lambton, Coldstream Guards, and Lieut. G. E. Cecil, Grenadier Guards, were buried together, and a cross was put up by the French with the following inscription:

Ici reposent
Quatre officiers de l'Armée Anglaise.
Le Colonel l'honorable GEORGE MORRIS. *R.I.P.*
Le Capitaine C. A. TISDALL, de la garde Irlandaise.
Le Lieut. GEOFFREY LAMBTON.
Le Lieut. GEORGE E. CECIL, des Grenadiers de la Garde.

it was found that all the supplies had gone on to Betz. This was at 11 o'clock at night, and it looked as if the men would have to bivouac foodless by the roadside.

Heroic measures were called for, and Major Jeffreys decided to brush aside the ordinary procedure and shortcircuit the usual channels of communication by going straight to the Divisional Commander, General Monro. He was instantly successful. On learning of the sad plight of the Battalion, General Monro undertook to supply it with food. He ordered his D.A.Q.M.G. to take the Battalion to his supply depot, and Major Jeffreys went back and fell in his weary men.

With the promise of a meal ahead they responded gamely, and marched off to La Villeneuve, the place indicated by the General, where rations of bully-beef, bread, and cheese were soon distributed.

Then the men were allowed two hours' sleep by way of a night's rest after one of the longest and most strenuous days they had ever had. They were more fortunate, though, than the men of the 2nd Battalion Coldstream Guards, who did not even manage to get any food that night, and who had to snatch what sleep they could lying down in the streets of Thury.

At 2 A.M. the Battalion marched off again—still retiring—through Antilly to Betz, where it was joined by No. 1 Company and 45 men of No. 4 under Lieutenant Stocks. Thence by Montrolle to Reez, where a halt was made for water, and on to Puisieux. Here the men

THE RETREAT FROM MONS 39

had a late breakfast, and then, in stifling heat, continued their march, with constant halts, through La Chaussée and Barcy to Meaux. They reached this village at 4 p.m., and, their long day's journey ended, they were refreshed by a bathe in the Ourcq Canal. This march was almost the hardest of the whole retreat, but, in spite of everything, the Battalion marched on, with scarcely a man out of the ranks, although the number of men who fell out in other regiments was by no means small.

Undoubtedly the men were by now beginning to feel the strain of this interminable retirement. However footsore and weary they may be, British troops will always respond when called upon to advance. But to ask them to make a special effort when retreating is quite another thing, even with the most highly disciplined. Besides, they were quite unable to see the necessity of it all. There had been no pitched battle, no defeat—in fact, whenever they had had a chance they had inflicted enormous losses on the enemy and driven him back. Of course they had seen no newspapers, and had no way of picking up any real idea of what was going on in France.

Next morning at 7 o'clock the march was resumed eastwards, and the Division crossed the Marne at Trilport, blowing the bridges up after them. This new direction was the result of the Germans moving along the north bank of the Marne, which they crossed near Sammeron. Then the Battalion moved southward again, through Montceaux and Forêt du Mans to Pierre Levée, where it bivouacked.

40 THE GRENADIER GUARDS

Chapter III.
2nd Batt. Sept. 1914.
Sept. 4.

The men had expected a rest on September 4, but the order soon arrived for the Brigade to continue the retirement. No. 3 Company of the 2nd Battalion Grenadiers under Captain Gosselin, and No. 4 Company under Captain Symes-Thompson, were sent out on outpost duty.

In the morning the Brigade marched to Les Laquais, where trenches were dug, joining up with the 5th and 6th Brigades on the right. At 5 P.M. the enemy shelled the right of the line, and at dusk the Brigade withdrew. It picked up No. 3 Company at Grande Loge Farm, and marched through Maisoncelles and Rouilly le Fay to Le Bertrand, where it bivouacked for the night.

Meanwhile Major Lord Bernard Lennox was despatched to Coulommiers to find the first draft that had been sent out from home—90 men under Captain Ridley. They arrived about midday after a train journey of thirty-six hours—they had been all round the country, constantly receiving fresh orders to go to different places. Lord Bernard Lennox had been instructed to remain at Coulommiers, but when he found the First Division retiring through the town all the afternoon, he decided to strike off westward with the new draft in search of the Battalion. This plan succeeded, and he found it about midnight.

Sept. 5.

It was a sadly tattered, unshaven, footsore body of men that marched at 3 o'clock next morning through La Celle and Malmaison Farm to Fontenay, where they went into billets. No Londoner seeing them would have guessed that these were the same smart Grenadiers whom he

THE RETREAT FROM MONS   41

had often admired on the King's Guard. But if their looks were gone, their spirit was indomitable as ever.

The Germans seem to have been genuinely under the delusion that by this time the long retreat had reduced the British Army, always "contemptible," to a mere spiritless mob, which it was no longer necessary to take into calculation in developing their plan of campaign. They little knew the British soldier. So far the 2nd Battalion Grenadiers had had no chance of showing its quality; it had just been marched off its feet from the start—in the wrong direction. But, in spite of all the men had gone through, they were ready at any moment to turn and fight like lions when they were allowed to.

And now at last the moment was close at hand. To their joyful surprise the officers of the Battalion found, on the morning of September 6, that the direction had been changed, and that an advance was to be made eastward against the German flank. At first it was thought that this meant the beginning of an offensive-defensive, the German attack having failed; but in reality, of course, the change was a much bigger one even than this. The French reserves were now available, and the Germans' greatest asset, superior numbers, was lost to them. And so a new phase of the campaign began to develop.

On the 6th Lieut.-Colonel Corry resumed the command of the Battalion, and Lieut.-Colonel G. Feilding took command of the Brigade.

Chapter III.
2nd Batt. Sept. 1914.

Sept. 6.

CHAPTER IV

THE BATTLE OF THE MARNE (2ND BATTALION)

Chapter IV.
2nd Batt.
Sept. 1914.

The German General Staff at this juncture realised that a retreating army is not necessarily a beaten one. For the last ten days, with their maps spread before them, they had had the satisfaction of moving the pins and flags representing their forces continually and rapidly nearer and nearer Paris. But if the French Army—the British Army, they thought, could be safely ignored—were to succeed in escaping south, it would remain a constant menace. It might even interfere with the Emperor's spectacular entry into Paris, every detail of which had been sketched out beforehand by the officials, whose business it was to stage-manage all the theatrical pageantry of their Imperial master's movements.

So a big *coup* was wanted—a smashing blow at the French. If the centre of the French line could be pierced by the combined efforts of Von Hausen's, the Duke of Würtemberg's, and the Crown Prince's armies, and if simultaneously Von Kluck's army, which had reached Senlis, and was only twenty-five miles from Paris, could execute a swift movement to the south-east, the Fifth French Army would be caught in a vice.

THE BATTLE OF THE MARNE 43

This strategic plan really menaced the whole of the interior of France, and had it succeeded might have resulted in her downfall. In all these calculations of the German Staff it appears to have been assumed that the British Army was practically out of action, and that whatever remained of it had in all probability been sent to reinforce the weak spot at Bar-le-Duc.

To accomplish his decisive stroke, Von Kluck had to execute that most dangerous of all manœuvres, a flank march with the object of rolling up the left of the French line. The German General Staff assumed that the left of the Fifth French Army was the left of the whole French line, and that nothing beyond a few cavalry patrols had to be reckoned with. Von Kluck was accordingly given orders to march his army to the left and attack the Fifth French Army under General Franchet d'Esperey. They knew nothing of the Sixth Army under General Maunoury, which had arrived with such dramatic suddenness in taxi-cabs from Paris.

The unknown and the despised elements proved Von Kluck's undoing. Before he had gone very far he found the completely ignored British Army on top of him, and the totally unexpected Sixth French Army on his right flank. Quickly realising his peril, he decided to retire. In the meantime, on the French side, General Foch, who was about in the centre of the French line, saw an opportunity, which he promptly seized, of driving a wedge between the armies of Von Hausen and Von Bülow. The situation was now entirely changed. The lately

Chapter IV.
2nd Batt. Sept. 1914.

triumphant German forces were no longer even moderately secure, and decided on a general retirement all along the line.

It was on September 5 that Sir John French and General Joffre conferred together and decided to take the offensive. To the British Army was assigned the space between the Fifth and Sixth French Armies. This meant a change of front, and hence that welcome order to the 2nd Battalion Grenadiers to move due east instead of south.

That evening Field-Marshal Sir John French issued the following orders :

(1) The enemy has apparently abandoned the idea of advancing on Paris and is contracting his front and moving south-east.

(2) The Army will advance eastward with a view to attacking. Its left will be covered by the French Sixth Army also marching east, and its right will be linked to the French Fifth Army marching north.

(3) In pursuance of the above the following moves will take place, the Army facing east on completion of the movement.

First Corps : right on La - Chapelle - Iger, left on Lumigny, move to be completed 9 A.M.

Second Corps : right on La Houssaye, left in neighbourhood of Villeneuve, move to be completed 10 A.M.

Third Corps : facing east in the neighbourhood of Bailly, move to be completed 10 A.M.

Cavalry Division (less 3rd and 5th Brigades) : to guard front and flanks of First Corps on the line Jouy-le-Chatel (connecting the French Fifth Army)—Coulommiers (connecting the 3rd and 5th Brigades). The 3rd and 5th Cavalry Brigades will cease to be under the orders of the First Corps and will act in concert under instructions issued by Brigadier-General Gough. They

THE BATTLE OF THE MARNE 45

will cover the Second Corps connecting with the Cavalry Division on the right and with the Sixth French Army on the left.

Sunday, the 6th, was the joyful day when there came this turn of the tide, and that morning Sir John French issued an order to his Army in which he said:

> After a most trying series of operations, mostly in retirement, which have been rendered necessary by the general strategic plan of the Allied Armies, the British Forces stand to-day formed in line with their French comrades, ready to attack the enemy. Foiled in their attempt to invest Paris, the Germans have been driven to move in an easterly and south-easterly direction, with the apparent intention of falling in strength on Fifth French Army. In this operation they are exposing their right flank and their line of communication to an attack by the Sixth French Army and the British Forces.
>
> I call upon the British Army in France to show now to the enemy its power and to push on vigorously to the attack beside the Sixth French Army. I am sure I shall not call on them in vain, but that on the contrary by another manifestation of the magnificent spirit which they have shown in the past fortnight they will fall on the enemy's flank with all their strength, and in unison with their Allies drive them back.

At 5.30 the same morning the 2nd Battalion Grenadiers marched to Le Mée, where trenches were dug. The men, for once, had had a good night's rest, and were in great spirits at the prospect of an advance. A sharp artillery attack was being carried on against Villeneuve, and the 1st Brigade was moved out to attack the place, while the 4th Brigade prolonged the line on the left. Being in reserve, the 2nd Battalion

CHAPTER IV.
2nd Batt.
Sept. 1914.

Grenadiers saw little of the day's fighting. In the event the artillery proved sufficient to shift the enemy, and the Battalion marched without further incident to Touquin, where it bivouacked for the night. That night the British Army occupied a line from Dagny on the right to Villeneuve-le-Comte on the left.

Sept. 7. Severe fighting went on all along the line next morning. Maunoury's taxi-cab army had been able to press Von Kluck as he retired, and the British Army had taken Coulommiers and La Ferté-Gaucher. As the German battalions retreated shells were poured on them by our artillery, who were kept well posted with information by the aircraft observers. Marching through Paradis, Mauperthuis, St. Simeon, and Voigny, the 2nd Battalion Grenadiers finally bivouacked at Rebais. Everywhere in the villages were staring evidences of the German occupation and hurried retreat. Shops had been looted, houses despoiled, and the contents — such as could not be carried away—had been wantonly destroyed, evidently under orders, and the fragments scattered to the winds. The advance-guard of the 4th Brigade (the 2nd Battalion Coldstream) was engaged with the German rear-guard during this march, and the Grenadiers who were in support came in for a certain amount of firing. The Germans could be plainly seen retiring by Rebais with masses of transport in great confusion.

Sept. 8. It became clear next day that Von Kluck's Army was in retreat, and Sir John French determined to press him and give him no rest—thus

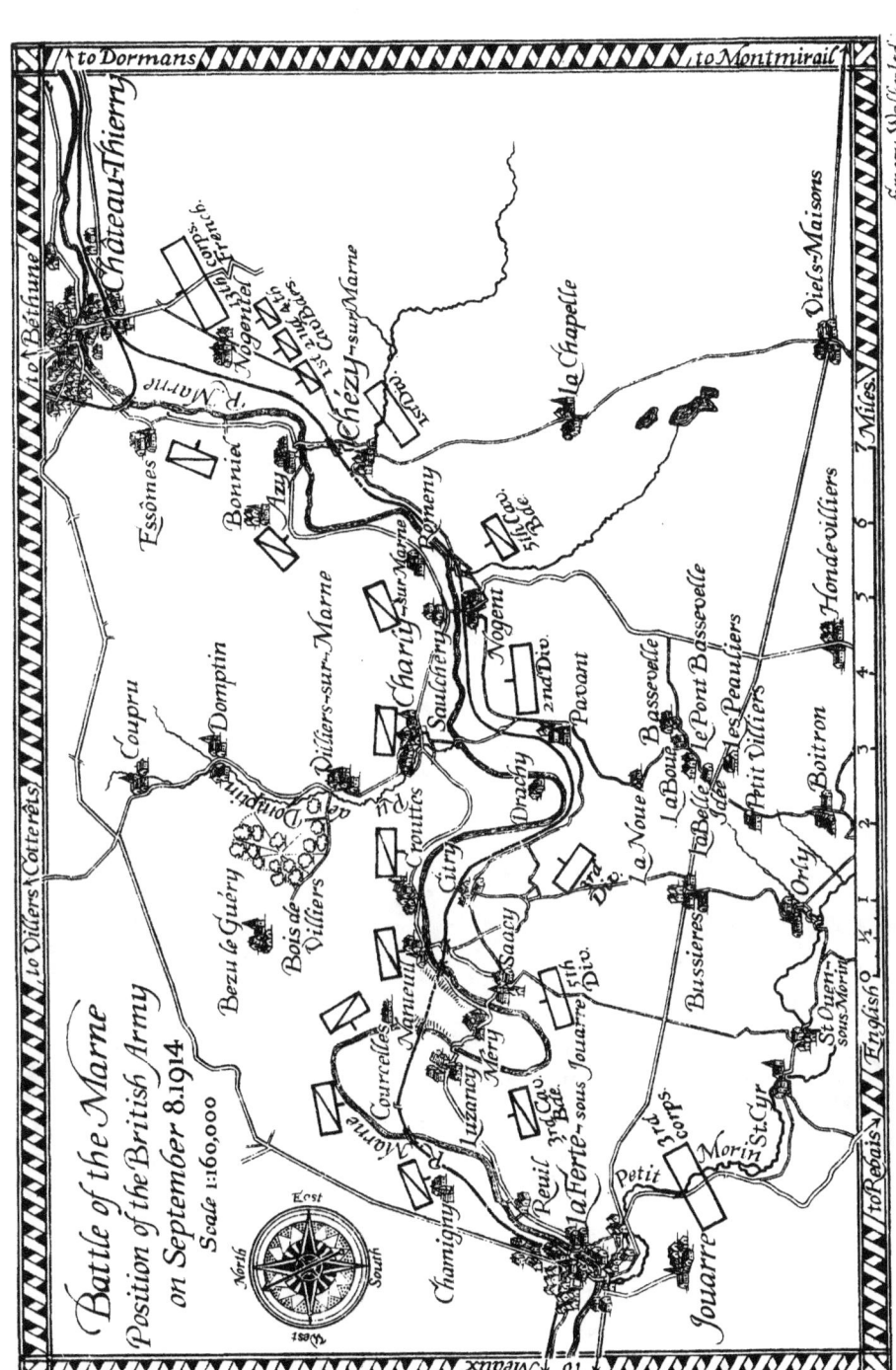

THE BATTLE OF THE MARNE 47

completely were the positions reversed. The First Corps advanced, and everything went well at first, but at La Trétoire it was held up by the German rear-guard, which had found a good position, and the 3rd Battalion Coldstream, which formed the advanced guard, was checked for a time by the German machine-guns hidden in the houses round the bridge over the Petit Morin. Meanwhile, a German field battery posted near Boitron shelled the high ground over which the main body of the 4th Brigade had to pass.

The Germans were evidently fighting a delaying action, and were employing their cavalry with great skill to hold the river as long as possible. In front of the British Army, the cavalry covering the retreat of Von Kluck's Army was commanded by General von der Marwitz, who showed no intention of abandoning his position without a struggle.

Thick woods run down to the river for the last half-mile here, but right through them goes one big clearing about eighty yards wide. This was swept by the German machine-guns, and it was a problem how to get the men across. No. 3 Company Grenadiers under Captain Stephen was sent on to support the Coldstream, followed later by No. 4 under Captain Colston. Both companies reached the edge of the wood, but were there stopped by a hail of fire from the machine-guns. Our field-guns could not reach the houses where these had been placed, and the howitzers were unaccountably slow in coming up. It was while he was endeavouring to find some way of advance that Captain Stephen was

Chapter IV.
2nd Batt. Sept. 1914.

shot through both legs; he was taken to hospital, and died of his wounds four days later.

Urgent messages to push on kept arriving meanwhile from Sir Douglas Haig. Lieut.-Colonel Feilding, who was temporarily in command of the Brigade, sent the 2nd Battalion Coldstream by a circuitous route to try and effect a crossing at La Forge, farther to the right. No. 1 and No. 2 Companies Grenadiers were then ordered to go round by a covered route to avoid the clearing in the wood, and had actually started when Lieut.-Colonel Feilding gave the order for them to turn about. Major Lord Bernard Gordon Lennox, who had raced off at their head, was so far in front that the order did not reach him. He rushed across the clearing, and just managed to get into a ditch on the other side, the shower of machine-gun bullets churning up the ground almost at his heels.

So deafening was the noise of the firing that it was impossible to pass orders simultaneously to the men scattered about in the woods, who at the same time were all on edge to advance. And soon it became very difficult to keep the troops together.

Lieut.-Colonel Corry had already gone off with these two companies, Nos. 1 and 2, to follow the 2nd Battalion Coldstream, when Lieut.-Colonel Feilding thought he saw the Germans retiring, and shouted to Major Jeffreys to turn the Grenadiers about and take them across the clearing straight down to the river, but No. 2 Company had got a good way ahead through the woods, and Major Jeffreys was only able

THE BATTLE OF THE MARNE 49

to get hold of half of No. 1 Company, which followed him across the clearing. Unfortunately, however, the German guns were still there, and opened a heavy fire on them. By this time the 2nd Battalion Grenadiers was hopelessly split up, different parts of the Battalion having gone in three different directions, and the 3rd Battalion Coldstream was also scattered all over the woods. In the meantime the howitzers came up, and soon drove the Germans out of their position. No. 3 Company had done well in the fighting, having succeeded in capturing one of the enemy's machine-guns and many prisoners.

The various parties then made their way through the wood to the edge of the stream, but as there was no bridge to be seen they worked along the banks to La Trétoire. Without further opposition, a party of the Irish Guards under Major Herbert Stepney, together with half of No. 1 Company under Major Jeffreys and Lieutenant Mackenzie, crossed the bridge, and advanced up the opposite side towards Boitron. In every direction the ground was strewn with dead and wounded Germans, and after advancing 1000 yards the party of Grenadiers reached the position which had been occupied by the German Battery; the guns had all been got away, but dead horses, overturned limbers, and dead gunners showed how this Battery had suffered at the hands of the 41st Brigade R.F.A.

As the enemy retired our guns and howitzers kept up a heavy fire, and inflicted severe losses. The whole Brigade had by now debouched from the woods, and gradually collected behind Boitron, while the Divisional Cavalry went on ahead so as to keep in touch with the retreating enemy. The 2nd Battalion Grenadiers was then ordered to advance in artillery formation over the open country north of Boitron, and met with no resistance.

But there was one incident that might have proved disastrous. In its eagerness to get at the enemy, No. 2 Company got rather ahead of its time, with the result that our own guns planted some shrapnel into it, luckily without doing much damage. On the left the Irish Guards and the 2nd Battalion Coldstream found in a wood a number of Germans with machine-guns, who had apparently got separated from the main body. Our men charged, and immediately up went the white flag; seven machine-guns and a large number of prisoners were taken, mostly men belonging to the Guard Jäger Corps.

Rain had been falling for some time in a steady downpour, and as the light was failing the Battalion assembled to bivouac near Les Peauliers. An extremely wet sainfoin field was chosen for the purpose, and there, in a misty September evening, the men lay down to sleep. Altogether the Grenadiers had lost forty men in the day's fighting, besides Captain Stephen.

Sept. 9. Dismally the raindrops trickled through the trees as the men roused themselves in the early morning. It was very cold, too, and the great-coats that had been so lightly flung away during the sweltering days of retreat were now bitterly regretted. And it was a particularly chilly

THE BATTLE OF THE MARNE 51

task that lay before the Battalion, for it was in reserve, which meant constant standing about—often even more tiring than a march. However, about midday it cleared, and a very hot sun soon got every one dry again.

CHAPTER IV.

2nd Batt. Sept. 1914.

On this day the passage of the Marne was forced; the Third Corps, under General Pulteney, bore the brunt of the fighting, whilst the First Corps on its right drove the Germans before it with some ease and took numerous prisoners. The 2nd Battalion Grenadiers, starting off at 7.30, eventually crossed the Marne at Charly, after innumerable halts and checks. Before it got over it had to wait some hours at Pavant, where it could watch various divisions crossing the river. This bridge at Charly was the only one in the neighbourhood left standing; it had been carefully prepared for demolition, and no one knew why, fortunately for us, it had escaped. Rumour said that the German engineers entrusted with the task got so drunk that, when the appointed moment arrived, they were quite incapable of carrying out their orders.

During the day Lieut.-Colonel Corry received orders to return home. He had been relieved of his command on account of the decision, already recorded, which he took at Mons.

The Battalion bivouacked that evening—rain was again falling—on the side of a wet hill near Villiers-sur-Marne, and woke up to more rainy, cold weather. The battle of the Marne had been won, and the Germans were retreating in perfectly orderly fashion, though we captured 13 guns, 7 machine-guns, and 2000 men. The

Sept. 10.

CHAPTER IV.
2nd Batt.
Sept. 1914.

prisoners said they had been officially informed that a large German army was investing Paris, and that their division was engaged in " drawing off" the French Army eastwards. The 2nd Battalion Grenadiers was again in reserve, and was constantly marched backwards and forwards throughout the day. It passed through Domptin, Coupru, Marigny, and Veuilly to Hautevesnes, where it bivouacked.

Sept. 11.

The pursuit continued during the two following days. Through heavy showers, which gave them a thorough soaking, the Grenadiers marched on the 11th by the way of Priez, Sommelans, Latilly, La Croix, and Breny to Oulchy, where they got into billets, and fires were lit to dry their clothes. Such inhabitants as were left eagerly helped to supply all the men's wants, and placed all they possessed at their disposal. The usual signs of recent German occupation were to be seen in every house. Drawers had been turned out, cupboards ransacked, and tables overturned, and the floors were thickly strewn with such things as the Germans had been unable to take away with them—clothes, smashed gramophone records, broken glasses, and other debris. But, in spite of the pitiable surroundings and their own soaked condition, the officers and men were soon put in the best of spirits by the cheerful fires and the appetising smell of bacon and eggs, put on to cook for them.

Sept. 12

Next morning's parade was at 5 o'clock, but the town was so crowded with supply wagons that it was 9 before a move could be made. It rained at intervals during the day, and in the evening another steady downpour set in, which once more soaked the men to the skin before they got to their billets at Courcelles, having marched through Beugneux, Arcy, Cuiry-Housse, Lesges, Limé, and Braine.

CHAPTER IV.

2nd Batt. Sept. 1914.

CHAPTER V

THE PASSAGE OF THE AISNE (2ND BATTALION)

<small>Chapter V.
2nd Batt.
Sept. 1914.</small>
For a week now the Germans had been steadily retiring, and there was no apparent reason why they should stop doing so. Each time they held a position the question naturally arose whether they were really making a determined stand, or whether this was just a case of a rear-guard doing its best to hold up the advance. The only way to find out was to attack them and make them show their dispositions.

At the Marne, where it might well have been supposed that the Germans had a good enough position to make a stand, their resistance had proved to be merely in the nature of a rear-guard action. It did not at first dawn on our Army that at the Aisne, on the contrary, the enemy had occupied a carefully chosen and sedulously prepared position which suited their purpose in every way.

An ideal position it was, indeed. Sir John French, in his despatch of October 8, 1914, thus describes it :

<small>The Aisne valley runs generally east and west, and consists of a flat-bottomed depression of width varying from half a mile to two miles, down which the river</small>

THE PASSAGE OF THE AISNE 55

flows a winding course to the west at some points near the southern slopes of the valley and at others near the northern. The high ground both on the north and south of the river is approximately 400 feet above the bottom of the valley and is very similar in character, as are both slopes of the valley itself, which are broken into numerous rounded spurs and re-entrants. The most prominent of the former are the Chivres Spur on the right bank and the Sermoise spur on the left. Near the latter place the general plateau on the south is divided by a subsidiary valley of much the same character, down which the small river Vesle flows to the main stream near Sermoise. The slopes of the plateau overlooking the Aisne on the north and south are of varying steepness and are covered with numerous patches of wood, which also stretch upwards and backwards over the edge on to the top of the high ground. There are several villages and small towns dotted about in the valley itself and along its sides, the chief of which is the town of Soissons.

The Aisne is a sluggish stream of some 170 feet in breadth, but, being 15 feet deep in the centre, it is unfordable. Between Soissons on the west and Villers on the east (the part of the river attacked and secured by the British Forces) there are eleven road-bridges across it. On the north bank a narrow-gauge railway runs from Soissons to Vailly, where it crosses the river and continues eastward along the south bank. From Soissons to Sermoise a double line of railway runs along the south bank, turning at the latter place up the Vesle valley towards Bazoches.

The position held by the enemy is a very strong one, either for a delaying action or for a defensive battle. One of its chief military characteristics is that from the high ground on neither side can the top of the plateau on the other side be seen, except for small stretches. This is chiefly due to the woods on the edges of the slopes. Another important point is that all the bridges are under either direct or high-angle artillery fire.

Until the afternoon of the 12th September it was still uncertain whether the enemy meant business this time or not, and then Sir John French came to the conclusion that, for the moment at any rate, they had stopped their retreat and were preparing to dispute vigorously the passage of the river. The presence of Germans had been reported by our cavalry south of Soissons and in the neighbourhood of Braine, but these were merely patrols.

The opposing forces were posted as follows: The German Army occupied the high ground north of the river, with Von Kluck still on the right flank. From the reports that came in, it appeared that the right of Von Kluck's army was resting on the forest of L'Aigle, and the left on the plateau of Craonne, while Von Bülow prolonged the line to the left. The French Army was now extended in an immense line from Compiègne to the Argonne, the British Army holding a portion of the front—about twenty miles—between Maunoury's Sixth Army and Franchet d'Esperey's Fifth Army.

On the left of our part of the line were the Third Corps, which was allotted the section from Soissons to Venizel, the Second Corps, which was between Venizel and Chavonne, and the First Corps between Chavonne and Bourg. In this last section there was a canal as well as a river to cross.

Sept. 13. Rain was pouring down when the Battalion paraded at 5.30 A.M. on the 13th, but it cleared

THE PASSAGE OF THE AISNE 57

up later, with sunshine and a strong cold wind, which soon dried the men again. The 4th Brigade marched towards Chavonne, and stopped under the brow of a high hill overlooking the river Aisne. Here there was a halt of several hours in the middle of the day, during which the commanding officers went on ahead with Lieut.-Colonel Feilding, the acting Brigadier, to reconnoitre the opposite heights from the high ground above St. Mard, whence the movements of the Germans could be clearly seen. Meanwhile, the 2nd Battalion Coldstream went forward under the cover of our guns to make good the passages over the canal and the river, the bridges naturally having all been blown up by the Germans. After about two hours it succeeded in driving off the enemy, who were seen running up the hill and disappearing over the sky-line.

In support of it, the 2nd Battalion Grenadiers advanced towards the river, but was then sent off to try and make the crossing about a mile to the east of Chavonne. The only means of getting over, apparently, was by three or four small boats of doubtful buoyancy, and it was clear that for the whole Battalion to cross in this way would be a lengthy business. Pushing ahead, however, to reconnoitre, Lord Bernard Lennox and Major Hamilton found a bridge which they thought at first the Battalion could use, but the moment they were seen on the bridge they were greeted with shrapnel, so well aimed that it was obvious the enemy had got the exact range. So they retired to report the result of their observations.

As it was now getting dark, and no foothold on the opposite bank could be obtained, Colonel Feilding decided to withdraw the 4th Brigade. The 2nd Battalion Grenadiers and 2nd Battalion Coldstream were therefore recalled, and sent into billets at St. Mard. Rain was again falling heavily, and the men were glad to be under cover, while the inhabitants cooked their rations and supplemented them with omelettes and vegetable soup.

Thus began the battle of the Aisne, and had the men only known that it was to go on, not for months but years, and that the same ground would be occupied by the Allies during all that time, they would hardly, I imagine, have shown quite the same dash as they did during the days that followed.

The morning of the 14th broke cold and wet. A thick mist hung over the valley of the river—fortunately for us, since this made artillery observation by the enemy impossible, and enabled the men to cross the river without coming under shell-fire. During the night the R.E. had managed to build a pontoon bridge over the river at Pont-Arcy, and at 5.30 A.M. the brigade moved off to this point. As this bridge was the sole means of crossing for all arms, there was naturally some little delay, and during the period of waiting Colonel Feilding sent for all the commanding officers; he explained the dispositions he had made, and instructed them to make Ostel their objective.

The 2nd Battalion Grenadiers was to form the advanced guard to the Brigade, and Major

THE PASSAGE OF THE AISNE 59

Jeffreys received orders to secure the heights about La Cour de Soupir, and then to push on and make good the cross-roads at Ostel, about a mile farther on. Accordingly the Battalion moved off, crossed the river, and marched to Soupir—without opposition. Had some German officer blundered, or did the enemy not intend to dispute the passage of the river? It seemed inconceivable that, if they intended to hold the position, the enemy should allow a whole battalion to cross unmolested.

At Soupir the road ran uphill through a dense wood, and it was impossible to see very far ahead. Progress was necessarily very slow, and the advanced guard had orders to move with the utmost caution. No. 1 Company, under Major Hamilton, formed the vanguard, and half of No. 2 Company, under Captain Symes-Thompson, was sent as a flank guard to the left, where the ground rose steeply above the road, and the trees were very thick. About half-way the vanguard came into touch with the German outposts. At the same time they were joined by some men of our 5th Brigade, who had gone too far to their left, and in consequence had narrowly escaped being captured by the enemy.

Word was sent back by Major Hamilton that he was not at all happy about his left flank, which was on the high ground towards Chavonne, and Major Jeffreys despatched the rest of No. 2 Company to support Captain Symes-Thompson and strengthen that flank. Two platoons of No. 1 and one platoon of No. 2 were sent off to the left, and, having got into touch with the cavalry on that flank, took up a position in the woods above Chavonne, where they remained for the rest of the day. Meanwhile, the leading men of the advanced guard, under Lieutenant Cunliffe, pushed on, and near La Cour de Soupir ran right into the enemy, who were in superior numbers. All the men were taken prisoners, and Lieutenant Cunliffe was wounded.

But the rest of the advanced guard were also pressing forward, and soon the positions were reversed. Faced with the alternative of capture or retiring before a stronger force, the German officer in command decided on the second course. This meant perforce abandoning the prisoners; but there was one thing at any rate that a German officer still could do. Remembering the teachings of his Fatherland, that the usages of war were a mere formula, and the most dastardly crime excusable if any advantage could be got from it, he deliberately walked up to Lieutenant Cunliffe, who was lying wounded on the ground, pulled out his revolver, and shot him dead.

As to what eventually happened to the German officer there is some conflict of evidence. Some of the men of the Battalion swore that they recognised him among the prisoners who were led away that evening. Another story, which was generally believed at the time, is that Captain Bentinck, with a company of Coldstream, happened to come up just in time to see this cold-blooded murder, and that the men were so infuriated that they bayoneted the German on the spot. But this version can hardly be true,

THE PASSAGE OF THE AISNE 61

for the Coldstream did not arrive till a good deal later.

Shells were now screaming through the trees with monotonous regularity, and the hail of bullets grew ever thicker as the advanced guard came up to La Cour de Soupir. It became evident that the Germans were not only in strength at the top of the hill, but were advancing across the open against our left flank, and at the same time trying to surround the advanced guard by working through the woods on the right flank. No. 3 Company, under Captain Gosselin, was sent off to the right with instructions to clear the enemy off some rising ground and protect the right flank. This it succeeded in doing, but found vastly superior numbers opposed to it, and could not make any farther progress. It was here that Lieutenant des Vœux was killed, being hit through both lungs by a chance shot in the wood.

Urgent appeals from the firing line induced Major Jeffreys to send two platoons of No. 4 to help No. 1 Company, and one to the right for No. 3, while the remaining platoon, with the machine-guns, under Lieutenant the Hon. W. Cecil, was posted on the edge of a clearing in case those in front were driven back.

The advanced guard had now done its part. It had ascertained where the enemy was posted, but if an advance was to be made, it was clear that it would have to be strengthened considerably. Colonel Feilding therefore sent the 3rd Coldstream up to the left of the road and the Irish Guards to the right. Pushing through

Chapter V.

2nd Batt.
Sept.
1914.

Chapter V.
2nd Batt. Sept. 1914.

the woods and picking up platoons of No. 1 and No. 2 Companies Grenadiers, these troops came up to the hard-pressed No. 1 Company on the open ground near La Cour de Soupir.

Here the Germans' attempt to cross the open was effectively stopped by our rifle-fire, and the whole of their firing line was wiped out. But even with these reinforcements we were still outnumbered, and an advance remained impossible.

On the right the Irish Guards had come up to No. 3 Company, and, carrying it on with them, managed gradually to clear the wood. As they did so they disposed of the German snipers, who had shot many of our officers. Lord Guernsey and Lord Arthur Hay of the Irish Guards were killed, and several other officers wounded. In the Grenadiers Lieutenant F. W. des Vœux was killed, while Captain Gosselin was wounded in the hand and Lieutenant Welby in the shoulder, but they refused to retire, and gallantly stuck to their posts.

During this wood-fighting a young soldier of the Grenadiers, Private Parsons, collected twelve men belonging to a battalion in another brigade, who were lost and had no officer or N.C.O. He got them together and commanded them for the rest of the fight, giving his orders clearly and coolly, and never making a mistake. He was promoted to Corporal on the field, and was mentioned in despatches of October 18, 1914. To the general regret of the Battalion, he died of wounds some ten days later.

By now the firing line was fairly well estab-

THE PASSAGE OF THE AISNE

lished behind the banks of some slightly sunken roads north and east of La Cour de Soupir; it was composed of Grenadiers, Coldstream, and Irish Guards, all mixed up together, as they had come through the woods by companies or platoons, just as the situation demanded. Though the German shells were still crashing into the trees and searching the woods, our own guns were answering back, in spite of having hardly a tenth of the ammunition.

During this time Lieutenant Walker, Lieutenant Harcourt Vernon, and Lieutenant MacKenzie were all badly wounded.

But while a satisfactory foothold had been obtained here, Sir Douglas Haig found that there was a gap between the First and Second Corps. Being very hard pressed, with no reserves available, he sent back for help to the Commander-in-Chief, who at once placed the Cavalry Division at his disposal. On foot, the cavalry was despatched to the left to prolong the line occupied by the 4th Brigade, and succeeded in repelling the German attacks.

A steady fire was being kept up by the 4th Brigade at the German front line, which was lying down close in front of it in a mangel and beet field, and therefore very hard to see. The German fire suddenly began to slacken, and the moment seemed to have arrived for a charge, when, without any warning, the men in the German leading line ran forward with their hands over their heads in token of surrender, and at the same time white flags appeared in various parts of the line. At once a large number of

Chapter V.
2nd Batt.
Sept. 1914.

our men leaped up and ran to meet them. Major Jeffreys and Major Matheson, fully alive to the possibilities of danger, shouted and yelled to them to stop, but the men ran on, eager to capture so many prisoners, and soon British and Germans were mingled together in a confused mass.

At this point the German supports opened fire on them all, mowing down friend and foe alike, and killing a large number of both sides. Most of those who were unhit dropped down at once where they were in the root field, and when it got dark many of the Germans walked into our lines and surrendered. It must be added that there is no evidence that this treachery was deliberately planned. It would seem that the leading line had had enough, and genuinely meant to surrender; the supports had no such intention, and there is thus perhaps some justification for their action. But it was a lesson to the 4th Brigade which it never forgot. Thenceforth the white flag was looked on with suspicion, and whenever it was used, not a man moved from his place.

After a hurried consultation between Major Matheson, Major Jeffreys, and Major Lord Bernard Lennox, it was agreed that, while Major Jeffreys held the enemy in check in front, the other two should take some men with them, and try to work round the German flank. This operation took some time, but evidently it surprised the Germans, who were holding a ridge about 500 yards in front of our firing line. Many of them could be seen running from right to left

THE PASSAGE OF THE AISNE

across the front, and offered a fine target for our men posted at the edge of the wood—the shooting was good and hardly a man escaped. Lieutenant Stewart was ordered to advance with a platoon of No. 4 Company, and managed to get on another 300 yards when he was wounded.

The difficulties of the situation were now borne in on Major Jeffreys and Major Matheson. It was getting dark, and they could get no orders from Brigade Headquarters, as the telephone wires had all been cut by bursting shells. Signalling was out of the question owing to the density of the woods. Meanwhile, the Germans were still shelling the road, and it seemed only too probable that the orderly who had been bringing instructions from the Brigade had been killed on his way. The men were dead-tired, having had nothing to eat all day, and Major Matheson, who had found it a very hard matter to get through the wood to the right, came to the conclusion that no advance could be made in this direction without reinforcements.

Therefore it was decided that the only thing to do was to re-sort the battalions and to dig in where they were. A point of junction was arranged, and the much mixed battalions were reorganised; digging started, and the men, tired out as they were, set to work with a will, and soon produced a trench. Thus was the beginning made of that long line of trenches which was eventually to stretch from the Argonne to the Belgian coast, and which formed the battle-ground of the two armies for years to come.

Converted into a dressing-station, the farm

CHAPTER V.

2nd Batt. Sept. 1914.

of La Cour de Soupir was filled with wounded, British and German. The ground in front of our trench was covered with dead and wounded Germans, but though as many stretcher-bearers as possible were sent out and worked all night long, it was not easy to find them in the darkness. It was a striking point of difference that while our wounded hardly made a sound, the Germans never stopped groaning and crying out : there was a continuous chorus all through the night of "Kamerad, Kamerad," and "Wasser, Wasser." A regular pile of Germans was discovered round two haystacks, while in a stubble-field close by was an almost complete firing line, laid out in a row, and all dead. Shelling began again at dawn before all the German wounded could be brought in.

Soon the farm was crowded, and the men for whom there was no room were put in the outbuildings. The removal of the wounded from the farm to the rear proved a great difficulty. The pontoon bridge at Pont-Arcy had been smashed, and on that side of the river, unfortunately, there were only four horse ambulance-wagons ; these, with their fagged-out horses, had to plod throughout the night up and down the steep hill which led to the farm, taking only a few wounded at a time.

Behind the farm was a deep quarry with several caves in it ; here the men not actually required for the firing line were stationed—comparatively safe except for an occasional shell from a German howitzer. The three or four hundred prisoners the Battalion had taken

THE PASSAGE OF THE AISNE 67

were herded together in the quarry under a guard and sent downhill next day. They made no attempt to hide their pleasure at escaping from the battle.

While Major Jeffreys was superintending the digging, a man of the Irish Guards arrived and said that as he was searching for the wounded, a German officer had come up to him and expressed a wish to surrender, but added that he would only give himself up to an officer. Thereupon Major Jeffreys told the man to find the German, if possible, and bring him in. When the man came back he reported that the original officer had refused to come so far, but that he had met another, who as willingly accompanied him. Out of the darkness stepped a tall, smart-looking Ober-Leutnant, who clicked his heels, saluted, and said in perfect English, "I wish to surrender." Major Jeffreys was at no pains to conceal his contempt for this poor specimen of an officer, and handed him over to one of the junior officers of the Grenadiers to take to the quarries.

That night the position of the 4th Brigade was as follows. On the left, in touch with the Cavalry Division, was the 2nd Battalion Coldstream, then the 3rd Battalion Coldstream and the 2nd Battalion Grenadiers, with the Irish Guards on the right. The 2nd Battalion Coldstream had been in reserve, but when there seemed a danger of the enemy getting between the First and Second Corps, the two companies of this battalion were sent off to strengthen the left flank.

CHAPTER V.

2nd Batt. Sept. 1914.

68 THE GRENADIER GUARDS

CHAPTER V.

2nd Batt.
Sept.
1914.

The First Corps had managed to establish itself across the Aisne on a line running from Chemin des Dames on the right, through Chivy and Soupir to the Chavonne—Soissons road, the latter portion being held by the 1st Cavalry Brigade. But the Fourth and Fifth Divisions had not been so successful, and had been unable to do more than maintain their ground. On the extreme left the Sixth French Army had got some distance over the Aisne, but the Fifth French Army had made no headway.

In his account of the day's achievements Sir John French wrote:

> The action of the First Corps on this day under the direction and command of Sir Douglas Haig was of so skilful, bold and decisive a character that he gained positions which alone have enabled me to maintain my position for more than three weeks of very severe fighting on the north bank of the river.

Sept. 15.

On the 15th Sir John French made an endeavour to strengthen the line, and consequently there was no need for the 4th Brigade to advance. All day it was shelled, and had to meet vigorous counter-attacks. It was holding a line which was really too long for it with its scanty reserves, and it is inexplicable why the enemy did not take advantage of this and drive it back to the river.

The morning was spent by the 2nd Battalion Grenadiers in improving the trenches. About noon it was heavily shelled, and as the enemy seemed to have the range of the trench, the men were withdrawn into the wood, a certain number being left to keep watch. They proceeded to watch, not without some quiet satisfaction, the empty trench being plastered with shrapnel that did no harm to any one.

More parties were sent out at dawn next day to collect the wounded, some of whom must have been lying out between the lines for nearly two days. A good many were brought in, but the work had to be stopped as soon as it was light, as the Germans deliberately shelled our stretcher parties. About 11 A.M. a shell set fire to a large stack, on the right of the farm, occupied by Captain Ridley and two men—they had been posted on top of it to snipe the German fire observation post, more than 1100 yards away. Captain Ridley had taken no notice of the shells that had been bursting all round him, but coolly stuck to his work, but now he was forced to abandon it, dazed by the explosion, and unhurt, though both the men with him were wounded.

Helped by the blazing rick to locate the farm, the German artillery now began to plaster it with common shell, shrapnel, and H.E. It is possible that if they had known it was full of their own wounded they would not have gone for it quite so furiously. However that may be, they finally got it alight, and then followed a scene of hopelessly illogical chivalry, our men risking their lives to save the German wounded from their own shells. The wounded were eventually carried out of the burning building and put in a safer place. At the same time, the Battalion Headquarters and the horses were moved down into the quarry.

Chapter V.
2nd Batt.
Sept. 1914.

As this violent shelling seemed to portend an attack, the trenches were fully manned, with the result that there were many casualties. One shell landed right in the trench and killed Lieutenant Welby and the men near him. He had been slightly wounded in the shoulder a couple of days before, but had refused to go to hospital. Although our gunners replied gamely, they could not compete with the lavish German expenditure of ammunition.

A report having come in that the enemy were advancing, Major Jeffreys ordered No. 2 Company to come up from the quarry, and line its northern edge, so as to be available as a support. It had hardly been there a quarter of an hour when an 8-inch high explosive just missed the farm, and, grazing the roof, pitched right on the edge of the quarry. A terrific explosion followed, and out of the 103 men who had been brought up, only 44 were left, all the rest being killed or wounded.

This same shell also killed three officers and a large number of men of the Oxfordshire Light Infantry, and Lieutenant Huggan of the R.A.M.C., but Major Jeffreys, Major Lord Bernard Lennox, Captain Powell, and Captain Pike escaped untouched, for some unaccountable reason, though they were sitting within a few yards of where it exploded, and men were killed and wounded on every side of them, some of them under cover. The trees on the bank fell down with a crash, and the whole quarry itself was filled with a dense yellow-black smoke.

It was a most disastrous shot, and, to make matters worse, the only medical officer on the spot had been killed, and there was no qualified person to attend to the wounded, with whom the caves in the quarry — seemingly the only safe spot — were now packed. The scene there was terrible. There was no light of any sort until a single candle was procured from somewhere. By its faint and uncertain glimmer ghastly glimpses could be caught of men writhing in pain, with their limbs smashed to pieces. Into one corner were crowded the German prisoners, glad of any shelter from the German shells, and there were also a large number of German wounded, who moaned and cried through the night. The officers and N.C.O.'s of the Grenadiers, who had just left the trenches to get a rest, had to give up all idea of that: they set to work and bound up with such skill as they possessed the wounds of friend and foe.

In the front trenches, meanwhile, shelling went on incessantly, and there were many counter-attacks, directed against the part of the line held by the Coldstream. During the evening two companies of the Oxfordshire Light Infantry were sent up to take over the trenches next morning. After dark the supports were brought from the quarry to the garden at the back of the farm, so as to be near at hand in the event of an attack.

One of the Battalion's much-regretted losses this day was Captain the Hon. W. A. Cecil. He had been in the thick of every engagement since the start, and had gained a great reputation in the past three weeks for the effective way in which he handled the machine-guns. On more than one occasion his keenness had led him into very dangerous corners, and it was while he was reconnoitring for a good position for his machine-guns that he was killed. Lieutenant Stewart was wounded, and Captain Gosselin, who had pluckily stayed with his company, though he was in great pain from the wound he received two days before, was now obliged to go into hospital.

Sept. 17. The Battalion was relieved just before dawn, and went into billets at Soupir. Officers and men alike were dead-beat, and slept through most of the day. The cold, wet nights had begun to tell on many of them, and some went sick. Among these was Prince Alexander of Battenberg, who got a bad chill, and had to be sent down to the base.

Sept. 18. On the 18th the Battalion went back to the trenches to relieve the Coldstream, to the left of the position it had held before. No. 1 and No. 2 Companies were in the firing line, and No. 3 and No. 4 in reserve. The moment they arrived they started digging and deepening the trenches, knowing that they would be under constant shell-fire during the day, and in places they could see the Germans doing the same, some 700 yards away. But before they could get through very much, the shelling began, and shrapnel came bursting all over them.

All through the day the roar of shells and rifle-fire went on, varied now and then by high-explosive shells from the howitzers, which made holes big enough to bury three or four horses in. Major Jeffreys, with Captain Howell, R.A.M.C., came to inspect the trenches, but at that moment the shelling became particularly vigorous and accurate, and they were obliged to accept the hospitality of Lord Bernard Lennox, who placed at their disposal the hole he had dug for himself. But as it had only been made for one, the owner was not altogether sorry when a lull in the firing made it possible for the visitors to continue their tour.

It should be mentioned here that the trenches during the first few months of the war consisted not of continuous lines of trench, but of a series of deep holes holding three to four men apiece, and separated from the next by some 10 feet of undug earth, which formed a natural traverse. There was hardly any parapet, and the earth was scattered to the front. The advantage of this type of trench was that it was difficult to locate and destroy by artillery, but if the enemy was near at hand vigilant communication either laterally or to the rear was practically impossible.

The supports and reserves were all hidden in caves very like those they had occupied in the quarry behind their first position. They were well rationed, with plenty of fresh meat, vegetables, and jam. They were, indeed, very much better off than the men in the trenches, for it turned very cold again at night, and rain fell heavily.

It was not hard to guess the reason for the severe bombardment and continual counter-attacks. This was one of the few positions where the Allies had succeeded in obtaining a foothold across the river, though why the Second Division

CHAPTER V.
2nd Batt.
Sept.
1914.

was allowed to get over at Pont-Arcy unmolested has never been explained. The Germans were not only far superior in numbers, but had a supply of shells and ammunition out of all proportion to that of the Allies; moreover, they had chosen an exceptionally good position and possessed heavy guns, such as were unknown in the British and French Armies. Though General Maunoury's Sixth French Army had at first advanced some distance on the extreme left, it had afterwards been held up, and was now only just holding back the enemy counter-attacks, which threatened to drive it back on the river. The British Army's task was the hardest of all, and the Second and Third Corps had been unable to establish themselves securely on the other side.

After the first few days of the battle, the German General Staff determined to direct its energies against the Sixth French Army and the right of the British Army, and to force back over the river the troops which had crossed. So the line occupied by the 4th Brigade came in for more than its share of artillery fire. This hurricane of shells was no doubt intended to prepare the way for the infantry counter-attacks, but wherever the Germans attempted an attack they found our men coolly waiting for them, and absolutely unshaken by the bombardment.

Our artillery's work in this battle aroused the greatest admiration among the Guards Brigade. Vastly outnumbered, with none of the heavy guns the enemy had, and in obviously inferior positions, it fought on gallantly

THE PASSAGE OF THE AISNE 75

in spite of great losses, and often succeeded in silencing the batteries which were shelling our trenches.

Brigadier-General the Earl of Cavan (an old Grenadier) arrived on the 19th, and took over the command of the Brigade, while Lieut.-Colonel Wilfred Smith assumed command of the 2nd Battalion Grenadiers. The Battalion remained in the trenches till the 21st and repulsed several attacks. Though the German infantry never seemed anxious to come to close quarters, their artillery made up for this hesitation by a prodigal expenditure of shells. Lieut.-Colonel Smith described in a letter a calculation he made during a bombardment which went on continuously for six hours; he timed the rate of the falling shells, and found that it came to an average of fifty shells a minute.

The nights were constantly disturbed by false alarms. It was the German practice to send out specially selected snipers to keep the whole line from having any rest. There is nothing more contagious than night firing; the snipers would start the men in front of them firing, and soon it would spread till there was a dull roar all down the line. Supports and reserves would stand to arms until it had died down, and then the Germans would start all over again in another part of the line, with the same result. By this time, too, the trenches were beginning to fill with water in places, which added to our men's hardships.

Every day there were some casualties, but considering the amount of ammunition expended

CHAPTER V.

2nd Batt. Sept. 1914.

Sept. 19–20.

Chapter V.
2nd Batt.
Sept. 1914.

they were really very slight. Lord Congleton had a lucky escape. He was sent for to Battalion Headquarters to make a report, and on his return found that his shelter had been blown to atoms. On the same day Lord Bernard Lennox had an even narrower shave. Taking off his greatcoat, he laid it on the back of the trench, but had hardly gone two or three paces when there was a terrific explosion. When he looked round, he saw that the right arm of his coat was gone altogether and the left cut to ribbons.

Sept. 21. At 4 A.M. on the 21st the Battalion was relieved by the Irish Guards under Lieut.-Colonel Lord Ardee, who, with Captain Lord Francis Scott, had been attached from the Grenadiers, and retired to Soupir. Captain Ridley was sent to inspect the trenches occupied by the 3rd Battalion Coldstream with a view to taking them over next morning, but this order was afterwards cancelled, and Lieut.-Colonel Smith, Captain Symes-Thompson, and Captain Colston went with the same object to the trenches west of Chavonne.

Sept. 22. Next day the Battalion marched at dawn to Chavonne, and took over the trenches held by the 1st Cavalry Brigade, which was very glad to relinquish its position. Cavalry at that time had no bayonets, and so were at a serious disadvantage in a night attack. A company being so much stronger than a squadron, only two platoons of each company were needed for the front trenches, the other two being kept in reserve. No. 3 and No. 4 Companies went into the trenches, No. 1 and No. 2 into billets. Though

THE PASSAGE OF THE AISNE 77

there was continual shelling here too, it was nothing compared with what the Battalion had got accustomed to; in fact, the universal opinion was that it was quite a quiet spot.

For nearly three weeks the 2nd Battalion Grenadiers remained in the trenches, two companies at a time. The general impression in the firing line seemed to be that the centre was waiting till the flanks could push on. There were also constant stories about the Russians. What really happened was that, with inferior numbers, General Joffre was unable to turn the enemy out of their positions. On the other hand, the Germans had given the Allies time to entrench themselves, and found it equally impossible to advance. Trench warfare had begun, and had come to stay. Months of comparative inaction were to follow, while the artillery pounded away at the infantry in the trenches.

"No man's land" between the trenches was covered with unburied bodies, but for either side to venture out merely meant adding to their number. The trenches were gradually improved and deepened, and communication trenches were dug in every direction. Rabbit netting was procured from the neighbouring woods and converted into wire entanglements, but at that time, with the exception of the Minenwerfer, there were none of the specially constructed infernal machines which later were to play such a large part in trench warfare. The infantry crouched in the trenches, while the artillery tried to reach it with every kind of shell; and though the casualties were sometimes considerable, on the

CHAPTER V.

2nd Batt. Sept. 1914.

Sept. 22–Oct. 11.

whole the infantry succeeded in keeping itself protected.

Occasionally an extra heavy dose of shelling warned the firing line that a counter-attack was in view, but when it came to the point of cold steel the German troops showed no inclination to close with our men. Another indication of a coming attack was the playing of the band of some German regiment, which was heard on one or two occasions—evidently as a stimulant for the men who were to take part. Raids were periodically made to catch the enemy's snipers, hidden in trees and hay-ricks. Some N.C.O.'s showed themselves particularly clever and resourceful in carrying out these excursions, but rashness cost a good many lives.

A welcome end was at last put to the continual night firing in which the German snipers had succeeded in involving us. Lieutenant Donald Miller, who was in command on the left, which was their favourite approach, gave orders that no one was to fire without his leave. He took upon himself the responsibility of distinguishing between sniping and a regular attack, and with entire success. Isolated shots were ignored, and the supports and reserves had a quiet night; the other companies soon learnt the trick, and before long there were no more false alarms.

On September 27 Captain Colston was seized with appendicitis, and had to be sent home for an operation. Captain Ridley took his place, but on the same day was hit on the head and between the shoulders by fragments of a shell which exploded near him. Fortunately his

THE PASSAGE OF THE AISNE 79

wounds were not serious, and after having them dressed he went back to the firing line.

In the first week of the battle of the Aisne the losses had been exceptionally heavy, but during the latter part of the time in which the British occupied the position, they were comparatively light. Sir John French estimated that from the start of the battle to the day the British Army left we lost altogether—in killed, wounded, and missing—561 officers and 12,980 men. On October 5 Captain Robin Grey, an officer of the Grenadiers attached to the Royal Flying Corps, was brought down while flying over the enemy's lines and made a prisoner.

Now the situation again changed. All along the French line there had been very heavy fighting, but while the Germans had been unable to pierce the line our Allies had equally failed to advance, though Maunoury had managed to extend his flank up to the Oise, while the new armies of Castelnau and Maud'huy were gradually lengthening the line in a northerly direction. Simultaneously the Germans had grasped that as nothing could be done on the Aisne the only possible chance of success was to turn to the French left.

So they at once began to stretch out their forces to the right, sending out huge masses of cavalry, and in their endeavour to find the French left pushed farther and farther north. They were not content with merely parrying French moves; they determined to outstrip them. They had shorter lines of communication and many more men than the Allies, and it is therefore

CHAPTER V.
2nd Batt.
Oct. 1914.

all the more to the credit of the French and British Armies that they should have won this race for the coast by a short head.

Having come to the conclusion that an advance on the Aisne was impossible, General Joffre decided that the first-line troops should be gradually replaced by Territorials and sent up to prolong the line on the left. Curiously enough, precisely the same instructions were at the same time issued to the German Army, and Landwehr troops were gradually brought into the trenches.

This decision was to alter the fortunes also of our own troops. When the French Army began its various moves, Sir John French went to General Joffre, and pointed out the difficulties in which the British Army was placed by being in the centre of the line. All the supplies in coming from England had to go through Paris and cross those intended for the left of the French line, with the risk of probable confusion. The right place for the British Army, therefore, was clearly on the left, where supplies could reach it with the least possible delay. He also put forward the purely sentimental advantage to be gained by our army operating as a separate unit and expanding on its own front.

General Joffre saw the force of these contentions, and agreed to the British Army being moved up to Belgium, French Territorials taking up its former position. It should be explained that Territorials in France are in no way the equivalent of our own; they are all men who have served in the Army, but are over the age for active fighting. In fact, they correspond to the German Landwehr.

The necessary arrangements for withdrawal and relief were made. The operation began on October 3, and the Second Cavalry Division under General Gough marched from Compiègne en route for the new front. The Army Corps followed in succession at intervals of a few days, and the move was completed by October 19, when the First Corps detrained at St. Omer. This transfer of hundreds of thousands of men from one point of the country to another without a hitch was a striking testimony to the qualities of the French General Staff.

On the night of the 12th the French Territorials arrived, and took over the trenches of the 2nd Battalion Grenadiers. Though a sturdy lot of men, they had not exactly the inches of a Guardsman, and so found great difficulty in reaching the loopholes, with the result that alterations had to be made all along the line.

Next morning at about 1 A.M. the Battalion marched by way of St. Mard and Vauxcéré to Perles, where it went into billets at a big farm, and had its first real rest out of the range of shell-fire for a very long while. It was generally thought that when the Germans discovered the change which was being made they would send a few high-explosive shells well to the rear of the trenches to catch the retiring troops. But as it happened, the enemy were far too busy with their own movements to pay any attention to what was going on in front, and the Battalion marched away unmolested.

Chapter
V.

2nd Batt.
Oct.
1914.

Oct. 14.

It started off again at 4 o'clock on the 14th and marched to Fismes, where it was to entrain for the north. After the usual long wait for the transport it got off at 7.30. The men were very closely packed, thirty-five or forty having to be put into each small covered truck, so that there was hardly room even to sit down. Through Paris, Beauvais, Amiens, Étaples, and Calais the train slowly wandered on, and finally the Battalion reached Hazebrouck at 7 o'clock next morning.

CHAPTER VI

THE FIRST BATTLE OF YPRES (1ST BATTALION)

MEANWHILE the 1st Battalion Grenadiers remained at Warley until September 1914. In the middle of the month the Seventh Division was formed, and the 1st Battalion Grenadiers was sent to Lyndhurst, near Southampton, where the Division was assembling, and placed in the 20th Brigade.

Major-General T. Capper, C.B., D.S.O., commanded the Division, which was composed as follows :

20th Infantry Brigade. Brigadier-General H. G. RUGGLES-BRISE, M.V.O.
    1st Batt. Grenadier Guards.
    2nd Batt. Scots Guards.
    2nd Batt. Border Regiment.
    2nd Batt. Gordon Highlanders.

21st Infantry Brigade. Brigadier-General H. WATTS, C.B.
    2nd Batt. Bedford Regiment.
    2nd Batt. Yorkshire Regiment.
    2nd Batt. Royal Scots Fusiliers.
    2nd Batt. Wiltshire Regiment.

22nd Infantry Brigade. Brigadier-General S. LAWFORD.
    2nd Batt. Queen's.
    2nd Batt. Royal Warwickshire Regiment.
    1st Batt. Royal Welsh Fusiliers.
    1st Batt. South Staffordshire Regiment.

CHAPTER VI.
1st Batt. Sept. 1914.

Brigadier-General H. G. Ruggles-Brise, who commanded the Brigade in which the 1st Battalion served, was himself an old Grenadier.

It was generally considered that the Seventh Division was one of the finest sent out. Most of the men in it, except the two Guards battalions, had served for several years in India and the Colonies, and were bronzed, seasoned men, thorough professional soldiers.

For artillery the Division had one brigade of horse and two of field artillery, Brigadier-General H. K. Jackson, D.S.O., being in command. The brigade of horse artillery consisted of two batteries only. No howitzer brigade had been provided, but a heavy battery of old 4·7's was added at the last moment. The transport had to be supplemented by farm-carts, afterwards painted grey. The Divisional Cavalry consisted of the Northumberland Hussars, originally commanded by Lord Ridley; unfortunately he became too ill to go to the front, and Lieut.-Colonel Cookson took his place.

The centre of interest was now shifting from France to Belgium. Confused by the conflicting accounts which filtered through, the people at home only grasped that the German advance on Paris had failed, and that there was consequently a stalemate. But Sir John French knew that, even though the Allies had won the race to the sea, there was every danger of the German Army concentrating somewhere in the north and breaking through the line, necessarily weak, of the Allied armies.

Although the Germans were in possession of

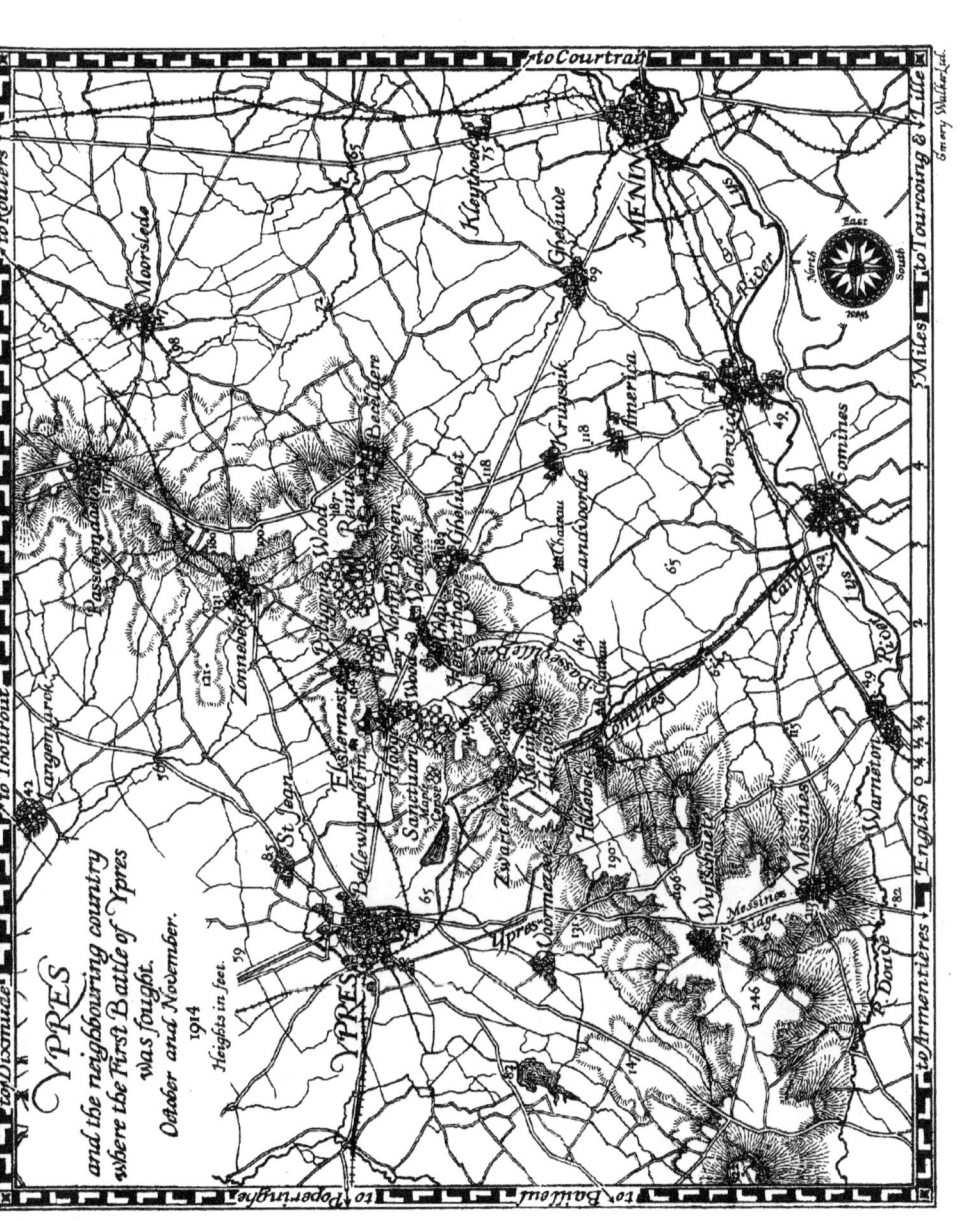

THE FIRST BATTLE OF YPRES 85

the greater part of Belgium, in their hurry to get to Paris they had been unable to dispose entirely of the Belgian Army, which had been so troublesome in the first stages of the war, and which had now retired into Antwerp. Consequently the German General Staff determined to make good the lines of communication by taking Antwerp and reducing all Belgium to ruins. As soon as this had been done all the available troops were to force their way through the Allied line and seize the northern part of France.

The capture of one of the largest towns in Belgium would be hailed with the greatest enthusiasm in Germany, and would also nip in the bud any scheme for sending British troops and guns to help the besieged Belgian Army. Germany knew that at present we had no guns capable of competing with hers, but if she delayed there was no reason why we should not manufacture them up to any calibre.

But, undeterred by our lack both of men and guns, the British Government had made up its mind to do *something*, at any rate, and the Naval Division, which had been intended as a Reserve for the Fleet, were accordingly despatched to Antwerp. This expedition was a glaring instance of our lack of preparation in the early stages of the war. Totally untrained, the men, many of them, knew nothing of the mechanism of the rifles they were armed with; they had no transport, and were given for their conveyance London motor omnibuses, with the familiar advertisements still on them.

This force was greeted with wild enthusiasm

when it arrived in Antwerp on October 4. Major J. A. C. Quilter, Captain A. E. Maxwell, and Lieutenant W. R. C. Murray, all officers of the Grenadiers, were lent to the Naval Division. Captain Maxwell was severely wounded in the subsequent fighting, and afterwards died, but the other two returned safely to England. Major Quilter, who remained attached to the Naval Division, was killed later in the Dardanelles while in command of the Hood Battalion.

With the monster German guns brought up against the town, the fall of Antwerp was a foregone conclusion. The Belgian artillery was quite outranged, and could make no sort of a reply, and the Naval Division had no heavy guns at all. So one-sided was the contest that for the defenders it was merely a matter of looking on while the huge shells fell and gradually devastated the town. On October 8 Antwerp capitulated, and there was a wild, confused rush by the inhabitants to get away. The Belgian Army and the greater part of the Naval Division managed to escape from the town, but about 18,000 Belgian troops and 15,000 British were forced up into Holland and interned.

Suddenly, when it had settled down to a sort of peace-manœuvre life at Lyndhurst, the Seventh Division received its marching orders. The Government had decided to send it to help the Belgian Army. It was practically the only available unit, except the Third Cavalry Division, which was sent off a few days later.

It was a quiet, peaceful Sunday when the

THE FIRST BATTLE OF YPRES 87

summons came. There had been so many rumours and alarms that no one took much notice of them, and the idea of departure had faded to a remote possibility. Passes had been given to the men to remain out till 9.30, and a field-day was arranged for the next day. Then came the order to embark at once from Southampton. In an instant there was feverish bustle and energy throughout the camps. The 1st Battalion Grenadiers marched off to Southampton, and was joined there by many men who were out on pass, but by the time the ship sailed all the Battalion was reported present.

Chapter VI.
1st Batt. Oct. 1914.

Embarking on October 4, the Seventh Division succeeded in avoiding the enemy's mines and submarines on its voyage to Zeebrugge, but the Cavalry Division was unable to follow, and was diverted to Ostend instead.

Oct. 4.

The following is a list of the officers of the 1st Battalion Grenadier Guards, who went out with the Battalion—all but a few of them were killed or wounded:

Lieut.-Colonel M. Earle, D.S.O. .	Commanding Officer.
Major H. St. L. Stucley . . .	Second in Command.
Lieut. Lord Claud N. Hamilton .	Machine-gun Officer.
Capt. G. E. C. Rasch . . .	Adjutant.
Lieut. J. Teece	Quartermaster.
Major the Hon. A. O. W. C. Weld-Forester, M.V.O. . . .	King's Company.
Captain the Hon. L. P. Cary (Master of Falkland)	,, ,,
Lieut. W. S. Pilcher . . .	,, ,,
Lieut. H. L. Aubrey-Fletcher, M.V.O.	,, ,,
Lieut. J. H. Powell . . .	,, ,,
2nd Lieut. R. O. R. Kenyon-Slaney	,, ,,

88 THE GRENADIER GUARDS

CHAPTER VI.

1st Batt.
Oct.
1914.

Captain the Hon. C. M. B. Ponsonby, M.V.O.	No. 2 Company.
Capt. G. C. G. Moss . . .	,, ,,
Lieut. G. E. Hope	Signalling Officer.
Lieut. T. E. R. Symons . .	No. 2 Company.
2nd Lieut. R. S. Lambert . .	,, ,,
2nd Lieut. M. A. A. Darby . .	,, ,,
Capt. Lord Richard Wellesley .	No. 3 Company.
Capt. G. Rennie	,, ,,
Lieutenant the Hon. A. G. S. Douglas-Pennant	,, ,,
Lieut. P. Van Neck . . .	,, ,,
Lieut. L. G. Ames	,, ,,
2nd Lieut. W. R. Mackenzie .	Transport Officer.
Major L. R. V. Colby . . .	No. 4 Company.
Capt. R. E. K. Leatham . .	,, ,,
Lieut. E. Antrobus . . .	,, ,,
2nd Lieut. S. Walter . . .	,, ,,
2nd Lieut. N. A. H. Somerset .	,, ,,
2nd Lieut. Sir G. Duckworth-King, Bart.	,, ,,

Attached—Lieut. J. G. Butt, R.A.M.C.

The crossing was made in the s.s. *Armenian*, which was fairly comfortable, and the *Turcoman*, just a cattle-boat, with no accommodation at all. The transports did not move out into the Solent till after dark on the 5th, and reached Zeebrugge at six o'clock on the morning of the 7th. Disembarking was none too easy a task, for the jetty was much too small for ships of that size, and there were no cranes or other appliances for unshipping the horses, which just had to be pushed down gangways.

Oct. 7.   Entreaties were made to General Capper by a Belgian colonel and two Staff officers, who had come as a deputation from Antwerp, that he

THE FIRST BATTLE OF YPRES   89

would bring the whole of the Seventh Division into that city. But Sir Henry Rawlinson had already sent orders for the Division to go to Bruges at once. The 1st Battalion Grenadiers made the journey in two trains, and was billeted in the suburb of St. André. Crowds lined the streets, and cheered each battalion lustily as it arrived. All the billeting was arranged without any difficulty, as the Belgian authorities knew to a man how many troops each village would hold.

That evening there was a "procession of humiliation" through the streets of Bruges, a long train of old men and women following in the wake of the priests, who were headed by acolytes swinging their censers. As they walked slowly through the streets, chanting a litany, they made an odd contrast with the masses of fighting men in khaki, and their array of wagons and guns.

Next day the whole Division was ordered to march to Ostend, to cover the landing of the Cavalry Division—a hot, tiring journey it was of fifteen miles, over the usual paving-stones. At Leffinghe, on the outskirts of Ostend, a defensive position was taken up and an attempt made to dig trenches, but the men could not go very deep, as at three feet below the surface they reached water.

Fortunately the Battalion was not called upon to hold them. Just before daybreak it left the trenches and marched into Ostend, where it entrained for Ghent. Sir Henry Rawlinson's plan was to operate on the Germans' left flank

CHAPTER VI.
1st Batt.
Oct. 1914.

and divert their attention from the Belgian Army, which might thus, he hoped, be able to escape from Antwerp.

Indescribable confusion reigned in Ostend. The whole country-side had swarmed in to see what was going on; the Cavalry Division was landing while the Seventh Division passed through to get to the railway station, and their movements were naturally hampered by the throngs of people which surged over the streets and quays. General Capper took with him the 20th and 22nd Brigades under Brigadier-Generals Ruggles-Brise and Lawford, leaving the 21st, under Brigadier-General Watts, to march back to Beernem, where it was to remain in reserve. Meanwhile, the Cavalry Division was to operate in the direction of Thourout.

When the two brigades arrived at Ghent, they found that a small force of French Marines and Belgian cyclists were already holding an outpost line in front of the town. The Germans, it was reported, had just crossed the Scheldt about ten miles to the east, and were moving north-west, with the object of cutting off the Belgian Army and the British and French Naval Divisions, which were evacuating Antwerp.

A second outpost line was taken up by the two brigades in rear of the French Marines, the 1st Battalion Grenadiers being in reserve. There were no machine-guns, and the only ammunition was the 200 rounds carried by each man. Though the artillery had been sent on the night before, it did not arrive at Ghent till twenty-four hours after the infantry, owing to the confusion

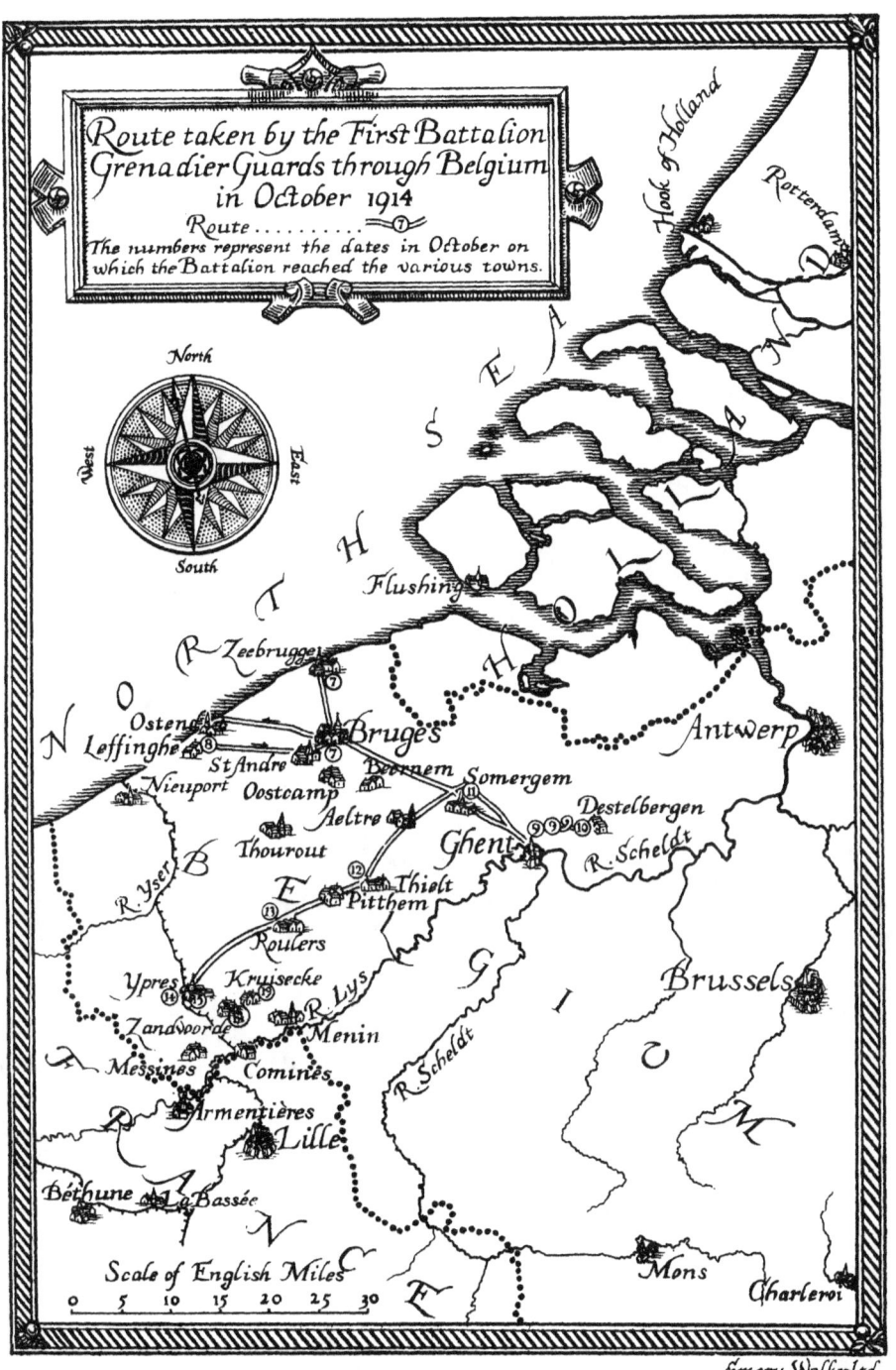

THE FIRST BATTLE OF YPRES 91

there was on the railway line, part of which was in the hands of the Germans.

No. 2 Company of the Grenadiers found one or two piquets blocking the main road, and had a very busy time with the Belgian refugees who were streaming out of Ghent all night long. The other three companies were sent into billets in some large dye-works, but there were so few exits that it was found it would take quite half-an-hour to evacuate the place, so that it was nothing but a death-trap. Accordingly No. 4 Company billeted in a timber yard close by, while the King's and No. 3 bivouacked in an orchard by the roadside.

The nights were cold, and when the Battalion requisitioned for blankets, huge rolls of velvet from the dye-works were issued by the Belgian authorities. Some ten thousand francs' worth of velvet, it was estimated, was damaged in this way. The men naturally did not mind what they looked like as long as they kept warm, but as they lay asleep in the yard, with rich velvet such as Velasquez might have painted wrapped round their khaki, they presented a spectacle decidedly incongruous.

Nothing much happened during the next day, though there were occasional alarms. Firing could be heard in the distance, but no shells or bullets came in the direction of our troops. When it was dark the Battalion was ordered to report to the commander of the outpost line. On the march they met scattered bodies of the French Marines, who had presumably been driven in, and when they got to Destelbergen it appeared

Chapter VI.

1st Batt. Oct. 1914.

Oct. 10.

that the Marines had been withdrawn from this section, which was now only thinly held by such men as could be spared by the Border Regiment on the left.

The King's Company was told to take over this section—by no means an easy task in the dark. The frontage was nearly a mile, with the platoons about six hundred yards apart, and the trenches were useless, being merely shallow rain-shelters, hastily covered over. By working all night the men succeeded in making some sort of a trench by dawn. Orders were received that there could be no retirement in case of attack, and that no support could be looked for.

It was a remarkable situation into which this quixotic operation had forced us. Here was an isolated British Division, with practically no base and with no available reinforcements, operating entirely by itself, while large bodies of the enemy were reported in every direction. But for the information, which was regularly supplied by the aircraft, such a position would have become impossible. The aeroplanes were most active, constantly spying out the enemy's movements, and the armed motor-cars also did very useful work.

Oct. 11. Spades and shovels were obtained from neighbouring cottages at daybreak on the 11th, and the men managed to make really good trenches. But in the afternoon the Battalion was withdrawn, and marched through Ghent. The whole force was retiring, and No. 2 and No. 3 Companies formed the rearguard to the two brigades. It was hardly expected that the Germans would

THE FIRST BATTLE OF YPRES 93

allow the force to get away without a severe fight, but nothing happened, though the enemy was close at hand, and entered Ghent soon after the mixed force of British, French, and Belgians had left the town. Passing through Ghent at dead of night after the cordial reception they had had from the inhabitants two days before, and with the knowledge that the Belgians were being left to the tender mercies of the Germans, was anything but a pleasant experience for the British Force.

Antwerp having fallen, the Seventh Division now got orders to make its way back as fast as it could to Ypres, and there join up with the rest of the British Army. This meant long marches and few intervals of rest, but with the German force that had been freed by the capture of Antwerp close behind, any delay was dangerous.

By dawn on the 12th, Ruggles-Brise's and Lawford's Brigades reached Somergem, and in the afternoon they marched to Thielt by way of Aeltre. At Oostcamp Watts's Brigade joined in and followed the others to Thielt. As the Division drew near that place the halts became more and more frequent—there were constant checks of as much as ten minutes, followed by moves of less than a hundred yards. This was a very trying climax after being up all night and marching all day. The last mile took two hours, and it was not till 1 A.M. that the men reached their billets.

A burst of very heavy rifle-fire at 6 o'clock next morning in the very centre of the town brought every one scrambling out of their billets,

94 THE GRENADIER GUARDS

CHAPTER VI.
1st Batt.
Oct.
1914.

with visions of outposts rushed and Germans in their midst. But it turned out to be only a Taube, at which every one who had a rifle was taking a shot. Eventually it was brought down about a mile off, the Grenadiers, Scots Fusiliers, and Pom-Pom Detachment all claiming the hit.

The whole Division started off for Roulers, followed by the Germans. On its arrival at Pitthem, a force of the enemy was reported to be advancing from the north and north-east. The baggage was therefore sent on, and the 20th and 22nd Brigades were ordered to take up a position in order to cover this change in the order of march. The Germans, however, did not come on, and the march was continued. The Division reached Roulers after dark—with the usual irritating and fatiguing halts. At each village, as the Battalion marched through, the whole population turned out and gave the men apples, cigarettes, and any other offerings they could, but the lion's share naturally fell to the advance guard and the leading battalion, and by the time the tail was reached the supplies had generally given out.

By now the Germans had grasped that this was an isolated Division, and were straining every nerve to catch it, so that the position at Roulers was very precarious. The reports from the aeroplane scouts were disquieting, and General Capper realised that every moment was precious.

Oct. 14. Early next morning the Division marched out of Roulers, and not long afterwards the Germans arrived; in fact, it was said that the rear-guard

THE FIRST BATTLE OF YPRES 95

was hardly clear of the town before the Uhlans were in it. No. 3 and No. 4 Companies, under Captain Lord Richard Wellesley and Major Colby, formed the advance-guard.

Rain fell heavily all the way, and the roads were in a terrible state, but the men's spirits were raised by the news that they were nearly in touch with the Expeditionary Force. These forced marches had told on the troops, and though in the Grenadiers not a man fell out, in some of the battalions men were left behind—never to be seen again. Others, determined not to fall into the enemy's hands, limped doggedly on in a pitiable plight, some having even taken off their boots and tied their puttees round their feet.

They reached Ypres at 2 P.M. on the 14th, and the King's, No. 3, and No. 4 Companies were detailed to find the outposts on the Menin and Messines roads. As the companies moved out to take up their positions they encountered several parties of Uhlans, which caused a good deal of excitement among the men, as they were the first of the enemy's troops actually seen. Some ammunition was expended without much result. But No. 4 Company at any rate accounted for four of these advanced cavalry.

In the evening a report was received that a German force of all arms, estimated to be an Army Corps, was advancing on Ypres from the direction of Comines. Their road was blocked by a platoon of the King's Company, and most of the men were delighted at the prospect of a fight, although those who knew the composition of a German Army Corps were not quite so enthusiastic. Two platoons of No. 2 Company under Lieutenant T. E. R. Symons were despatched to Voormezeele, about a mile in front of the outpost line, to block the road and report at once any movements by the enemy.

These were the first trenches dug on the Ypres battle-ground. The men at that time imagined that they had only to scrape out temporary shelters which would be sufficient protection for a night or two. They little thought that they were laying the foundation of an intricate network of trenches which would be constantly used for the next four years.

The first battle of Ypres which was now about to begin may be said to fall into four clearly marked stages:

A. *Up to October 19*: the operations of the Second and Third Corps from the La Bassée Canal in the south to Armentières and Ploegsteert Wood, in which they forced their way forward in the face of always increasing opposition; the Second Corps establishing itself on the high ground south-west of Lille ("the Aubers Ridge"), although it was being held up on its right by the strong German position of La Bassée; the Third Corps continuing the line northward astride of the Lys. On their left the enemy's cavalry threatened the passages of the Lys from Warneton downward, but could not cross the river. Its operations connected up those of the Second and Third Corps with those of the Seventh Division and Third Cavalry Division, with which General Rawlinson, after advancing eastward to assist in the retirement of the Belgian Army from Antwerp,

THE FIRST BATTLE OF YPRES 97

had fallen back to a position a few miles east of Ypres.

By the evening of October 19 the line of the Second Corps ran approximately from east of Givenchy — Violaines — Lorgies — west of Illies — Herlies to Le Pilly, while between it and the Third Corps was General Conneau's French Cavalry Corps, somewhat to the left rear of the Second Corps. The Third Corps had reached the line Radinghem—Ennetières—Prémesques—Frélinghien—Le Gheer. The British cavalry continued the line down the Lys to the Ypres—Comines Canal, and was in touch with the right of General Rawlinson's command, which, after attempting to advance on Menin on the morning of October 19, had been forced to fall back to the position Zandvoorde—Kruiseik—Zonnebeke by the appearance on its left of large forces of Germans, before which the French cavalry (connecting General Rawlinson's force with the Belgians) was falling back.

The situation, as it then stood, seems to have offered Sir John French two alternatives for the employment of Sir Douglas Haig's Corps, which had then completed its concentration in the area St. Omer—Hazebrouck : he might utilise it to reinforce Generals Smith-Dorrien and Pulteney, who were holding a long front, and whose troops had had over a week of difficult, if on the whole successful, fighting, and lacked the numbers needed for any further advance. Reinforcements thrown in on this quarter might have saved Lille, and enabled the French, in co-operation with whom the British were acting, to outflank the

VOL. I H

Germans opposed to them in the neighbourhood of Loos and Arras. Ever since the battle on the Aisne had reached a deadlock in the middle of September, it had been the object of the Allied forces to outflank the German right, while the Germans had by continually reinforcing and prolonging their threatened flank succeeded in thwarting this effort. It is this double prolongation of the opposing lines, first by one combatant, then by the other, which is called " the Race to the Sea," and of which the first battle of Ypres was the culminating point.

The other alternative was to send in this force farther to the left to carry out a wider turning movement than the mere move round what seemed then the German right south of Lille, and by pushing forward east of Ypres in the direction of Bruges to outflank the German line far more effectively. It is a little difficult to ascertain from the evidence at present available what exactly was known as to the opposition to be expected in such a movement. It would seem that the full strength of the German force available, consisting of several of the newly formed Reserve Corps (raised since the beginning of the war), was hardly appreciated. The idea, prevailing at the British Headquarters, was that if used on the extreme left flank in this way Sir Douglas Haig's part would be essentially offensive; but as things turned out, he was speedily thrown on the defensive, and forced to fight a most desperate battle to prevent greatly superior forces of Germans forcing their way through Ypres to the Channel ports. Badly as the Second

THE FIRST BATTLE OF YPRES 99

CHAPTER VI.

1st Batt. Oct. 1914.

and Third Corps needed help, it was most fortunate that, when the German attack began, it found the First Corps, advancing past Ypres, in its path.

B. *From October 20 to October 28* : the operations in this phase have a two-fold character. On the left Sir Douglas Haig endeavoured to advance first of all north of, and then through, General Rawlinson's troops; and, though to some extent successful, he encountered ever-increasing opposition, so that by October 28 the British in this quarter (east of Ypres, north of the Ypres—Comines Canal) had been definitely thrown on the defensive, and were hard put to it to hold their own against the repeated attacks of considerably superior forces. Meanwhile, on October 20, the Germans had developed a powerful counter-attack against the long and attenuated line held by the Second and Third Corps. The left of the Second Corps at Le Pilly was driven in, and simultaneously General Pulteney's troops were ousted from Ennetières and Prémesques, and these losses, coupled with the great superiority of the German forces opposed to them, compelled the Second and Third Corps to retire. Thus the valuable tactical position of the Aubers Ridge was lost, and the Second and Third Corps compelled to retire to the line Givenchy—Richebourg l'Avoué—Neuve Chapelle—Bois Grenier—Houplines—Le Gheer. At the same time the cavalry north of the Lys was gradually pressed back to the line St. Yvon—east of Messines—Hollebeke—Zandvoorde. Fortunately at this critical time the arrival of the Lahore Division of the Indian Corps provided a much-needed assistance, but, despite this, the village of Neuve Chapelle was lost on October 27, and a counter-attack on October 28 failed to regain possession of it.

C. *From October 29 to November 10* : in this period the operations north of the Lys, where the German attacks reached their maximum in force, were of the greatest importance, fresh troops being constantly put in. South of that river the fighting gradually diminished in intensity, the German attacks being held up by the Second Corps, part of which was relieved by the Indian Corps (the Meerut Division, which arrived in the line on October 31), and the Sixth Division of the Third Corps. A little ground was lost, but nothing of real importance. North of the river the intensity of the fighting increased greatly, and on October 29 the Germans attacked in great strength, but were only able to gain a little ground. Two days later, on October 31, they renewed the attack with the utmost vigour, and made a determined effort to reach the Channel ports. The line of the First Division about Gheluvelt was broken, and the Division fell back. General Lomax and the greater portion of his staff were killed, while the casualties in the rank and file were enormous. The day was saved by Brigadier-General Charles FitzClarence, V.C., who, quickly realising the peril of the situation, ordered the 2nd Battalion Worcestershire Regiment to retake Gheluvelt, although they were not under his command. The First Division gallantly rallied, and regained some of the ground that had been lost, but not without desperate fighting and very heavy losses. At the same time the Fourth

THE FIRST BATTLE OF YPRES

Division of the Third Corps was very hard pressed at Le Gheer, but managed to retain its ground after hard fighting and a successful counter-attack. On November 1 the cavalry, after a most magnificent resistance at Messines and Wytschaete, was finally dislodged from the Messines Ridge. By this time French reinforcements were arriving in large numbers, and they took over the line between the left of the cavalry and the right of Sir Douglas Haig's command (into which the Seventh Division had now been absorbed), but their repeated counter-attacks on the Messines Ridge, and between Wytschaete and the Ypres—Comines Canal were unsuccessful. After October 31 the fighting north of the Ypres—Comines Canal did not reach the same intensity till November 11, but the Germans made repeated attacks, and forced the line back a little at several points. It became necessary to relieve the Seventh Division, whose infantry had been reduced to about a quarter of its original strength, and this was done by putting in about a dozen of the scarcely less exhausted battalions of the Second Corps, which had just been taken out of the line north of La Bassée for a well-earned rest. By November 5 the right of Sir Douglas Haig's line, south of the Ypres—Menin road, was held by the equivalent of a division from the Second Corps, the First Division being in his centre, and the Second on his left, though all three divisions were much intermingled.

By November 10 the cavalry, upported by a few battalions of the Second Corps, had taken over a line west of the Messines Ridge, and on the left of the Third Corps. From the Douve southward to La Bassée the line was approximately established as it remained through the winter of 1914–15, the Third Corps being astride the Lys, while the Fourth Corps (the Eighth Division, which had by this time arrived) continued the line from about Bois Grenier to beyond Neuve Chapelle, the Indian Corps being on the right.

D. *November 11 to 20*: November 11 was the next most critical moment of the battle after October 31; on this day took place the great attack of the Prussian Guard, which broke through the line of the First Division near Veldhoek and penetrated into the Nonne-Bosschen, but was checked there, and then dislodged by a counter-attack by the 52nd Oxfordshire Light Infantry, perhaps the most dramatic of all the individual episodes of the battle. On this day the line of the Third Division south of the Ypres—Menin road was also violently assailed, and some ground was lost; but the net result of the day was the failure of the great German effort to break through, and from that moment the fighting north as well as south of the Lys tended to diminish in intensity. The Germans made a few more attacks, but none in such strength or determination as those of October 31 and November 11, and about November 15 the French began to take over the positions in "the Ypres salient," so obstinately defended by Sir Douglas Haig for nearly four weeks. It may be gathered from the accounts of the fighting of the subsequent months that the Germans were for the moment exhausted, that their supplies of am-

THE FIRST BATTLE OF YPRES 103

munition were running low, and that the attack of November 11 represented their last bolt—until more could be forged. Thus if the Allied effort to outflank the German right and roll up their line had been unsuccessful, defensively the first battle of Ypres was a great success, the German effort to break through being definitely and decisively defeated. November 20 may be taken as the end of the battle, as it was on that day that the last unit of Sir Douglas Haig's command was relieved by the French, the British line then extending approximately from Givenchy in the south to Keniwel in the north. During this fourth phase the operations on the line from the Douve to the La Bassée Canal had been of the character of " normal trench warfare," neither side attempting any major operation.

Ypres was to be held at all costs till the First Corps arrived—those were Sir Henry Rawlinson's orders. There were no other British troops in the neighbourhood when the Seventh Division arrived there, except the Third Cavalry Division, which had been sent on in the direction of Menin to reconnoitre. The Eighty-seventh French Territorial Division was at Ypres, and the Eighty-ninth at Poperinghe (both under General Bidon), while the Belgian Army had reached the Forest of Houthulst.

At first General Capper decided to post the Seventh Division from Zonnebeke to Langemarck, asking the Eighty-seventh French Territorials to hold, for the moment, the line from Zonnebeke to Hollebeke; there they would get into touch with Allenby's Cavalry Division,

CHAPTER VI.

1st Batt. Oct. 1914.

Oct. 15.

Chapter VI.
1st Batt.
Oct. 1914.

which was on the left of the Third Corps. Operating on the left of the Seventh Division, Byng's Cavalry Division would keep touch with the Belgians and French Marines.

But these orders were afterwards cancelled when it was clear that Menin would be the probable line of advance. General Capper made the Seventh Division change places with the Eighty-seventh French Division, so that it now took up the line from Zonnebeke to Hollebeke, with Ruggles-Brise's Brigade on the right, Watts's in the centre, and Lawford's on the left. Four German Army Corps were now rumoured to be operating somewhere in Belgium, but where exactly no one knew.

Oct. 16. A piteous sight confronted the 1st Battalion Grenadiers as it marched eastward towards Zandvoorde on October 16, after a quiet day in billets on the outskirts of Ypres. On the roads it met the whole civilian population of the neighbouring towns and villages, which was in flight before the advancing enemy. Old men and women ran breathless; children trotted by their mothers' sides; some had all their worldly possessions in carts drawn by ponies or dogs; others were pushing wheelbarrows loaded with all the goods they could carry away. All had a look of terror in their eyes, and all hurried madly to safety, spurred on by the thought of the blazing villages that lay behind them.

The advance-guard of the Brigade was formed by the King's and No. 4 Companies under Major Weld-Forester and Major Colby. Progress was

THE FIRST BATTLE OF YPRES 105

very slow, even after daybreak, as there was a fog, and every wood by the roadside had to be thoroughly cleared. A few shots were exchanged with Uhlans, but there was no serious resistance, and the Brigade entered Zandvoorde at 11 A.M. Two miles from Zandvoorde, meanwhile, No. 3 Company under Lord Richard Wellesley had been ordered to Hollebeke to protect the right flank of the Brigade; this Company rejoined the Battalion later on.

CHAPTER VI.

1st Batt. Oct. 1914.

At Zandvoorde a strong defensive position was taken up, facing east; it had a good field of fire, and there was a fairly wide stream two hundred yards from the trenches. The King's and No. 4 Companies were in the front trench, and No. 2 and No. 3 in reserve. That night the enemy played his old tricks, and kept every one awake, with a few snipers firing at intervals into different parts of the line. The men were then new to such devices, but it was not long before they learned to distinguish between sniping and an organised attack.

The following day the whole Brigade was ordered to advance and occupy the ridge Kruiseik — America, with its right bending back to Zandvoorde, the Scots Guards having occupied Kruiseik the night before. At night villages could be seen burning in every direction, set on fire by the Germans, and this was taken as an indication that the enemy was preparing to attack.

Oct. 17-18.

On the 19th orders were received for an advance by the Seventh Division on Menin and Wervicq; it was reported that the enemy was

Oct. 19.

in no great strength, and that his forces consisted principally of Landsturm, with no artillery. The attack was to take place in three phases:

First phase: by the 22nd Brigade on the left against an advance position at Kleythoek.

Second phase: by the 20th and 21st Brigades against Gheluwe.

Third phase: by the whole Division against Menin and Wervicq.

Sir John French, in his despatch of that date, said:

> I considered, however, that the possession of Menin constituted a very important point of passage, and would much facilitate the advance of the rest of the Army, so I directed the General Officer commanding the Fourth Corps to advance the Seventh Division upon Menin and endeavour to seize that crossing on the morning of the 18th.

It was no easy task that was allotted to Sir Henry Rawlinson, for he had nothing to fall back upon. The cavalry under Byng was hardly strong enough to do more than feel for the enemy, and there was therefore only the French Territorial Division at Ypres as a reserve. There was nearly twenty miles of front for the Seventh Division to operate on, and no one knew when the First Corps would arrive.

The advance of the Seventh Division began in the morning. The 1st Battalion Grenadiers deployed for an attack on Gheluwe and Kruiseik, with No. 2 and No. 3 Companies in the firing-line, and the King's and No. 4 in support. The men were extended to eight paces, and each company had a frontage of half a platoon; the Battalion

THE FIRST BATTLE OF YPRES 107

was thus in sixteen lines, with 200 yards between each line, during the preliminary advance under artillery fire.

When about half the Battalion was on the move, the order to advance was countermanded, for news had arrived that a large force of all arms was advancing from the direction of Courtrai. Lawford's Brigade, which had reached Kleythoek, was strongly attacked on its left flank and compelled to fall back with heavy losses. The advance on Menin had been found impracticable; Sir Henry Rawlinson suddenly realised that with a single infantry division it was sheer madness to attack an enemy force which, according to our airmen's reports, was far stronger than Sir John French had anticipated. Being the pivot on which the whole Division had to turn, Ruggles-Brise's Brigade had not gone far when the countermanding order came, but the left of the Division had to retire some distance before it was in line facing the right way.

Ruggles-Brise's Brigade retired to its former position, which consisted of a semicircular line running from Zandvoorde through Kruiseik to the cross-roads on the Ypres—Menin road. To the 1st Battalion Grenadiers was allotted a frontage of nearly a mile, from and including the village of Kruiseik to the cross-roads, on the left being the Yorkshire Regiment from Watts's Brigade and on the right the Border Regiment. No. 2 and No. 3 Companies were in the firing line, and No. 4 and the King's Company in support.

A circular salient is not easy to hold, and after the greater part of the day had been spent in

Chapter VI.
1st Batt.
Oct. 1914.

improving the trenches and putting out barbed wire under intermittent and ineffective shell-fire, orders were received to withdraw the line. This withdrawal was necessitated by the Divisional order to send back two battalions as Divisional Reserve. This left only the Grenadiers and Border Regiment to occupy the whole line. After consulting General Ruggles-Brise, Lieut.-Colonel Earle decided to withdraw Nos. 2 and 3 Companies and convert the support trenches into the firing line. This meant altering the trenches a good deal, as those used for the supports were too wide and shallow. The whole situation had, however, changed, and the Division was now on the defensive.

Oct. 20.

Improvements in the line generally were made next day. Besides being deepened, the trenches were made narrower by driving wash-poles into the bottom about three feet apart, closing up the intervals with doors, shutters, straw hurdles, etc., and then filling up the space behind with earth. This work was practically finished, when it had to be stopped because a reconnaissance was sent out in front with a battery of R.H.A. (13-pounders) to support it, and no sooner had the battery opened fire than it was itself attacked by much heavier artillery from the direction of Wervicq.

For an hour a constant stream of shrapnel and high explosive poured over our trenches. There was one short lull, when our R.H.A. Battery ran short of ammunition, and the Germans, thinking they had knocked the battery out, also ceased fire. On realising their mistake,

THE FIRST BATTLE OF YPRES 109

they began again with renewed energy. High-explosive shells were bursting all down the trenches, back and front, but luckily none landed actually in them; and though a cottage by the side of the road caught fire, the removal of the wood and straw lying near the trench averted all danger. Very grateful the Grenadiers were for the close touch which F Battery under Major Head managed to keep with them during these anxious days' fighting. It was a perfect example of how artillery and infantry should co-operate.

In the afternoon the enemy launched his infantry attack, preceded by scouts and snipers, and covered by artillery and machine-gun fire. Almost for the first time the Germans were now distinctly seen, and there was something almost reassuring in the fact that they looked like ordinary beings. Hitherto they had seemed a sort of mysterious bogey, something far away on the black horizon, an evil force associated with burning houses and fleeing inhabitants. Though their attack was all according to the book, they never succeeded in reaching our trenches. In many places they managed to advance under cover to within 200 yards of our position, but the attack was half-hearted and therefore failed.

The machine-guns under Lord Claud Hamilton were posted on the right of the Battalion, and remained there for seven days, day and night, without relief, under continual fire from the enemy's artillery and machine-guns. During this strenuous time they fired 56,000 rounds, and inflicted considerable loss on the enemy.

CHAPTER VI.

1st Batt.
Oct.
1914.

By dusk the Germans had established a considerable force within striking distance, and the whole British line stood to arms till about 9 P.M., expecting an assault any moment. Why with such enormous advantages the enemy did not make a more determined attack it is difficult to understand. They outnumbered our troops by four to one, and had an overwhelming superiority in artillery. But while the Seventh Division were all seasoned professional soldiers, the German Corps consisted mostly of Landwehr, that is, second-line troops or men retired from the active army.

Nothing happened till midnight, when the enemy suddenly opened a heavy fire, and in places began half-hearted assaults, which were easily repulsed. He kept up a continuous and comparatively useless fire for an hour, but with our men the control of fire was excellent. During these spasmodic attacks the R.H.A. Battery, which was just behind the village of Kruiseik, did most effective work, bursting groups of shrapnel with great accuracy and rapidity over the German lines, at a range of only eight hundred yards. The Seventh Division was occupying more ground than it could properly hold, but with so few troops General Capper had no alternative. Two platoons of No. 2 Company were furnished during the night to support the King's Company in the fire trenches, but even with their help it found the greatest difficulty in filling its part of the line.

Oct. 21.

There was some shelling in the early morning of the 21st, but nothing serious happened till the

THE FIRST BATTLE OF YPRES 111

afternoon, when the enemy at last attacked, apparently, all along the line. So long was the line General Capper was now holding that he found it impossible to keep any reserves. At first the 2nd Battalion Scots Guards was in Divisional Reserve, but it was soon wanted, and was sent up into the firing line in the morning. When appeals for help came afterwards from various quarters, General Capper had only the cavalry to send. The Northumberland Hussars were despatched to fill the gap between the 20th Brigade and the Third Cavalry Division, and when the right flank of the Division needed strengthening the Divisional Cyclist Company was sent thither.

CHAPTER VI.

1st Batt.
Oct.
1914.

By this time the First Corps had arrived, and had been sent up to the north of Ypres. As it turned out, that spirit of dash which won Sir John French his reputation in South Africa proved the saving of the situation. Had he been of a more cautious disposition, he would undoubtedly have sent the First Corps to reinforce General Smith-Dorrien, who was in great difficulties farther south. Its despatch north of Ypres, originally with the idea of a general advance, saved the Seventh Division from utter destruction.

The position of the line was now as follows: the First Corps from Bixschoote to Zonnebeke; the Seventh Division from Zonnebeke to Zandvoorde; then Byng's Cavalry and Allenby's Cavalry up to the left of the Third Corps.

About mid-day the 21st Brigade was heavily attacked, and Brigadier-General Watts sent back for reinforcements. There were none. Some

Chapter VI.
1st Batt.
Oct. 1914.

companies had to be sent in support, and General Ruggles-Brise ordered No. 2 and No. 3 Companies of the Grenadiers to go to its help. Two companies of Scots Guards had already been sent to Zandvoorde to fill up a gap on the right, occasioned by the withdrawal of the 5th Cavalry Brigade, while the remaining two companies were with the Divisional Reserve at Gheluvelt. These continual demands for reinforcements naturally weakened the 20th Brigade considerably. Under heavy shell-fire the Scots Guards started off, but the attack on the 21st Brigade died away, and after they had gone about a mile they were ordered to return, as they might be wanted any moment to support their own Brigade.

Meanwhile the line held by the Grenadiers was heavily shelled, not only by the Germans but by our own guns, which were firing short. The men naturally were infuriated by this, but fortunately the mistake did not last long, as the artillery was soon able to correct its own distance. During the night the German machine-guns had been brought up close, one at least being placed in a house 150 yards from our trenches, and the covering fire from these was most disconcerting. It was generally oblique, and enabled the German infantry to approach with far fewer losses than on the previous day. An infantry attack was made, but was not pressed home, and except for spasmodic bursts of rifle-fire the night was again fairly quiet.

Oct. 22.
Having been in the trenches for four days and nights, the King's and No. 4 Companies were relieved by No. 2 and No. 3 Companies. Air-

THE FIRST BATTLE OF YPRES

craft reports that the enemy was massing troops near America seemed to presage an attack, but except for the inevitable sniping nothing happened in that part of the line, the attack that day being directed against the 22nd Brigade and also against the First and Second Divisions farther north. The relieved companies had not been long in their dug-outs, however, before two platoons of No. 4 Company under 2nd Lieutenant Walter and 2nd Lieutenant Somerset were ordered to occupy some trenches vacated by the 21st Brigade on the left, while the King's Company was sent up to Kruiseik to reinforce No. 2 Company.

CHAPTER VI.

1st Batt. Oct. 1914.

The position of the Seventh Division was now becoming most precarious, holding doggedly on as it was to a line seven miles long, with every man in the trenches. General Lawford's 22nd Brigade had been attacked by a large force and obliged to give ground; this made an ugly dent in the line, and placed the 21st Brigade in an acute and perilous salient. To help the hard-pressed Seventh Division Sir Douglas Haig now sent along the Second Division, which had been relieved by the French Ninth Corps.

Oct. 23.

Owing to the heavy mist on the 23rd neither side could use artillery till 9 A.M., when the enemy began to bombard the Kruiseik salient. The day's attack was directed against the 21st Brigade, and the Wiltshire Regiment had some desperate fighting. The two platoons of the Grenadiers which had been sent up the night before were attacked by two battalions of Germans, but they held their ground and never

114   THE GRENADIER GUARDS

Chapter VI.
1st Batt.
Oct. 1914.

gave an inch. They suffered severely, however, and 2nd Lieutenant Walter and 2nd Lieutenant Somerset were both killed before these platoons were withdrawn. The whole line of trenches was bombarded incessantly, and all day the German guns swept the rear of the line so as to catch the supports as they came up.

A message was sent to the Grenadiers about 2.30 from the Border Regiment on the right to say that their trenches had been blown in, and they might want help. Accordingly the King's and No. 4 Companies were ordered to move across to a position in rear of the Border Regiment, so as to support them if necessary. No sooner had they left their dug-outs and fallen in than they were heavily shelled, though they were well out of sight of the German gunners.

Incidents like this gave rise to stories of spies behind the British lines, who could telephone to the enemy's gunners the exact position of bodies of our troops. But had the Germans had any means whatever of obtaining information they could hardly have failed to know that, instead of the large forces they imagined to be opposed to them, there was nothing to bar their way to Calais but a single unsupported British Division.

When the leading platoons of the two companies of the Grenadiers reached the position indicated, which was the ridge in rear of the Borderers' trenches, they came under the concentrated fire of batteries from three different directions, and suffered some loss. So heavy was the fire that they found it impossible to remain on the ridge, and as the Border Regiment had not

THE FIRST BATTLE OF YPRES 115

definitely asked for support the King's Company was ordered to retire. It retired in good order and in slow time, though under heavy fire all the way. Lieutenant H. L. Aubrey Fletcher and several men were wounded, but the casualties were not so heavy as might have been expected. Fortunately the enemy burst their shrapnel too high, and the ground was so soft that the high-explosive shells did little damage except when they got a direct hit.

A violent attack was made next day on the salient formed by the British line, which at last began to show signs of giving way. After some desperate fighting the Wiltshire Regiment was driven in, and the Germans got possession of Polygon Wood. Ruggles-Brise's Brigade was heavily engaged, as the enemy's attack was being pressed home with great vigour, especially on the left of the Battalion, where the Germans were trying to break through between the Grenadiers and the Yorkshire Regiment. No. 4 Company, under Major Colby, was therefore ordered to counter-attack. Great difficulties were added to its task by the tobacco-drying grounds —ready-made wire entanglements on which the men's packs and accoutrements caught while the German machine-guns were practically enfilading them. But, in spite of everything, Major Colby succeeded in driving back a much larger body of the enemy, and thus making that part of the line secure.

It was a brilliant bit of work, and was specially mentioned by General Capper in his report. But it was very costly: Major Colby, Lieutenant

CHAPTER VI.

1st Batt. Oct. 1914.

Oct. 24.

116 THE GRENADIER GUARDS

Chapter VI.
1st Batt. Oct. 1914.

Antrobus, and a hundred men were killed, and Captain Leatham was wounded. The only officer of this company who escaped unhurt was Lieutenant Sir G. Duckworth-King.

In the evening news arrived that the First Corps was attacking the enemy on the left, and this somewhat relieved the situation. The reserve trenches came in for severe shelling during the night, but, as it happened, there was only a platoon of No. 2 in reserve at the time. It had a curious experience, which might have had serious results. Two companies of the Queen's had been sent up to the reserve dug-outs. Somehow the report was spread that the Germans had got into Kruiseik, and an alarm was raised. The platoon from the Grenadiers stood to arms, and as it waited saw in the moonlight a line of men with fixed bayonets advancing on their flank. They were preparing to meet them with the bayonet when they suddenly realised that they were friends. Major Stucley leaped from the trench, and went himself to explain matters to the two companies, which returned to their original position.

Oct. 25.

The Germans were reported next day to be entrenching all along our southern front and opposite Zandvoorde. About sunset the Grenadiers were attacked, and one platoon from No. 2 Company under Lieutenant Lambert became isolated, the enemy having taken the trench on its right and also the houses behind it. Three messengers were sent back to Battalion Headquarters for help, but only one got through, and he was wounded. Lieut.-Colonel Earle sent up a platoon of No. 3, and

THE FIRST BATTLE OF YPRES 117

the houses in the rear of the line were partially cleared.

A determined attack developed later that night, and a mass of men was seen advancing on the left. A voice called out, "Don't shoot! We are the South Staffords." But the German helmets could be distinctly seen against the glow from a burning farm; a heavy fire was opened on them, and slowly they disappeared. As a matter of fact two companies of the South Staffords had come up to the Battalion as a reserve that night, and the Germans must have known it. In the morning forty or fifty dead Germans were counted in front of the platoon under Lieutenant Lambert, and 200 prisoners were captured by the Scots Guards in a house in rear of the line. Viscount Dalrymple and Captain Fox, with two companies of the Scots Guards, cleared all the Germans out of the village, and restored the line.

During the night Lord Claud Hamilton, whose guns were in action all night, saw a body of men moving in fours down the road behind him, and naturally thought they were men of the Brigade. But as they passed a burning house he saw the German helmets, and turned one of his guns on them, while the other gun continued to engage the enemy in front. He was relieved before dawn by Lieutenant Gladwin of the Scots Guards with a fresh team of men, who took over the Grenadier machine-guns. Soon after he took charge Lieutenant Gladwin was killed.

The First Division had now taken over the line from Reutel to the Menin road, so that the Seventh Division held only the section from the

Chapter VI.

1st Batt. Oct. 1914.

Oct. 26.

Chapter VI.
1st Batt.
Oct. 1914.

Menin road through Kruiseik to Zandvoorde. But this salient had become more and more acute and dangerous, and General Capper decided to readjust the line and reduce the salient as far as he could. To withdraw from a position when at close grips with the enemy was a task requiring careful staff work, but it was successfully carried out that night.

Before dawn the King's Company took over the fire trenches with a platoon of No. 3 under Lieutenant Van Neck, while a platoon from No. 2 under Sergeant Boyles occupied a trench about 200 yards to the left. One platoon of the King's Company was 300 yards to the right of the rest of the company, and another 300 yards farther to the right were the Scots Guards.

A terrific shelling of our trenches began early in the morning, and reached such a pitch that the men counted as many as sixty shells a minute on each small trench. The whole of the enemy's artillery fire was concentrated on Kruiseik. Gallantly our men held on, in spite of the fact that again and again the shells blew in the trenches and buried half-a-dozen men at a time, all of whom had to be dug out with shovels. Some of them had as much as three feet of earth on top of them, and many were suffocated before they could be rescued.

So violent were these attacks that by mid-day the Germans had broken through the line held by two companies of the South Staffords, which had been sent to relieve the Border Regiment. By 2.30 P.M. the enemy had gone through the gap, and had managed to get in rear of two companies

THE FIRST BATTLE OF YPRES 119

of the Scots Guards, which suddenly found themselves surrounded and fired at from all directions. Although the Scots Guards still fought on, they were captured by degrees in small parties, and the survivors were finally made prisoners, including Lieut.-Colonel Bolton, Major Viscount Dalrymple, and Captain Fox. Finding his flank exposed, Lieut.-Colonel Earle at once gave orders to the Grenadiers to retire, but this order did not reach the fire trenches for a long time, and was never received by the King's Company at all. Meanwhile, General Ruggles-Brise ordered the guns back to their old position on the Zandvoorde Ridge, and having collected the remainder of the Scots Guards, the Gordons, and the Borderers, he returned to the hollow west of Zandvoorde.

The position now seemed hopeless for the King's Company and the other two platoons, for the Germans had got round both flanks, and the rest of the Battalion was retiring. Lieutenant Pilcher, one of the officers of the King's Company, managed to get back to Battalion Headquarters, only to find that the Battalion had retired. He started to return at once, but the Germans were closing in on the company, and as there were no communication trenches, he had to advance in the open with the enemy on each side of him. However, he got through to Major Weld-Forester, and told him of the retirement. Meanwhile, Lieutenant Hope, the signalling officer, who had been ordered to retire with the rest of the Battalion, turned back on his own initiative to warn the King's Company, and even got some of the First Division to come to its assistance.

CHAPTER VI.

1st Batt.
Oct.
1914.

Chapter VI.
1st Batt.
Oct. 1914.

At first Major Weld-Forester had determined to hold on grimly to his bit of the line, but it now seemed clear to him that he ought to join in the retirement. To do this meant going clean through the Germans, who were now firmly established in the village and outhouses—but on the other hand to remain meant being surrounded and captured. So he quickly decided to retire and join the rest of the Battalion. He knew he could rely on his men to do anything or go anywhere, and trusted to their discipline to carry through even such a desperate plan as this of forcing a way through the Germans.

Having explained the whole situation to his officers and N.C.O.'s, he sent an orderly to Lieutenant Van Neck, and told him to retire at the same time. But the message never reached this officer, nor did the platoon of the King's Company which was 800 yards away receive the order. The result was that these two isolated platoons continued to fight on until they were overwhelmed by the advancing German masses.

Meanwhile, through the village came the King's Company, with Major Weld-Forester at their head, bayonets fixed and in perfect order. On they came, straight through the Germans, who were at first dumbfounded by the reckless daring of the enterprise. Soon the enemy collected themselves, and the machine-guns began rattling from the windows; but friend and foe were so intermingled that it was difficult for them to fire, and it would have taken better men than the Germans to stop the men of the King's Company, when they had made up their minds

THE FIRST BATTLE OF YPRES 121

to get through. Many casualties there were, of course, but Major Weld-Forester succeeded in joining the Black Watch that night, and linked up with the rest of the Battalion next morning.

Chapter VI.

1st Batt. Oct. 1914.

The same night the retirement of the whole Division was carried out successfully, and it took up a second position running through the cross-roads near Gheluvelt. The remainder of the Grenadiers, under Lieut.-Colonel Earle, retired in good order through the First Division and went into billets on the outskirts of Ypres, where they were joined next morning by what was left of the King's Company. After five days and nights in the trenches without relief the men were utterly worn out, but in spite of their hard fighting and heavy losses their spirits were not depressed nor their discipline in any way relaxed.

On the 27th the 1st Battalion Grenadiers moved from billets outside Ypres to a bivouac in Sanctuary Wood, just south of the Menin road. Ruggles-Brise's Brigade was withdrawn from the Basseville River, and the battalions were re-organised. When the roll was called, it was found that the losses in every battalion had been considerable. The 1st Battalion Grenadiers had lost 9 officers and 301 men, the 2nd Battalion Scots Guards 17 officers and 511 men, the 2nd Gordon Highlanders 3 officers and 159 men, and the 2nd Border Regiment 17 officers and 431 men. What remained of the Seventh Division was now transferred to the First Corps under Sir Douglas Haig.

Oct. 27.

A report was received that the Twenty-seventh German Reserve Division had been ordered to take the cross-roads south-east of Gheluvelt, and

Chapter VI.
1st Batt. Oct. 1914.

the 20th Brigade was ordered to relieve the 22nd Brigade just south of the Menin road. General Ruggles-Brise placed the Grenadiers in the front line next to the road, with the Gordons on their right, while the remnants of the Borderers and Scots Guards were left in support. Guides were furnished by the 22nd Brigade, and General Ruggles-Brise, who knew the ground well, since it was next to his old Headquarters, met them at the cross-roads. As the trenches were very inadequate, most of them mere scratches, and some even facing the wrong way, the Grenadiers were ordered to withdraw at daybreak, if there was no attack, so as to evade shell-fire. As the day dawned, General Ruggles-Brise returned to his Headquarters, where he was met by the Brigade-Major, who told him that an attack was expected at dawn, and that he had received instructions to bring up the two supporting battalions.

On the way up the Scots Guards were so unlucky as to have a shell burst right into one of their companies, causing some twenty casualties. 2nd Lieutenant Gibbs was killed, and Captain Kemble and Lieutenant Lord Dalhousie severely wounded.

It was a melancholy scene through which the Grenadiers marched off. Some ten days before, when they passed through Gheluvelt, they had been greeted by the inhabitants; now it was a deserted ruin. Most of the houses and the church had been demolished, and such buildings as remained looked like dolls' houses, when the fronts have been removed. The roadway was full of

THE FIRST BATTLE OF YPRES 123

great shell-holes, and some carcasses of horses added to the dreariness of the picture. Arrived at their destination, Nos. 2, 3, and 4 Companies were put in the firing line, and the King's Company in support. It was practically dark, and as the trenches were very bad they had to dig themselves in as well as they could.

The German General Staff was now getting impatient. In spite of their immense superiority in numbers and in guns, the Germans had succeeded only in making dents in the line, and had not yet broken through. So they determined to mass their guns and infantry at certain parts of the line, and drive a wedge through—one of the points selected being the left of the line held by the 1st Battalion Grenadiers near the cross-roads. Every one on the British side knew of the projected attack, from General Headquarters down to the latest-joined drummer boy, but foreknowledge was of little use, as there were no reserves available.

At 5.15 A.M. on the 29th—a densely foggy morning—the Battalion was heavily shelled by our own guns; presumably the fire was intended for the German infantry, which was known to be somewhere near. Although every possible precaution had been taken against an attack at dawn, there was no sign of any movement on the part of the enemy, and after the Battalion had waited for an hour and a half, the report of an intended attack was dismissed as untrue. The question then arose as to what should be done to obtain food for the supporting battalions. They had been hurried up in the dark, and no

CHAPTER VI.

1st Batt.
Oct.
1914.

provision had been made for their rations, nor was it possible to bring food up in wagons to positions in such close proximity to the enemy. The Brigadier decided that, as the expected attack had not been made, it would be best to send these two battalions back to get their food, so that on their return they would be prepared to remain in the front trench, and meet any attack that might come later in the day.

They had been gone hardly half-an-hour when the Germans opened a very heavy fire, and in the mist which was still clinging to the ground rifle-fire was poured upon the Grenadiers from the left rear. It was at once realised that the enemy had managed to penetrate the line between the two Divisions. To meet this enfilade fire the left flank of the line turned back, and before long the whole Battalion was forced to leave the fire trenches and occupy the support trenches, which were far too deep for the men to fire from.

Major Stucley, the second in command, dashed off at once with Captain Rasch, the Adjutant, to bring up the King's Company, the only support available. In place of the shell-fire, which had practically ceased, there now arose a steady rifle and machine-gun fire from the houses to the left and even the left rear of the Battalion. Swinging round to the left, the King's Company, headed by Major Stucley, steadily advanced for about two hundred yards, when it came to the support trench occupied by No. 2 and No. 3 Company. Major Stucley at once grasped the gravity of the situation. The King's Company had already suffered many casualties, as it came

THE FIRST BATTLE OF YPRES 125

up across the open, and the enemy's machine-guns were pouring a murderous fire into the other two companies—No. 4 Company under Captain Rennie still remained in the fire trenches on the right. The problem was how, with three companies and no reserve, to stop a force ten times as numerous. The Germans had taken all the houses near the Menin road, and the thin line of Grenadiers, with their left turned back to face the road, was all there was to stop the rush of the enemy.

And indeed it was a formidable rush. They came on in such numbers that an officer afterwards said the attacking force reminded him of a crowd coming on the ground after a football match. Shoulder to shoulder they advanced, much in the same way as their ancestors fought under Frederick the Great, and though for spectacular purposes at Grand Manœuvres their mass formations were very effective, in actual warfare against modern weapons they proved to be a costly failure.

The German General Staff had studied the question of the attack with the usual German thoroughness. It had carefully considered whether it should adopt the formation evolved by the British Army from the South African war or not, and had come to the conclusion that the personal equation played too large a part in an advance in extended order, and that for a conscript army the only possible formation was close order, in which the small percentage of cowards would be carried forward by the great majority of brave men. Nevertheless, in spite of their solid phalanxes,

Chapter VI.
1st Batt. Oct. 1914.

it was said that the German officers advanced with revolvers in their hands, to shoot men who lagged behind.

For our men the difficulty was to shoot the Germans quick enough. Ever since the South African war the men had been taught to fire at a little brown smudge on a green background painted on the target, an artistic triumph of the musketry authorities, supposed to represent all that a man would be able to see of his enemy in a modern battle. But here were full-length Germans not a hundred yards off, alarmingly visible, and in such numbers that even for the worst shot there was not the slightest difficulty in hitting them, especially as they were often three or four deep. In spite of this, however, the apparently hopeless impossibility of stopping so many, and the futility of killing a few out of such a crowd, made some of our men sometimes shoot very wildly.

Major Stucley disdained all cover and dashed forward at the head of the King's Company, determined to save the situation. In the hail of bullets he fell shot through the head, and soon afterwards Captain Lord Richard Wellesley was killed in the same way. Major Weld-Forester, Captain Ponsonby, and Lieutenant the Hon. A. G. S. Douglas-Pennant, who had necessarily to expose themselves, were wounded. Captain Ponsonby recovered, but Major Weld-Forester and Lieutenant Douglas-Pennant died two days later.

Finding it impossible to stay in the front trench any longer, No. 4 Company retired to the

THE FIRST BATTLE OF YPRES 127

brickyard. Captain Rennie, who commanded them, was never heard of again. Still the Grenadiers held doggedly on to their support trench for another hour, until it was found that the Germans had got round their left and were enfilading the whole trench. Bullets seemed to be coming out of the mist from all directions, and the enemy to be on every side. Captain Rasch, who was now the only officer left above the rank of lieutenant, decided to get out of the trench and retire to the small wood near the brickyard. The order was given, and the Grenadiers—what was left of them—retired to the wood and formed up on the other side.

In the meantime the First Division on the left, almost annihilated by superior numbers, had been forced back. This made the position of the Grenadiers still more untenable, but General Capper was gathering together what reinforcements he could to save the line.

Seeing what straits the Grenadiers were in, the Gordon Highlanders on the right sent what reserves they had to help, and a company arrived under Captain Burnett. The Grenadiers and Gordons formed one line, and advanced gallantly, but when they got near the wood they came under the fire of a German machine-gun, which enfiladed them. Undaunted by this bad start, and determined to regain their former trenches, Captain Rasch and Captain Burnett led their men on through the wood. There was something particularly gallant in the way this remnant of a battalion, with one reinforcing company, was not content to hold its own, but actually undertook a counter-

Chapter VI.

1st Batt.
Oct.
1914.

attack when it knew the enemy was in vastly superior numbers. It was the men themselves, inspired by the few remaining officers, that were carrying out this counter-attack.

Back through the wood they went, and gained the north side of the brickfields, but the Germans, at first taken by surprise at this bold stroke, rallied and drove them out. A second time our men counter-attacked, and this time they forced their way past the brickfields to a hedge running parallel with the road. They got into the ditch on the south side of the Menin road, and were joined there by two platoons of the Gloucester Regiment, which came up as a reinforcement. In that ditch they remained till the order came to retire. Captain Rasch and Lieutenant Pilcher took their handful of men—all that remained out of the splendid Battalion nearly 1000 strong, which had marched out from Ypres less than a fortnight before—and got into a trench some three hundred yards east of the windmill.

The Scots Guards meanwhile, supported by the Queen's, were sent through the south of Gheluvelt, and succeeded in driving the enemy back and almost regaining the ground originally held by the Grenadiers and Gordons. When night fell, the 20th Brigade was holding precisely the same ground that it had occupied in the morning.

There can be no doubt that the Germans were completely deceived as to our strength, and that what misled them was the more than gallant manner in which the Grenadiers held on to the trenches in the morning, and the almost reckless

THE FIRST BATTLE OF YPRES 129

audacity with which the Grenadiers and Gordons attacked later. The enemy was apparently quite unaware how threadbare this part of the line was. These continual counter-attacks gave the impression that there must be large reserves in rear, which made the Germans think it unwise to push on. Had they only known that there were no reserves at all, and that all that lay between them and Ypres were just the remains of a battalion, with hardly an officer or non-commissioned officer left alive, the result of the battle, and all that depended on it, would undoubtedly have been very different.

The losses among the officers of the Grenadiers were very heavy. Lieutenant-Colonel Earle was severely wounded during the engagement, and, while dressing his wounds, Lieutenant Butt, R.A.M.C., was shot through the head. Colonel Earle was afterwards reported to be lying in a house some two hundred yards in rear of the Battalion Headquarters dug-out. Several men volunteered to carry him back, but as the enemy were within a couple of hundred yards of the house this would have meant certain death, not only for the stretcher-bearers but for Colonel Earle himself. So it was decided to leave him where he was. The total list of casualties among the officers of the Battalion was:

Lieut.-Colonel M. Earle . (Commanding Officer) wounded and prisoner.
Major H. St. L. Stucley . (Second in Command) killed.
Lieut. J. G. Butt . . (Medical Officer) killed.
Major the Hon. A. O. W. C. Weld-Forester . (King's Company) killed.

130　THE GRENADIER GUARDS

Chapter VI.
1st Batt.
Oct. 1914.

Lieut. H. L. Aubrey-Fletcher	(King's Company)	wounded.
Lieut. J. H. Powell	,, ,,	wounded.
2nd Lieut. R. O. R. Kenyon Slaney	,, ,,	wounded.
Captain the Hon. C. M. B. Ponsonby	(No. 2 Company)	wounded.
Lieut. G. E. Hope	(Signalling Officer)	wounded.
2nd Lieut. R. S. Lambert	(No. 2 Company)	wounded.
Captain Lord Richard Wellesley	(No. 3 Company)	killed.
Captain G. Rennie	,, ,,	missing, reported killed.
Lieutenant the Hon. A. G. S. Douglas-Pennant	,, ,,	killed.
Lieut. P. Van Neck	,, ,,	killed.
Lieut. L. G. Ames	,, ,,	wounded.
Major L. R. V. Colby	(No. 4 Company)	killed.
Capt. R. E. K. Leatham	,, ,,	wounded.
Lieut. E. Antrobus	,, ,,	killed.
2nd Lieut. S. Walter	,, ,,	killed.
2nd Lieut. N. A. H. Somerset	,, ,,	killed.

That night the Battalion went into billets at Hooge, half-way to Ypres, with only four officers and a hundred men left, exclusive of transport. The officers were Captain Rasch, Lieutenant Pilcher, Second Lieutenant Darby, and Second Lieutenant Sir G. Duckworth-King.

Oct. 30.　Men who had been left in the trenches, not knowing of the order to retire, kept arriving in driblets during the night, and the strength of the Battalion had risen by next morning to 250 men. But, with most of the officers and N.C.O.'s killed or wounded, the whole machinery of the Battalion had disappeared, and Captain Rasch had to do what he could to reorganise the remnant into a fighting unit. Ruggles-Brise's Brigade—with the exception of the Gordon Highlanders, who had been ordered to report themselves to General Bulfin—were placed in reserve to the other two brigades of the Seventh Division.

CHAPTER VI.

1st Batt. Oct. 1914.

Repeated attempts to penetrate the line were made by the Germans throughout the day. For each attack preparation was made by very heavy shell-fire, and the ground in rear of our forward line was thoroughly searched, apparently with a view to harassing any reinforcements that might be sent up to the firing line.

The Grenadiers had just settled down for the night when the Battalion was ordered to fall in and move off with the rest of the Brigade to occupy a new defensive position. Later in the war, when a battalion had been knocked to pieces as the Grenadiers had been the day before, it was picked out and given a rest, but in those early days this was impossible, as every man was continually wanted to check the renewed attacks of fresh enemy troops. The Germans were constantly throwing into the attack fresh battalions at full strength, whereas in the British Army the term " Battalion " meant two or three hundred worn-out men who had been fighting daily for the last ten days or so.

Eventually, after a long, circuitous march, the Battalion was put into dug-outs in Brigade Reserve at 3 A.M. Orders were received that the First and Second Divisions, with the Cavalry Brigade, were attacking the following day, and that the 20th Brigade was to remain in its position until 6.30 A.M., when it was to leave one battalion

Chapter VI.
1st Batt.
Oct. 1914.

in support of the left portion of the line, and move the rest to a central position where it could rapidly support any part of the line held by the Seventh Division.

Oct. 31.

On the 31st, the day that Sir John French described as the most critical in the whole battle of Ypres, the remnant of the Seventh Division was holding a line from the Ypres—Menin road, in front of the cross-roads at Veldhoek, to a point 500 yards north of Zandvoorde. At 1 A.M. it was decided to push the Scots Guards and Borderers up, and entrench them close behind the left of the 21st Brigade.

Directly day broke the Germans began a terrific shell-fire all along the front, and by 8 o'clock shells were bursting ceaselessly on and over the line. Towards noon word came that the 21st and 22nd Brigades had been shelled out of their position and forced to retire. In rear of the 21st Brigade the Scots Guards and Borderers still held their line, and General Ruggles-Brise himself led up the Grenadiers in prolongation of this line, with the hope of stemming the German advance.

This movement had to be carried out very hurriedly, with no opportunity of reconnaissance, and the Battalion lost rather heavily in crossing the reverse slope of a hill in front of gun position. When it had gained the ridge through the woods, it was found that to be of any use the Grenadiers would have to push forward, and occupy the trenches vacated by the 21st Brigade. This they managed to do, in spite of very heavy shell-fire, and three or four of the

THE FIRST BATTLE OF YPRES

most forward trenches on the right of the 21st and the left of the 22nd Brigades were occupied just in time to meet a portion of the German attack, now being delivered on the Gheluvelt—Zandvoorde frontage.

By the time it had reached and occupied the trenches, the strength of the Battalion was scarcely fifty of all ranks, and this handful of men had to confront thousands of Germans, with the additional handicap of having its right flank exposed, as the enemy had gained the 22nd Brigade's trenches. It was fortunate for us that the attack, wonderfully brave as the Germans were, was apparently quite disjointed and unorganised. No officers could be seen leading the men, who advanced in dense masses to within three hundred yards of the trenches, and were simply mown down by the fire of the Grenadiers.

Things now seemed to be going better for us, when suddenly the right-hand trench reported that the Germans were streaming through a wood, and, crossing the Veldhoek—Zandvoorde road, were working their way immediately to our rear. All our reserves had been used up by this time, and the only thing to do was to hang on somehow till nightfall, sending word at once to the Division of what had happened. As no communication had been established since the re-occupation of the trenches, Captain Brooke, the Staff Captain on the 20th Brigade Staff, who had come up to see how things were, got out of the trench and, finding a loose horse, galloped off, and told General Capper. General Capper

CHAPTER VI.
1st Batt.
Oct.
1914.

went off to ask General Bulfin for help, but already the 4th Guards Brigade—which included the 2nd Battalion Grenadiers—was advancing to make a counter-attack through the wood.

When he got back to the Grenadiers in their trenches, Captain Brooke was surprised to find them still holding their own and quite happy. They were successfully beating off repeated German attacks to their front. The 4th Guards Brigade evicted the enemy from the wood, and it was then decided to withdraw the Grenadiers, the 21st Brigade being ordered to take over their trenches.

Thus ended one of the most desperate days of fighting in the whole war. As has been already said, it seems incredible that the Germans, with their vast numbers of men and their great superiority in guns, should not have broken through the line. They were very near doing it; indeed, so critical did the situation become at one time, that General Capper issued a provisional order that, if the line became untenable, the Brigade was to fall back on a new line extending from one mile east of Zillebeke to the fifth kilo on the Ypres—Menin road.

As the Battalion marched back with the Scots Guards, two guns were seen in the rear of the trenches, standing all by themselves. It looked at first as if they had been abandoned. But closer inspection showed that every single man and horse of the team was there—dead. The gunners had remained gallantly at their posts to the last. Men from the Grenadiers, the Scots Guards, and the Bedford Regiment

THE FIRST BATTLE OF YPRES 135

were sent to rescue the guns, and bring them to a place of safety.

The Grenadiers returned to the shelters at the Château Herenthage, which they had occupied during the morning. There the officers found that their shelter had during their absence been blown to pieces by a high-explosive shell, and it was plain that, had they remained in reserve that day, there would have been no officers left at all in the Battalion.

The action of the 1st Battalion Grenadiers on this day was afterwards described by the G.O.C. Seventh Division in his report as mainly instrumental in restoring the battle south of the Ypres—Menin road.

The total strength of the 20th Brigade was now reduced to 18 officers and 920 men, constituted as follows : the 1st Battalion Grenadiers, 5 officers (the four previously mentioned and the transport officer, Lieutenant Mackenzie) and 200 men, commanded by Captain Rasch ; the 2nd Battalion Scots Guards, 5 officers and 250 men, commanded by Captain Paynter ; the 2nd Border Regiment, 5 officers and 270 men, commanded by Captain Warren ; and the 2nd Gordon Highlanders, 3 officers and 200 men, commanded by Lieutenant Hamilton.

Very heavy shell-fire opened the morning of November 1. One high-explosive shell stripped off the whole back of the house occupied by the Brigade Headquarters, which was thereupon moved to shelters in the Château Herenthage wood. An infantry attack followed, but it was only feeble, and the Grenadiers remained in a

CHAPTER VI.

1st Batt.
Oct.
1914.

Nov. 1.

CHAPTER VI.
1st Batt.
Nov. 1914.

Nov. 2.

Nov. 3.

wood south of Herenthage in Brigade Reserve. There they prepared a second line of fire-trenches, and improved the existing dug-outs, while the wood was shelled at intervals with high explosives.

The brunt of the attack at that part of the line was borne next day by the Border Regiment, which held on to its trenches so gallantly and unflinchingly, in spite of a murderous enfilade fire, that it received a special message from General Capper. In the evening it was relieved by the Grenadiers. During the heavy shell-fire, with which the enemy searched the ground in rear of our trenches, General Ruggles-Brise was severely wounded, and Major A. Cator, the Brigade-Major, took over command of the Brigade.

The men had now managed to put out a little wire in front, and it seemed unlikely that the Germans would be able to make much impression on the line. The trenches, which were good and continuous, were held by the Grenadiers on the right and the Scots Guards on the left. There was a weak spot on the right of the Grenadiers near the wood, but this was well covered by the Gordon Highlanders in rear.

In the afternoon of the 3rd, the Scots Guards reported the enemy to be massing in the woods in front of them, while parties were observed moving towards our right, and our guns turned a heavy fire on to them. Though no attack developed, a few parties of the enemy advanced in a half-hearted way, more as if they were carrying out a reconnaissance. The Brigade suffered some casualties during the day from shells and snipers, and Lieutenant Sir G. Duckworth-

THE FIRST BATTLE OF YPRES 137

King, who had almost miraculously come unhurt through the last ten days' fighting, was at last wounded.

A draft of 100 men under Lieutenant C. Mitchell arrived next day, and considerably added to the strength of the Battalion. There was a great deal of indiscriminate shelling and sniping, and Lieutenant G. E. Hope was wounded in the head by a sniper.

On the 5th there was heavy shell-fire as usual, and some trenches were blown in. The 20th Brigade was relieved on that day by the 7th Brigade, and marched through Ypres, which was being shelled as far as Locre. The men found the march very fatiguing, for they had had little sleep for many days, and had been digging or fighting all the previous night. Owing to the incessant shell-fire, it had been found impossible to organise the Battalion into any recognised formation during the period from October 29 to November 5. If fifty men were wanted for the trenches, some one had to go round the dug-outs and collect them. There was no company, platoon, or even sectional organisation. In spite of this everything went well, a result due to the splendid spirit shown by the men themselves.

At daybreak the Brigade reached Locre, weary with the long march, but very glad to get away from the constant roar of shells and rifle-fire. As every available house and shed was already occupied by the French, the church was opened and the Grenadiers and part of the Scots Guards billeted there. The march was resumed in the

CHAPTER VI.

1st Batt. Nov. 1914.

Nov. 4.

Nov. 5.

Nov. 6.

138   THE GRENADIER GUARDS

Chapter VI.
1st Batt. Nov. 1914.

afternoon through Bailleul to Meteren, where the Brigade went into billets.

The Grenadiers were now reorganised into a single Company as follows :

HEADQUARTERS

Officer Commanding and Adjutant	Captain RASCH.
Quartermaster	Lieut. J. TEECE.
The King's Company . .	Lieut. Lord CLAUD HAMILTON.
No. 1 Platoon . . .	Lieut. MITCHELL.
No. 2 ,, . . .	2nd Lieut. M. A. A. DARBY.
No. 3 ,, . . .	Lieut. W. R. MACKENZIE (Transport Officer).
No. 4 ,, . . .	Sergeant C. JONES.
Company Sergeant-Major . .	Drill-Sergeant J. L. CAPPER.
Company Q.-M. Sergeant . .	Colour-Sergeant T. W. BROWN.

Nov. 7–8.   On November 7 the Battalion did an hour's steady drill. There was something very fine and at the same time pathetic in the remnants of this decimated Battalion going through their drill with the determination to maintain the high standard of discipline no matter how small their numbers might be. Next day the whole Brigade attended divine service for the first time since they had left England, and as there was no chaplain, the Brigadier, Major Cator, read the service. In the afternoon the Brigade was drawn up in square facing inwards, and General Capper addressed it. He expressed his admiration of the way in which it had fought round Ypres, and told the men that they had upheld the splendid traditions of their regiments.

THE FIRST BATTLE OF YPRES

The fact that the flower of the German Army was defeated by the British Expeditionary Force, that is to say, the original army that existed before the war, will always make the first battle of Ypres particularly interesting to students of military history. Although it can hardly be claimed as a decisive victory, there is small doubt that the result influenced the whole course of the war, for had the Germans, when they turned their whole strength on Ypres, been able to force their way to the coast, the subsequent operations of the British Army would have been considerably affected.

Two battalions of the Grenadiers fought at Ypres, and each covered itself with imperishable glory. Never before in the long history of the regiment had so many casualties befallen them in a single action; never before had so large a force of the Grenadiers been almost annihilated.

Each battalion had gone into battle with a great reputation to maintain—a reputation won in centuries of fighting, carried forward in almost every campaign in which the British Army has taken part, and all the officers and men were fully conscious of their responsibility. Old Grenadiers well knew that every nerve would be strained to uphold the traditions of the regiment; but no one dared to hope that the illustrious past could be enhanced, and that these two battalions of the regiment would increase their fame in divisions in which every battalion distinguished itself.

The part taken by the 1st Battalion in the defence of Ypres, when with the Seventh Division

Chapter VI.

1st Batt. Nov. 1914.

CHAPTER VI.
1st Batt.
Nov. 1914.

they repelled attacks from forces eight times their number, will ever remain a precious memory to be handed down to future generations.

Major-General Sir Henry Rawlinson, in an order which he issued to the Seventh Division, said :

After the deprivations and tension of being pursued day and night by an infinitely stronger force, the Division had to pass through the worst ordeal of all. It was left to a little force of 30,000 to keep the German Army at bay while the other British Corps were being brought up from the Aisne. Here they clung on like grim death with almost every man in the trenches, holding a line which of necessity was a great deal too long—a thin exhausted line—against which the prime of the German first-line troops were hurling themselves with fury. The odds against them were eight to one, and when once the enemy found the range of a trench, the shells dropped into it from one end to the other with terrible effect. Yet the men stood firm and defended Ypres in such a manner that a German officer afterwards described their action as a brilliant feat of arms, and said that they were under the impression that there had been four British Army Corps against them at this point. When the Division was afterwards withdrawn from the firing line to refit, it was found that out of 400 officers who set out from England there were only 44 left, and out of 12,000 men only 2336.

Major-General Capper, in a report on the 1st Battalion Grenadiers, which he sent later to Lieut.-General Pulteney, commanding the Fourth Corps, wrote as follows :

This Battalion fought with the utmost tenacity and determination in a most exposed position at Kruiseik in front of Ypres, being subjected to an almost ceaseless heavy artillery fire and repeated attacks by the enemy

THE FIRST BATTLE OF YPRES

for a week. Owing to the length of front to be held, no relief could be found for troops in the trenches. During this fighting Major Colby's Company of this Battalion counter-attacked the enemy, who had almost successfully attacked the line. In the counter-attack this Company lost four officers killed and wounded, only one officer and forty-five men returning unhurt, but this Company succeeded in driving back a very much larger hostile force. This Battalion lost very heavily in the three weeks' fighting before Ypres. I consider that the resolution and gallantry of this Battalion, obliged to take its share in holding a height which was the pivot of all the operations in this part of the field, was most noble and devoted and worthy of its highest traditions.

CHAPTER VI.

1st Batt. Nov. 1914.

Later on, in the same operations, though weakened in numbers, and with few officers, the Battalion exhibited gallantry in a counter-attack near Gheluvelt, where it was mainly instrumental in restoring the battle south of the main Ypres—Menin road; and subsequently the same tenacity as it had shown at Kruiseik in holding a very difficult and exposed part of the Brigade line in the final position in front of Ypres.

The Battalion remained at Meteren until the 14th, and spent most of its time in reorganising and re-equipping. On the 10th a draft of 401 men arrived with the following officers: Major G. W. Duberly, Captain the Hon. R. Lygon, Lieutenant E. S. Ward, and Lieutenant C. A. V. Sykes; and on the 11th, 133 men originally intended for the 2nd Battalion arrived from the Base Camp under Lieutenant C. L. Blundell-Hollinshead-Blundell and Lieutenant C. V. Fisher-Rowe. These additions brought the strength of the Battalion almost to its usual proportions.

Meanwhile Field-Marshal Sir John French had

visited the Brigade, and saw the remnants of the battalions which had formed the original Seventh Division. He congratulated both officers and men on the fine work they had done round Ypres.

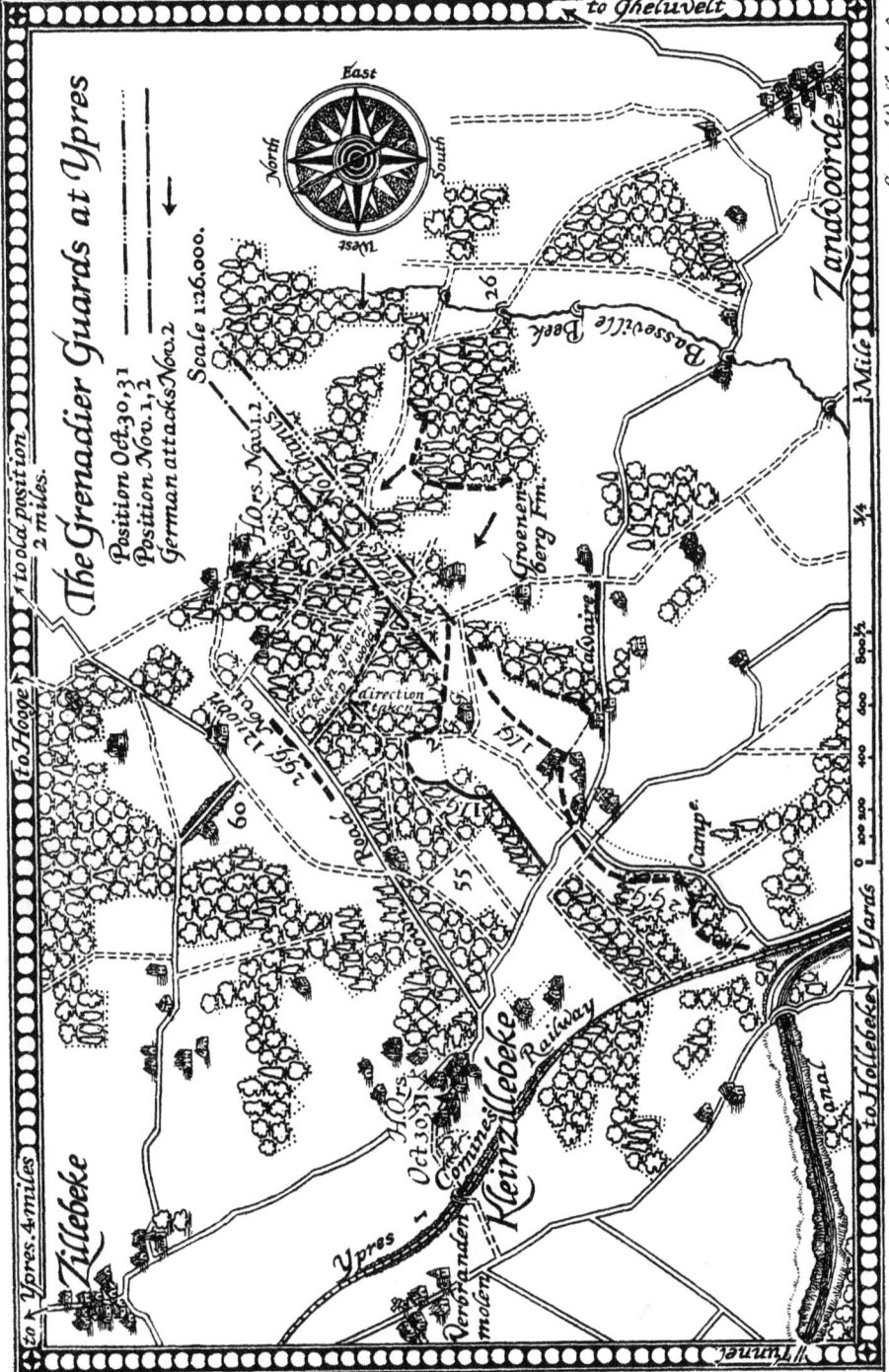

CHAPTER VII

THE FIRST BATTLE OF YPRES (2ND BATTALION)

HAVING completed its detrainment, the First Corps, under Sir Douglas Haig, was concentrated between St. Omer and Hazebrouck. Sir John French had now to make up his mind whether he would use it to strengthen his line, which was much longer than his numbers warranted, or send it to the north of Ypres. He decided that the greatest danger was that the Germans might carry out a wide turning movement on his left flank, and he sent the Corps north of Ypres accordingly. The French cavalry were to operate on Sir Douglas Haig's left, and the Third Cavalry Division, under General Byng, on his right.

After two nights in billets at Hazebrouck, the 2nd Battalion marched on the 17th to Boeschepe. Two days afterwards arrived Captain M. E. Makgill-Crichton-Maitland, Captain R. H. V. Cavendish, M.V.O., Lieutenant J. S. Hughes, Lieutenant I. St. C. Rose, and Captain C. R. Champion de Crespigny, who was appointed Staff Captain to the 4th Brigade.

The officers of the 2nd Battalion were now as follows :

144   THE GRENADIER GUARDS

CHAPTER VII.
2nd Batt.
Oct. 1914.

Lieut.-Colonel W. R. A. Smith	Commanding Officer.
Major G. D. Jeffreys	Second in Command.
Capt. E. J. L. Pike	Adjutant.
Lieut. C. W. Tufnell	Machine-gun Officer.
2nd Lieut. A. K. S. Cunninghame	Transport Officer.
Lieut. J. H. Skidmore	Quartermaster.
Major G. C. Hamilton	No. 1 Company.
Capt. C. Symes-Thompson	,, ,,
Lieut. J. S. Hughes	,, ,,
Lieut. the Hon. W. R. Bailey	,, ,,
Major Lord Bernard Gordon-Lennox	No. 2 Company.
Lieut. I. St. C. Rose	,, ,,
Lieut. C. M. C. Dowling	,, ,,
2nd Lieut. F. W. J. M. Miller	,, ,,
Capt. E. G. H. Powell	No. 3 Company.
Capt. R. H. V. Cavendish, M.V.O.	,, ,,
Lieut. Lord Congleton	,, ,,
Lieut. F. G. Marshall	,, ,,
2nd Lieut. C. R. Gerard	,, ,,
Capt. M. E. Makgill-Crichton-Maitland	No. 4 Company.
Capt. E. D. Ridley	,, ,,
Lieut. F. G. Beaumont-Nesbitt	,, ,,
Lieut. M. G. Stocks	,, ,,

It was a cold raw morning on the 20th, when the Battalion marched at 5 A.M. to St. Jean, a small village to the north of Ypres, where it was ordered to take up an entrenched position, with the Coldstream on the right, and the 5th Brigade on the left. Matters were complicated by the fact that the French looked upon this part of the line as theirs. However, eventually matters were arranged, and British and French troops settled down together to a pouring wet night.

Oct. 21.   There was another move next morning. The Battalion assembled at 5.30, and marched to a position near Hanebeek Brook, about two miles

Lieutenant-Colonel W. R. A. Smith C.M.G.
Commanding 2nd Battalion
Died of wounds received at Festubert 19 May 1915

THE FIRST BATTLE OF YPRES

west of Zonnebeke, where the 4th Brigade concentrated. Then the whole Brigade advanced about half a mile towards Passchendaele with the 3rd Battalion Coldstream on the left, and the 2nd Battalion Coldstream on the right—each battalion having two companies in the firing line, and the rest in support, while the 2nd Battalion Grenadiers was in reserve.

About 2.30 Lord Cavan, finding that the two Coldstream battalions had drifted somewhat apart, ordered up the 2nd Battalion Grenadiers into the centre of the line. As they made their way across ploughed fields, they came in for a great deal of unaimed rifle-fire, but suffered very little loss.

About 400 to 500 yards east of Zonnebeke—Langemarck road the three battalions dug themselves in for the night, since news had been received that large German forces were advancing through Houthulst Forest. Before long the sky was lit up in all directions by the farms which the enemy was burning. By this illumination the Germans attempted a counter-attack, and came on shouting, "Don't fire, we are the Coldstream." It was characteristic of the German thoroughness of method to master this regimental idiosyncrasy, and say Coldstream and not Coldstreams. But the Battalion had not fought for two months without learning the enemy's tricks, and as spiked helmets could be distinctly seen against the glow of the burning farms, they fired right into the middle of the Germans, who hastily retired.

Before daylight next morning the companies in the firing line were relieved by those in support.

CHAPTER VII.
2nd Batt.
Oct. 1914.

The whole Brigade then set itself to improving the trenches and consolidating the position. It turned out that on the left the First Division had been held up, while on the right the 22nd Brigade was in a tight place. Consequently the situation was distinctly uncomfortable. The trenches, composed of isolated holes which held two or three men apiece, were exposed from the left to enfilade fire, but there the Battalion had to remain for two days, shelled intermittently. They suffered many casualties. While making his way down the firing line, Captain Maitland was forced to walk a great deal in the open, and was wounded in the head by a sniper, who succeeded in hitting several other men. In the evening Lieutenant Donald Miller, who had come out originally with the Battalion, and had fought all through the retreat, was killed by a high-explosive shell.

Oct. 24.

On the 24th the Second Division got orders to take up the ground occupied by the Seventh Division, from Poezelhoek to the Becelaere—Passchendaele road, and the First Division was relieved by French Territorial troops, and concentrated about Zillebeke.

At the same time the 4th Brigade was relieved by a Brigade from the Sixth French Army under General Moussy, and the men of the Grenadiers watched the French attack Passchendaele with much interest. Though the attack was met with a heavy artillery and rifle fire, and made but little progress, the personal gallantry of General Moussy himself and his staff, who exposed themselves freely while close up to the front trenches,

THE FIRST BATTLE OF YPRES 147

made a great impression on all the officers and men of the 2nd Battalion. After dark this French Brigade took over the trenches, and the 2nd Battalion Grenadiers moved back about two miles to a farm, where the men managed to snatch a couple of hours' sleep. At 5.30 A.M. it started off again, and after a circuitous march of about six miles reached Eksternest, where it formed the reserve of the 6th Brigade. Here, at last, it had a thorough rest in barns, outhouses, and elsewhere, with plenty of straw to lie on, while a fowlhouse constituted No. 3 Company Headquarters.

The Battalion paraded, much refreshed, at 6.30 next morning, but did not move off till 9. It advanced towards the Six Cross Roads, and halted behind Polygon Wood. In the afternoon it was ordered to attack the enemy's position near Reutel, passing over the trenches held by the 5th Brigade, while the Irish Guards were to advance on the same position from the northwest. The Orders were:

Chapter VII.
2nd Batt. Oct. 1914.

Oct. 25.

The attack will begin at 3 P.M. 4th Guards Brigade will have for its objective the Reutel Spur. The 1st Battalion Irish Guards will commence its advance at once as far as the line of trenches now held by the 5th Brigade. At 3 P.M. its scouts will pass that line, and the battalion will endeavour to establish itself in such a position that it can by its fire materially assist the main attack which will be delivered from the south and south-west.

The 2nd Batt. Grenadiers will work round the stream at once as verbally ordered until their right reaches a point one company's length beyond the forks of the two streams. At 3 P.M. it will be prepared to attack the R. of Reutel from S.W. During this operation the 2nd Battalion Grenadiers will specially detail a half company to protect its right. The 2nd Battalion Coldstream will follow the Grenadiers and act in close support of them. They must also give special orders about their right flank. The 3rd Battalion Coldstream will be in reserve in a covered position at Six Cross Roads. It is quite understood that the time is short, but this operation must be carefully carried out without hurry. Brigade Headquarters will be at Six Cross Roads at 2.45 P.M.

Advancing in artillery formation, the Battalion came in for a great deal of rifle-fire, but fortunately no shells. Major Lord Bernard Lennox had taken advantage of the halt in the morning to reconnoitre the line of advance thoroughly, and was able to lead the companies to their destinations. There was no great difficulty in reaching the trenches, but when the Battalion advanced another 150 yards it came under a very heavy cross-fire; only one platoon of No. 2 Company actually crossed the 5th Brigade trenches. The other companies were held up before they reached the firing line. The Bedfords on the right, unable to carry on the advance, retired again to the trenches, and the Irish Guards on the left were also held up.

Darkness was now coming on, and it seemed madness to attempt to take a strong position in a thick wood where no one knew precisely the position of the trenches, or how strongly they were held. So Lieut.-Colonel Smith directed No. 2 Company to fall back and take over a trench from the Oxfordshire Light Infantry, with the Highland Light Infantry on the left and the Royal Scots Fusiliers on the right. A

THE FIRST BATTLE OF YPRES 149

platoon of No. 1 Company was added to the right of No. 2. Its position was along the front edge of the private grounds of a fine château, which was then intact.

Three times during the night, which was very dark and windy and rainy, the Germans attacked—at 9 P.M., at midnight, and at 3 A.M. But the position was fairly secure, and each time they retired. It is doubtful whether they ever intended to press the attack home, and possibly they were only trying to locate the exact position of our trenches—not a very difficult task, as they were but 300 yards off.

That evening the following message was received from Sir John French:

The Field-Marshal Commanding-in-Chief wishes once more to make it known to the troops under his command how deeply he appreciates the bravery and endurance which they have again displayed since their arrival in the northern theatre of war. In circulating the official information which records the splendid victory of our Russian Allies, he would remind the troops that the enemy must before long withdraw troops to the East and relieve the tension on our front. He feels it is quite unnecessary to urge officers, N.C.O.'s, and men to make a determined effort and drive the enemy over the frontier.

Digging started with a will in the trenches early next morning. It had come to be a regular habit with the battalions which had been through those first months of the war, at once to dig themselves in deep in any new position, no matter how soon they might have to move on. They had learned by experience that the labour was well worth while. On this occasion the trouble

Chapter VII.

2nd Batt. Oct. 1914.

Oct. 26.

150   THE GRENADIER GUARDS

CHAPTER VII.

2nd Batt. Oct. 1914.

was that the deeper the men dug the wetter the ground became, and soon they were up to their ankles in mud. But the sun came out about mid-day, and helped to dry up the ground.

No regular attack was made that day, though there was constant shelling, and the Battalion therefore had comparatively few casualties. German snipers were very busy, but did little damage; our men took every opportunity of retaliating; and Lieutenant I. Rose was reported to have been particularly successful in accounting for the enemy marksmen. The howitzers paid less attention to the trenches than to the Château. On this unfortunate building the high-explosive shells dropped with monotonous regularity, but the little tower still remained standing. The Battalion Headquarters, which were behind the Château, had a decidedly warm time, getting the benefit not only of the shells from the howitzers, but of all the stray bullets that went wide of the trenches.

Oct. 27. Most of the next day was spent in mending the line and consolidating the position, for there were weak spots, which the Divisional Staff discovered, usually between Brigades. Barbed wire was now to be had, and orders were issued for entanglements to be put up in front of each trench. In the afternoon the companies of the 2nd Battalion Grenadiers in reserve were sent to take over the trenches of the 3rd Battalion Coldstream, and to stay there until they were relieved by the Black Watch at midnight. Both these reliefs were carried out successfully and without any casualties, though the task was by

THE FIRST BATTLE OF YPRES 151

no means easy, owing to the thickness of the wood and consequent bad communications.

Sir John French had now placed what remained of the Seventh Division and the Third Cavalry Division under the orders of Sir Douglas Haig, who redistributed the line thus :

(A) The Seventh Division from the Château east of Zandvoorde to the Menin road.

(B) The First Division from the Menin road to a point immediately west of Reutel village.

(C) The Second Division to near the Moorslede—Zonnebeke road.

The 2nd Battalion Grenadiers now moved back about a mile to Nonne-Bosschen Wood, and having slept there returned the next morning under howitzer fire across two fields to the northern edge of Polygon Wood, where it remained until the 6th Brigade passed through it to attack Reutel Ridge. Then it moved forward in support, and dug in round a farm. Before it had gone far the 6th Brigade was fiercely attacked, and succeeded in driving the enemy off with some loss, though unable to advance farther itself. The 4th Brigade was not wanted, and spent a quiet afternoon near the Farm—" quiet " in this case being a comparative term, denoting that they were not directly under fire, for our own howitzers were only twenty yards off, and kept firing ear-splitting salvos all day.

Having received orders the night before to be ready at a moment's notice, the Battalion was under arms soon after dawn next day. But it was not until much later that it got instructions

Chapter VII.

2nd Batt.
Oct.
1914.

Oct. 28.

Oct. 29.

152   THE GRENADIER GUARDS

CHAPTER VII.
2nd Batt.
Oct. 1914.

to move to the other side of the Racecourse Wood, and entrench a position almost at right angles to the line of trenches in front. It turned out that the Seventh Division on the right had been driven back, and though most of the ground had been regained there was still a risk of the Germans pushing through. Meanwhile, Captain Ridley was ordered to take No. 4 Company, and support the Cameron Highlanders near the Château. He sent up two platoons into the trenches on their right, and kept the rest in support. They came in for a good deal of shell-fire, but were not seriously attacked.

Oct. 30.

Except for No. 4 Company the Battalion was in Corps Reserve next day with the Irish Guards, while the 2nd and 3rd Battalions Coldstream were in the trenches. But about 3 P.M. the Brigadier, Lord Cavan, got news that there had been a serious break in the line about two miles to the right, *i.e.* the south, and was instructed to send up the battalions, which he had in reserve, to report to General Bulfin, commanding the 2nd Brigade.

Lord Cavan went himself to see General Bulfin at his Headquarters, and was directed to despatch these battalions southwards to protect the right flank of the 2nd Brigade. Accordingly the 2nd Battalion Grenadiers, Irish Guards, and Oxfordshire Light Infantry marched off from Polygon Wood towards Klein Zillebeke, and Captain Ridley was ordered to withdraw No. 4 Company and join the remainder of the Battalion as it moved off. The orders given to Lieut.-Colonel Smith were to reinforce the cavalry,

THE FIRST BATTLE OF YPRES 153

which was holding a line very lightly north of the Château de Hollebeke.

By dusk these battalions were astride of the Klein Zillebeke — Zandvoorde road, the Grenadiers on the right and the Irish Guards on the left, with their left thrown forward a little, to keep touch with the right of the 2nd Brigade. Lord Cavan went on ahead with his Staff, to see that the whole line was made continuous. On going forward to inspect the position which the cavalry was holding, Lieut.-Colonel Smith found that it was on a forward slope, which seemed to him untenable, and he thought this a good opportunity for making a fresh disposition. So he arranged with the cavalry that it should continue to hold its line, while the Battalion dug in, in its rear. A new line, which consisted as usual of a series of deep narrow holes with no parapet, was accordingly made, with the right on the railway, and the left on the Klein Zillebeke road.

Major Lord Bernard Lennox with No. 2 Company was on the right, Major Hamilton with No. 1 in the centre, and Captain Powell with No. 3 on the left; one platoon from No. 4 under Sergeant Hutchings was posted on the Klein Zillebeke road; and the rest of the company went to Battalion Headquarters, north-west of the wood between the railway and Klein Zillebeke. Supplies and ammunition were brought up, and by 1 A.M. the Battalion was well dug in. The cavalry then withdrew from the trenches in front and retired. Meanwhile the Irish Guards had dug trenches, prolonging the line to the left.

CHAPTER VII.

2nd Batt.
Oct.
1914.

Chapter VII.

2nd Batt. Oct. 1914.

Oct. 31.

Sir John French in his despatch describes the afternoon of October 31 as the most critical moment in the whole battle. By sheer weight of numbers the Germans endeavoured to break through the line, and their immense superiority in guns encouraged them to hope that they would be able to beat down any opposition. The greater part of the Second Division was still on the Moorslede—Zonnebeke road, on the left of the First Division, while the three battalions detached under Lord Cavan remained on their new line.

After a long wet night in the trenches, the 2nd Grenadiers were to have a still longer day's fighting—a day, too, in which they were most of the time " holding on by their eyelids." As soon as day dawned, they were deluged by a rain of shells, to which our artillery could make no sort of reply. Some troops of the French Ninth Corps tried to advance through the 2nd Battalion Grenadiers and Irish Guards, and attack the enemy's position, but the shell-fire was so intense that they never succeeded in getting beyond the line of trenches. Most of them took refuge in the trenches, while some dug new ones.

The shells came crashing through the trees continuously, and Lieut.-Colonel Smith decided to move the Battalion Headquarters back about one hundred yards. Particularly violent was the bombardment of No. 2 Company, of which the trenches, being near the railway, were no doubt easily located by the enemy's artillery, directed with deadly effect by a captive balloon. Two high-explosive shells landed in one trench, and killed and buried a number of men. Lieutenant

THE FIRST BATTLE OF YPRES 155

Rose had a marvellous escape. He was actually buried, but was dug out just in time. Major Lord Bernard Lennox wisely withdrew part of his company into the support trenches for a time, and no doubt thus saved many lives.

About 11 A.M. Lord Cavan sent the following message :

> Keep on repairing your trenches. If any quiet intervals, begin communication trenches zigzag to your rear, so that to-morrow infantry can keep out of main trench during heavy shelling hours and easily man it when required. Can you possibly push an Observation Post forward to any point from which it could see and report ?

It looked as if the Germans were going to attack this part of the position about mid-day, but eventually they moved northward. Early in the afternoon Lieut.-Colonel Smith received a message from Lord Cavan that the enemy had broken through the line to the left of the Irish Guards. Soon afterwards came this further message :

> The situation is extremely critical. You are to hold your ground at all costs. Sir Douglas Haig relies on the Grenadiers to save the First Corps and possibly the Army.

After such a call as that, Lieut.-Colonel Smith at once determined to put every available rifle in the trenches. The few men that still remained in reserve were accordingly sent up to the front trenches. No. 3 Company was very much extended, although a platoon from No. 4 had already been sent to support it. Captain Powell sent a

CHAPTER VII.
2nd Batt.
Oct. 1914.

message to say that he might not be able to stay without more support, and Colonel Smith replied that he must hold on at all cost. Lieut.-Colonel Smith then reported the measures he had taken to Lord Cavan, who replied :

Splendid. Hang on like grim death. You may yet save the Army.

It was undoubtedly a case of hanging on, while this terrific bombardment continued, but the Grenadiers had not wasted their time the night before, and had dug themselves in deep. It was to their good digging that Lieut.-Colonel Smith afterwards ascribed the fact that they never gave an inch, although it was certainly an advantage to them that the position was partly concealed owing to the nature of the ground. The enemy plastered the whole locality with shells, but only in a few cases were they able to locate the actual position of the trenches. The Germans were reported meanwhile to have driven back the First Division from Gheluvelt, thus exposing the left flank of the Seventh Division. The Headquarters of the First and Second Divisions had been shelled, General Lomax had been mortally wounded, and several Staff Officers killed. Such heavy casualties among the Staff, in the middle of a battle, naturally dislocated the machinery of the Higher Commands. However, about 2 P.M. Lord Cavan sent word that the situation was easier, and that he was sending up the Oxfordshire Light Infantry on the left of the Irish Guards.

Constant anxiety had been felt about the

THE FIRST BATTLE OF YPRES 157

right of the position occupied by the 2nd Battalion Grenadiers. A high railway embankment, beyond which was a small wood, made it very difficult to keep up communication, especially when the shelling was so severe, and Lieut.-Colonel Smith sent a message to Lord Bernard Lennox : " Is your right still in touch with 4th Hussars ? Brigadier pressing for a reply." To which Lord Bernard answered, " Yes."

At 2.40 Lieut.-Colonel Smith sent the following request to the Headquarters of the 4th Brigade :

> Wood just short of D E near Canal is full of Germans, also Château de Hollebeke. Can you turn on guns, please ? My advance posts have been driven in.

The Canal was dry, and formed no obstacle; and though there were a few British cavalry this side of the embankment, they were not enough to stop an attack. The French were said to be coming up to strengthen this part of the line, but they did not arrive. Of all this fortunately the Germans knew nothing, and instead of attacking this weak spot, they directed their energies to the centre of the section of the line held by the Grenadiers.

About 3 o'clock the enemy advanced in force through the wood near the railway, but was met with such a withering fire from No. 1 Company that he did not succeed in getting very far. An hour later Lord Cavan sent this message :

> Well done. If absolutely forced back, retire as on parade with your proper right, that is your left retiring,

on line of railway. Put up the best fight you can on edge of wood.

2nd Batt. Nov. 1914. There was no need to retire, however, although there was one moment at which the situation seemed critical, for the Germans brought up some field-guns, and plastered the trenches with every conceivable kind of shell.

The shelling stopped shortly after dark, and the men were able at last to look out over their trenches, and survey the scene by the lights of a farm which was blazing in the centre of the line. They saw a spectacle, which later on grew more and more familiar. What had once been a field was now a mass of trenches; the whole place had been ploughed up by shells, and the hedges were all torn up and burnt and blown to bits.

Nov. 1. During the night the 2nd Battalion Grenadiers was relieved by a regiment from the French Sixteenth Corps, and retired at 4 A.M. to the rear of Zwarteleen, where the men thought they were going to get some rest, but before very long they were on the move again. Sir Douglas Haig had sent a message which Lord Cavan circulated as follows:

The German Emperor will arrive in the field to-day to conduct operations against the British Army. The G.O.C. First Corps calls upon all ranks once more to repeat their magnificent efforts and to show him what British soldiers really are.

All the enemy's efforts were now concentrated on smashing the left of the Irish Guards' trenches with high-explosive shells, and firing with wonderful accuracy they gradually blew the trench in bit by bit, and knocked out their machine-guns. At 3 P.M. Lord Cavan heard a report that the Irish Guards were retiring, and that they had only about 200 men left. He sent orders at once that they were at all costs to hold on to the wood 200 yards in rear of their old line. The French were told to stay where they were, as in the event of a withdrawal the whole British line was to pivot on them on the elbow of the Canal. The highest praise was afterwards given by the British Generals to the French for the way in which they held their trenches all day, in spite of the fact that their left was in the air.

An urgent appeal for help now reached Lord Cavan from one of the Corps Staff, stating that the Northamptonshire Regiment was being driven back and needed support. The 2nd Battalion Grenadiers was immediately sent off with orders to report itself to General Bulfin, who was to be found in a wood three-quarters of a mile southwest of Herenthage. But by the time the Battalion arrived there General Bulfin had been wounded, and Lieut.-Colonel Smith could not find out what it was he was expected to do.

In the meantime Lord Cavan received orders to assume command of the whole section from the east edge of the wood to the French left. In these strenuous days it was no uncommon thing for an officer to be told in the middle of a battle to take over command of a force during a difficult operation—a war ordeal, for which peace training had supplied no practice. To take over the command of a Division is no easy matter at any time, but to do it at a critical moment, with heavy fighting going on, demands a man of more than ordinary

CHAPTER VII.

2nd Batt. Nov. 1914.

capacity. Lord Cavan galloped up with his Brigade-Major, Major the Hon. W. P. Hore-Ruthven; on arrival at General Bulfin's Headquarters he found that everything had been momentarily disorganised by the sudden departure of the wounded General. Officers of all sorts were asking for orders. The Germans were breaking through. Perplexing problems of every description were submitted for instant solution. Shells were falling in the immediate neighbourhood of the Divisional Headquarters. Very slowly Lord Cavan drew out his cigar-case, and having carefully selected a cigar, proceeded to light it, turning it round to see that it was evenly lighted. This had a wonderful effect on all present, for it not only enabled Lord Cavan himself to concentrate his thoughts on the problem, and to see clearly the most pressing needs of the moment, but it also inspired all the officers with confidence. As a Staff Officer, who was present, said afterwards, that cigar saved the situation.

On the left the Sussex Regiment was in touch with the Seventh Division, and stood firm. The Northamptonshire Regiment, Gordon Highlanders, and Oxfordshire Light Infantry had all been pressed back from their advanced trenches, though the enemy had not got beyond them. Lord Cavan at once ordered the Grenadiers to leave their packs at the farm in the rear of the Brown Road, and to clear the wood south-east of that road at the point of the bayonet.

Thereupon Lieut.-Colonel Smith launched the Battalion with fixed bayonets into the wood. It was very thick in places, and there was always a

THE FIRST BATTLE OF YPRES 161

risk of some company getting lost. The Germans, it was found, had left the wood, but only recently, as was evident from the number of dead. That the difficult manœuvre, entrusted to the Battalion, was carried out most successfully was due to the excellent manner in which the four Captains led their men. One platoon of Major Hamilton's company, which went beyond the wood and was enfiladed by machine-guns, had to remain under cover of a bank till dark, when it retired and joined the main line. With this exception the companies—No. 1 under Major Hamilton, No. 2 under Lord Bernard Lennox, and No. 3 under Captain Powell—all managed to reach the edge of the wood in perfect order. No. 4 under Captain Ridley was in support.

CHAPTER VII.

2nd Batt. Nov. 1914.

This advance had the excellent effect of establishing confidence. Lord Cavan was able to reorganise the line of defence for the night, and, by blunting the salients of the wood facing south-east, to reduce the garrison. The result was that he withdrew two battalions—one, the Sussex Regiment, was placed in reserve; the other, the Gordon Highlanders, was sent back to the 20th Brigade, to which it belonged.

As soon as it was dark, the Germans tried to set the wood on fire, but fortunately did not succeed, though there were isolated fires in various parts of it. It was an awkward position and very difficult to hold, as the Germans were so close, but orders were received for the battalions to dig in where they were. To officers, who had been taught from their early youth that one of the essentials of a trench line was a good field of

CHAPTER VII.
2nd Batt.
Nov. 1914.

fire, this digging in a thick wood, where the field of fire was never more than from fifteen to twenty yards, seemed an absurdity. But ideas on this subject had been considerably revised by the war—besides, in a long line of trenches running several miles, battalions of course must join up with each other, and cannot choose a position for themselves.

At 10 o'clock that night, No. 4 Company, under Captain Ridley, was directed to take over the position held by a company of the Gordons on the left, but finding that the trench had almost vanished after a day's work by the German artillery, it dug a new one slightly in rear, which was not finished until 3 A.M.

Nov. 2. This was the situation on the Monday morning: the Northamptonshire Regiment was in touch with the Seventh Division on the left; the Oxfordshire Light Infantry and Grenadiers, slightly intermingled, were in the centre, and the Irish Guards on the right—all holding the southeast edges of the wood. Four vigorous attacks on the line—at 8.45, 11, 2, and 5.45—were delivered by the Germans, preceded by heavy shelling, especially on the left. The attack at 11 looked dangerous at one time, when the Germans got within twenty-five yards of our trenches, but our fire was very steady, and they could make no farther headway. The 2 o'clock assault partially developed, but the one at 5.45, just after it got dark, was the most serious.

It was directed against Captain Ridley's Company and against the Oxfordshire Light Infantry, and the enemy advanced with a beating of drums

THE FIRST BATTLE OF YPRES 163

and blowing of horns. The night was cold, with some light from the moon. As the enemy came on, an incident that was never explained took place. The firing almost died down, and this message, sent from no one knew where, was passed along the line : " Don't fire. The Northamptons are going to charge." It so happened that Lieut.-Colonel Smith and Major Jeffreys were in that part of the trench at the time, and directly they heard the mysterious message they realised it was a German ruse. They yelled at the men to go on firing. The fire was at once taken up and continued, while the attack died away. Next day Lieut.-Colonel Smith tried to discover where the fictitious order started, but in vain.

All night the enemy could be heard digging away, in some places near to our trenches. At 1 A.M., No. 4 Company was sent back in reserve, being relieved by a company of the Oxfordshire Light Infantry, which next morning reported that 300 dead had been found in front of the trench. Some were found within a few yards of our line.

On Monday evening, the night of the attack, this special order from the Commander-in-Chief was circulated :

The Field-Marshal Commanding in Chief has watched with the deepest admiration and solicitude the splendid stand made by the soldiers of His Majesty the King in their successful effort to maintain the forward position which they have won by their gallantry and steadfastness. He believes that no other Army in the world would show such tenacity, especially under the tremendous artillery fire directed against it. Its courage and endurance are beyond all praise. It is an honour to belong to such an Army.

164   THE GRENADIER GUARDS

Chapter VII.
2nd Batt.
Nov. 1914.

The Field-Marshal has to make one more call upon the troops. It is certainly only a question of a few days, and it may be of only a few hours, before, if they only stand firm, strong support will come, the enemy will be driven back, and in the retirement will suffer losses even greater than those which have befallen him under the terrific blows by which, especially during the last few days, he has been repulsed.

The Commander-in-Chief feels sure that he does not make his call in vain.

J. D. P. FRENCH, Field-Marshal,
Commander-in-Chief to the British Army
in the Field.

Nov. 3.

A comparatively quiet interval followed. There was intermittent shelling next day, though nothing very serious, and the snipers on both sides kept up a lively fusillade. The trenches meanwhile were deepened and improved. Some new orders with regard to the coming fighting were also issued. Each battalion had two companies in the firing line and two in support, and the captains were told that they must rely on their own supports if they wanted any help. There was a Cavalry Brigade in reserve, but Lord Cavan did not wish to call on it unless it became absolutely necessary. Another warning against the enemy's tricks was sent to the men in this message from G.O.C. First Corps:

First Cavalry Division reports that in the attacks on them the Germans wore British uniforms, especially kilts, and when approaching our trenches shouted, "Don't fire; we are short of ammunition," and similar expressions. All troops in the trenches are to be warned of this practice by the enemy.

An instruction was issued also for the making

THE FIRST BATTLE OF YPRES 165

of circular redoubts, about twenty-five yards in rear of the existing line of trenches, with the object of stopping a rush if the line should be pierced.

An artillery duel—rather one-sided—occupied the next two days. A German aeroplane having located the trenches, the enemy's guns became very busy, though mostly against the support trenches, chiefly with the object of " searching the ground." Early in the afternoon the First Division reported that the enemy was attacking from the direction of the woods south of Gheluvelt. The artillery had been turned on them, and preparations were being made to meet the attack, but nothing came of it. The shelling stopped at nightfall, and the Battalion settled down to a pitch-dark, pouring wet night in the trenches, which were all in wet clay and marshy ground, and the men's sole consolation was that the Germans must be having just as bad a time.

By the 5th it began to be thought in the firing line that the enemy had abandoned all attempt to break through the line, but in reality he was waiting only for reinforcements. He had succeeded in making a dent in the line near Messines, and was now determined to throw the whole weight of his superior numbers on Ypres. He chose for his point of attack Klein Zillebeke, the junction between De Moussy's French Division and the 4th Brigade, or rather the four battalions under Lord Cavan.

Shelling began with renewed vigour as soon as the sun had cleared away the next morning's

Chapter VII.
2nd Batt.
Nov. 1914.
Nov. 4.

Nov. 5.

Nov. 6.

mist, and just before mid-day significant instructions were received from Lord Cavan:

"Your position must be retained at all costs," he said in a message sent out at 11.50. "Redoubts must be occupied, every spare man and tool employed to make secondary trench. I trust you after splendid defence of last few days to maintain it to the end."

And in a second message a few minutes later:

"Have asked Seventh Division to do everything possible to help you with artillery fire."

Evidently the Brigadier expected a determined attack on that part of the line, and Lieut.-Colonel Smith made his dispositions accordingly. Early in the afternoon he got a report from the Irish Guards that the French Division on their right had been driven in. Immediately afterwards came a message from Major Hamilton that the Irish Guards themselves had been driven in, and that his right was consequently in the air.

Major Hamilton's Company was now bearing the brunt of the attack, and was in a very critical position. Lieut.-Colonel Smith sent word to ask him whether he needed any help. He replied: "Hughes only wants a few men, and I have sent him up one section. Bailey is lining road 200 yards to my front. O.C. Oxfords promised support if necessary."

Shortly afterwards it was reported that the Germans had reached Brown Road, and were advancing round the right rear of the Battalion. Lieut.-Colonel Smith at once posted Lieutenant Tufnell with one machine-gun on the Brown Road, to guard the ride through the wood across which the enemy would have to pass, to get behind our line of trenches, telling him to use his own discretion as to the position he should take up. Lieutenant Lord Congleton was also sent with one platoon to stop the Germans from getting through a gap which was reported to the right rear of the Battalion. Lieutenant Tufnell apparently decided that he would be able to get a better target for his machine-gun, and at the same time guard the ride, if he accompanied Lord Congleton. He accordingly took up a position from which he could command the advancing enemy, but had not been there long before he was mortally wounded.

At this point Lieut.-Colonel Smith reported to Lord Cavan that it was urgently necessary that a farm to his front should be destroyed, as there were machine-guns firing from it. He received the reply that if it were humanly possible the howitzers would do as he asked.

Two companies of the Sussex Regiment were now sent up to support the right of the line, and helped to hold things together, but the situation was most critical. The enemy had driven back De Moussy's French infantry, and consequently there was a bad dent in the line. Lord Cavan's troops were still holding on with their right in the air when the Household Cavalry was called in to retrieve the situation. Lord Cavan sent off Captain R. C. de Crespigny, his Staff Captain, at full gallop to Sanctuary Wood with orders to the Household Cavalry to come up at once. Colonel Wilson immediately ordered his men to mount, and galloped round by Maple Copse to within 500 yards of Brigade Headquarters, where they dismounted and fixed bayonets. Into the midst of the Germans they dashed, headed by Colonel Gordon Wilson.

Throwing in the cavalry at the critical moment to save the situation has from time immemorial been a recognised tactical manœuvre, but in this case the Household Cavalry fought as infantry, and very splendid infantry they made. They swept forward to the attack with all the precision of an infantry battalion, and soon Klein Zillebeke was filled with British, French, and German troops fighting at close quarters. When it came to hand-to-hand fighting, the Germans could not stand up against the splendid men of the Household Cavalry, and they were gradually driven back till the line was restored. This gallant charge of the Household Cavalry on foot, Lord Cavan afterwards said, not only prevented the 4th Guards Brigade from being cut to pieces, but also saved Ypres. Colonel Gordon Wilson and Colonel Hugh Dawnay were killed, and the Household Cavalry lost a large number of men, but the situation was retrieved.

While this was going on, No. 1 Company Grenadiers, which was on the right, had been practically wiped out. Since the withdrawal of the Irish Guards, almost every man had been killed or wounded by shell-fire. Sergeant Thomas, who commanded the right platoon of No. 1, remained at his post after the Irish Guards had gone, until he had only three men left, when he withdrew to Brown Road. During that time he was twice buried by shells, and had three rifles broken in his

THE FIRST BATTLE OF YPRES 169

hand. Sergeant Digby was mortally wounded, and was never seen again.

Lord Cavan telephoned: "Hang on tight to Brown Road. Try and get touch with half battalion Sussex Regiment sent to farm at Irish Guards H.Q." Lieut.-Colonel Smith passed this on to Captain Powell, adding: "Are you in touch with the Sussex?" to which Captain Powell replied: "Yes, I am in touch with Sussex, who prolong my line to the right, bent back to right rear."

In the meantime, Lieutenant Lord Congleton, finding how weak the right of the line was, had moved his platoon to the right of the Sussex. He had lost a number of men, but at the same time had managed to collect several Irish Guardsmen. They had no rifles or ammunition, but he placed them at intervals among the men of his platoon, and went and collected rifles for them himself from the casualties. Then he went round a second time with an orderly and collected ammunition. By this means he was able to hold the gap all through that night, and next day was specially mentioned by Lieut.-Colonel Smith, who wrote that the intelligent way in which he handled his platoon on his own initiative was beyond all praise.

Much help towards keeping the right of the line intact was also given by Colonel Davies, commanding the Oxfordshire Light Infantry, who throughout the afternoon kept sending up any men he happened to have in reserve.

When darkness fell Lord Cavan gave Lieut.-Colonel Smith these directions:

CHAPTER VII.

2nd Batt.
Nov.
1914.

Chapter VII.
2nd Batt.
Nov. 1914.

Can you establish a line between the Brown Road and your original line so as to keep touch for certain with battalions on your left? I want to make sure that my line for the night is in touch all along. I have ordered two battalions to establish the line of the Brown Road up to south-west edge, where I hope to establish touch with the French. I have told General Kavanagh he can withdraw his Cavalry Brigade directly the whole of the Brown Road is established.

The new line was arranged about midnight, and at 1 A.M. the men began to dig, although they were dead tired. The trenches were completed by 4 A.M.—a fine performance on a pitch-dark night, with the additional handicap of the trees.

Nov. 7–9.
For three days the battalions remained in their trenches at Klein Zillebeke without any direct attack being made. Shelling went on all day with monotonous regularity, but on the whole little damage was done, though the German howitzers made spasmodic efforts to demolish the trenches, and occasionally managed to blow in a bit of trench and bury some men. The nights were comparatively quiet except for some sniping, and though the mornings were generally foggy, anything in the way of dirty weather was welcomed by the men, as it made artillery observation impossible.

Nov. 10.
The shelling increased enormously on the 10th, and owing to the right having been thrown back, that part of the trenches was open to enfilade fire from the German guns. By this time their artillery had the range of our trenches pretty accurately, and obtained a large number of direct hits. Further, the wood, always a trouble, became

THE FIRST BATTLE OF YPRES 171

more and more difficult to hold : trees cut down by the shells fell crashing to the ground, and made communication impossible. About mid-day the bombardment became terrific, and it seemed as if it would be impossible for any one to live under the storm of shells.

CHAPTER VII.

2nd Batt. Nov. 1914.

A heavy loss this day was the death of Major Lord Bernard Lennox, who was killed by a high-explosive shell. For three months he had been in the thick of every engagement, always cheerful, and making the best of every hardship. He was one of the most popular officers in the Brigade of Guards, and his death was very keenly felt by every one.

Lieutenant M. G. Stocks was also killed by a shell, and Lieutenant Lord Congleton, who had so distinguished himself only a few days before, was shot through the heart. Lieutenant H. R. C. Tudway was hit in the head by a shell, and died a few days later. Captain Powell was buried by another shell, and was only just saved in time and brought in. Captain Ridley was wounded in the back, but after being attended to in the dressing-station was able to return to his company.

There was considerable delay in collecting the wounded. It was impossible to attempt to work by day, and the difficulties of carrying stretchers by night were increased by the fallen trees.

That night the Battalion went into Corps Reserve, and bivouacked in dug-outs. Lord Cavan, in writing an account of the day's fighting, said :

The 2nd Battalion Grenadiers made a wonderful stand to-day against enfilade fire of the worst description. They stuck it out simply magnificently.

The King subsequently telegraphed to the Commander-in-Chief:

The splendid pluck, spirit, and endurance shown by my troops in the desperate fighting which has continued for so many days against vastly superior forces fills me with admiration. I am confident in the final results of their noble efforts under your able command.

GEORGE R.I.

Sir John French replied:

Your Majesty's most gracious message has been received by the officers and men of Your Majesty's Army in France with feelings of the greatest gratitude and pride. We beg to be allowed to express to Your Majesty our most faithful devotion and our unalterable determination to uphold the highest tradition of Your Majesty's Army, and to carry the campaign to a victorious end.

Lord Kitchener telegraphed:

The splendid courage and endurance of our troops in the battle in which you have been engaged during the last few days, and the boldness and capacity with which they have been led, have undoubtedly given the enemy a severe blow, successfully frustrating their efforts. Let the troops know how much we all appreciate their services, which worthily maintain the best traditions of our Army.

Having been placed in Corps Reserve for four days, officers and men of the Battalion were under the impression that they were going to have a quiet time for that period, sleeping in peace at night and resting during the day. But they were mistaken. In reality, they spent three of the nights marching about the whole time, and each day they were moved up in support of this or that

THE FIRST BATTLE OF YPRES 173

part of the line, to the invariable accompaniment of considerable shelling. To begin with, the relief took most of the first night, and it was not till 5 A.M. that the Welsh Regiment and Munster Fusiliers finished taking over the trenches. Then at last the Battalion was able to march over to the dug-outs at Bellewaardes Farm, north of Hooge.

The worst of it was that those placed in reserve were at the beck and call of any General who wanted reinforcements. At one time the Battalion was placed under four Generals, and received different orders from each, which came about because the units in front got hopelessly mixed, and the battalions were constantly changed from one brigade to another. For instance, when the 2nd Battalion Grenadiers arrived at Bellewaardes, Lieut.-Colonel Smith rode over to see General Monro, who congratulated him on the good work his men had done, and said he would come round later and say a few words to them. By the time Lieut.-Colonel Smith returned, he found that the Battalion had been ordered to move to a wood north-east of Hooge Château, in order to be in a position of readiness to reinforce the line near Polygon Wood, where the Prussian Guard was reported to have broken through. He sent one company up into the wood, and scattered the rest about the grounds of the Château. It was chiefly shrapnel-shelling that they were exposed to during this operation, and there were few casualties.

In the afternoon orders were received to support an attack which was to be carried out by the

CHAPTER VII.
2nd Batt.
Nov. 1914.

Sussex Regiment, Oxfordshire Light Infantry, and Gloucester Regiment. They were to retake the trenches which had been captured by the Prussian Guard in the morning, south-west of Polygon Wood. The Battalion was severely shelled, as it crossed the open ground towards the wood east of Hooge in artillery formation, and had thirty to forty casualties in a few minutes. Then Lieut.-Colonel Smith sent Major Jeffreys forward to find General FitzClarence, under whose orders the Battalion had been placed.

The enemy now began to shell this spot with shrapnel, and with every one underground it was no easy matter to find the General or his Staff. Major Jeffreys was joined by Lieut.-Colonel Smith; they searched and searched in vain, and came across Major Corkran, Brigade-Major of the 1st Brigade, who had been engaged on the same fruitless errand. Deciding to wait, Lieut.-Colonel Smith sent Major Jeffreys back to the Battalion, where he found Captain Pike, who was almost immediately afterwards wounded by a shell.

Meanwhile the Battalion had been waiting for hours under shell-fire, and had suffered about thirty further casualties. It was now night, pitch-dark, and pouring with rain; and to assemble the men, who were spread out in artillery formation, was by no means easy, but Major Jeffreys managed to get them together near Nonne-Bosschen Wood. Eventually Lieut.-Colonel Smith found General FitzClarence, and got permission to give the men a meal before taking them up to the front. Having returned to the Battalion, he marched it back to the Château grounds, where after some

THE FIRST BATTLE OF YPRES 175

delay the cookers arrived, and the men settled down to a meal in the pouring rain. Lieutenant the Hon. W. R. Bailey was appointed Adjutant in Captain Pike's place, and at once took over his duties.

Chapter VII.
2nd Batt.
Nov. 1914.

After an hour's sleep the Battalion started off again at midnight, and marched ankle-deep in mud and slush to the Headquarters of the 1st Brigade, where it received its orders for the attack in which it was to operate with the 1st Battalion Irish Guards, Royal Munster Fusiliers, and Gloucester Regiment.

Nov. 12.

These orders were:

The following move at 2.15 A.M., to position of readiness at S.W. corner of Polygon Wood—2nd Battalion Grenadiers, 1st Battalion Irish Guards, Royal Munster Fusiliers. Left of Grenadier Guards and right of Irish Guards at S.W. corner of Polygon Wood, both in column of route heading south. Royal Munster Fusiliers on edge of wood just in rear of centre. When ordered to move from position of readiness to attack, Grenadiers will lead in file, passing along western side of trench and shooting any enemy met with either in or out of it. Irish Guards to follow Grenadiers in same formation, Royal Munster Fusiliers to follow Irish Guards. When trench has been cleared, Battalions will occupy and hold it till further orders. Attack will be ready to start any hour after 4 A.M. All movements to be made quickly and silently. Reports to H.Q. 1st Guards Brigade. Captain Fortune, Black Watch, will act as guide to Grenadiers. Battalions in rear will keep touch with Battalions in front of them. Gloucesters will fill gap as at present.

At 3 A.M. these battalions started. It had been arranged that the Irish Guards should lead as far as Polygon Wood, and General Fitz-Clarence and his Staff walked at their head. In spite of the darkness the battalions kept well together. They were marching down a muddy lane when suddenly some shots were heard in front, and General FitzClarence halted his force and went to see what was going on. The advance began again slowly, they reached the west edge of the wood, and the Grenadiers got into the ditch at the edge. Then came the news that General FitzClarence had been mortally wounded. Colonel Davies arrived next with the Oxfordshire Light Infantry, having reconnoitred the positions; he had found that the Germans were in great strength, with wire entanglements in front and several machine-guns.

The question now arose: What should be done? Was it wise to carry on the attack with no General in command? Eventually the matter was referred to Brigadier-General Westmacott, commanding the 5th Brigade. He decided that it would be best to abandon the attack, as after this delay there would not be enough time for it to develop before daybreak. He therefore ordered the battalions back behind the wood, west of Nonne-Bosschen Wood, and determined to hold a new line. Colonel M'Ewen of the Camerons was sent for, to take command of the Brigade.

The work of digging the new line was entrusted to the Gloucesters, but as they were not strong enough to hold it, No. 4 Company Grenadiers under Captain Ridley was sent up to reinforce them. Tired as the men were, they dug for their lives, and by 6 A.M. had managed to dig them-

THE FIRST BATTLE OF YPRES

selves well in. The rest of the Battalion returned to the Château, where it was found that in the darkness one platoon of No. 1 Company and the Battalion Headquarters had gone astray. However, they arrived next morning.

After having been placed under several different Brigadiers, the Battalion was finally ordered by Colonel Cunliffe Owen to move with the Irish Guards to the wood on the Menin road, and there dig itself in. Off it went, and began digging again till the dawn broke, when the shelling started again as usual. This was the only day on which the Battalion had no rations, the constant moves having disorganised the transport, but enough bully beef was procured to give the men something to eat.

During the day the Battalion remained in its trenches. There was the inevitable shelling and sniping, but little damage was done. In the evening it moved back to within a mile of the Château, and was just settling down when it received orders to move on to Sanctuary Wood —so called because it had never been shelled. After some delay, it got to the wood in the middle of the night, finding there some howitzers which had been attracted by the name. The officer in command explained that they had been shelled out of every place they had visited hitherto by the bigger guns of the enemy. Before long, however, the German artillery located the howitzers, and at once began to shell the wood. While Major Hamilton was in his dug-out, a high-explosive shell brought the whole structure down on him, and he was dug out, unconscious, only just in time. Not long afterwards Lieutenant Dowling was wounded.

In the middle of the next night the Battalion was ordered to return to the trenches and join the 4th Brigade. Its four days' "rest" was over, and all ranks welcomed with enthusiasm the prospect of getting back to the trenches!

Next day the Battalion marched back through Zillebeke to Lord Cavan's Headquarters, and was at once sent back into the trenches, part of which it had held the week before. The companies were sent up on each side of the Cavalry Brigade, which was holding a line across Brown Road, and the Battalion was therefore split up into two portions. Nos. 4 and 2 Platoons of No. 3 Company were on the left of the cavalry, and Nos. 1 and 2 Companies on the right; the only reserve there was consisted of two platoons of No. 3 Company, and so they "carried on" for two days without any happenings of great importance. The weather meanwhile became very cold, and there were continual snow blizzards.

On November 17 the Germans made their last serious attack on Ypres. The day opened with a terrific bombardment, evidently heralding a determined attack. The shelling went on steadily all the morning, and about 1 P.M. the attack started, the brunt of it falling on No. 1 and No. 2 Companies. No. 2 in particular was very hard pressed. Captain Symes-Thompson was killed, and Lieutenant Lee-Steere, who took over the command, sent back word that they were running short of ammunition. There were but two platoons in reserve, and they numbered only thirty men, but Lieut.-Colonel Smith sent them up under Captain Cavendish with some ammunition. By the time they arrived Lieutenant Lee-Steere had been killed. Captain Cavendish sent back a message that the enemy was apparently entrenching in a spinney about four hundred yards to our front, and that his numbers were estimated at 500. About this time the enemy attacked in great force, but was quite unable to make any headway against our rifle-fire. The spirits of the men were wonderful, and they fought on, quite unaffected by the terrible casualties caused by the shell-fire amongst their ranks. Captain Cavendish was surprised at suddenly hearing a burst of firing intermingled with shouts of laughter. It turned out that some Germans, who had lain down in a slight fold in the ground when their attack failed, were trying to crawl back, and the men of Nos. 2 and 3 Companies were firing at them as they went. The enemy was now becoming very numerous in front, and the situation was reported to Lord Cavan by Lieut.-Colonel Smith, who received this reply:

Chapter VII.
2nd Batt.
Nov. 1914.

Call on 1st Battalion Coldstream for help if required at once. Brigade Headquarters knocked to bits, so have shifted to farm north-west of wood, on Figure 17 of K 17, in dug-out.

A little while afterwards the situation was easier, and on hearing that the line was still intact, Lord Cavan sent the message:

Well done. Hope you got my memo. *re* calling on 1st Battalion Coldstream at once if necessary, now in the wood alongside of you. You must use them to help both yourself and the Irish Guards. When called on let me know. Am turning all the artillery on the wood to your front. I have no means of communication left except orderlies.

The 1st Battalion Coldstream at that time consisted of a draft of 300 men under Captain G. Edwards, which had just arrived from England, the Battalion having been practically wiped out in the Prussian Guard attack of November 4.

No. 1 Company was now in a bad way, and Captain Hughes sent back an urgent request for more ammunition. But, as most of the pack animals had been killed in the morning's bombardment, it was a problem how to send it. Major Jeffreys collected as many orderlies as he could find, loaded them up with all the ammunition they could carry, and himself led them along to the trenches. This was no easy matter, as not only was the ground they had to cross under shell-fire, but the whole place was knee-deep in mud. The last fifty yards to the trenches they had to crawl.

The firing had been kept up practically all the afternoon, and some idea of the amount of ammunition expended may be gathered from the fact that No. 1 Company alone fired 24,000 rounds. This was the first time our men saw the hand grenades which were to play such a large part in trench warfare. Little puffs of smoke had been occasionally seen bursting on the bodies of the Germans, and these proved to be caused by hand grenades of a primitive type, which exploded when hit by our bullets.

By the evening the German attack had died down. The enemy had lost very heavily, and

THE FIRST BATTLE OF YPRES 181

realised, apparently, that the line was too strongly held for any frontal attack to succeed:

The casualties amongst the officers of the 2nd Battalion were unfortunately heavy:

Captain E. J. L. Pike	(Adjutant)	wounded.
Lieut. C. W. Tufnell	(Machine-gun Officer)	killed.
Capt. C. Symes-Thompson	(No. 1 Company)	killed.
Major Lord Bernard Gordon-Lennox	(No. 2 Company)	killed.
Lieut. I. St. C. Rose	,, ,,	wounded.
Lieut. C. M. C. Dowling.	,, ,,	wounded.
2nd Lieut. F. W. J. M. Miller	,, ,,	killed.
2nd Lieut. J. H. G. Lee-Steere	,, ,,	killed.
Capt. E. G. H. Powell	(No. 3 Company)	wounded.
Lieut. H. R. C. Tudway	(No. 3 Company)	killed.
Lieut. Lord Congleton	,, ,,	killed.
Captain M. E. Makgill-Crichton Maitland	(No. 4 Company)	wounded.
Captain E. D. Ridley	,, ,,	wounded.
Lieut. M. G. Stocks	,, ,,	killed.

The 2nd Battalion had been fighting incessantly from October 21 to November 16. Day and night it had been attacked by an enemy greatly superior in numbers. As it had never for a moment been able to leave the front line, its sleep had been broken and scanty. Yet well aware that no reinforcements were available, the Battalion had throughout realised that it must continue to hold the line, and had faced its task with the utmost determination. Even when it was in reserve, it had taken part in serious engagements, but this to a certain extent was an experience which it shared with the other battalions of the 4th Brigade.

CHAPTER VII.
2nd Batt.
Nov. 1914.

The 2nd Battalion Grenadiers had been most fortunate in its neighbours during these strenuous days, and the men soon found that the other battalions in the Second Division were as stout fighters as themselves. The 2nd Battalion Oxfordshire and Buckinghamshire Light Infantry in particular was known throughout the Division as one of the best battalions in the Expeditionary Force, and the Grenadiers knew from experience that it could be relied upon to hold a trench to the last man.

But perhaps the branch of the service which won the men's admiration most of all was the artillery. Outnumbered and outranged, the Second Division artillery fought on, and time after time saved the situation. Its supply of shells, compared to that of the German artillery, was ridiculously small, and yet never for a moment did it fail to respond when called upon to support the infantry attacks. According to all preconceived theories it should have been wiped out altogether, and in fact many batteries were annihilated. But the Grenadiers knew that as long as there were any men left alive the guns would be served.

Nov. 19.

The first battle of Ypres may be said to have ended on the 19th, although naturally the enemy continued his shelling. Some of No. 1 Company's trenches were blown in, but there were no infantry attacks. In the evening the 2nd Battalion Grenadiers was relieved by the 3rd Battalion Coldstream and marched to St. Jean, where one company went into billets, and the other three lay in the open and made themselves as comfort-

THE FIRST BATTLE OF YPRES 183

able as they could with straw, which they took from the ricks at the farm close by. Curiously enough, the farmer some twelve months later sent in a claim for compensation for the straw that had been taken. The few remaining officers managed to get into one room at the farmhouse.

CHAPTER VII.

2nd Batt. Nov. 1914.

It was bitterly cold, and there were several degrees of frost and two or three inches of snow on the ground. Before leaving, Lieut.-Colonel Smith sent the following message to Captain Cavendish :

If it is possible, will you try and identify some of the units which attacked you yesterday ? Perhaps you could get a few shoulder-straps after dark, but you are not to risk life to get them. I do not want to support you unless it is necessary, but I can send a platoon of the Coldstream to a place near Irish Guards' support if you would like it. You will be relieved by Coldstream to-night about 8 P.M. after your teas, and will come to Brigade Headquarters where you will get instructions. The men of the Coldstream now with you should come back at the same time.

The shoulder-straps referred to in this message were duly secured and forwarded to the Intelligence officer of the Division. The Germans who had attacked the day before were from the Fifteenth Corps.

Lord Cavan, in a private letter to Colonel H. Streatfeild, commanding the Regiment, wrote :

No words can ever describe what the devotion of the men and officers has been under the trials of dirt, squalor, cold, sleeplessness, and perpetual strain of the last three weeks. Their state of efficiency still can, I think, be gauged by the fact that twelve attacks have been repulsed and two companies of Grenadiers fired twenty-

THE GRENADIER GUARDS

CHAPTER VII.
2nd Batt.
Nov. 1914.

four boxes of ammunition on the 17th, so persistent were the enemy's assaults. We are told we are to be relieved very soon and sent right back for a good fortnight to refit and reclothe and reorganise. We came into this theatre 3700 strong, and we shall go back about 2000, but nothing finer to my mind has ever been done by human men. I really should cry if the Germans got into Ypres before we go. On the 17th before the attack they threw over 200 big shells in and around my Headquarters and for one and a half hours it was pretty horrible, but the dug-outs saved us, though my signal officer and 13 men were wounded and 2 killed at the door of my dug-out. The smell of the explosion was horrible. One shell pitched in our signal cart and blew the limber 55 yards away from the body.

The 2nd Battalion remained at St. Jean the next day, and in the evening received orders to move back and refit on the following night:

The Brigadier is directed by Sir Douglas Haig to inform the 4th Guards Brigade that their relief will definitely take place to-morrow night 20th/21st for certain. He also wishes it to be explained that by sticking to their positions for an extra day, the whole British Expeditionary Force has benefited to the extent that their front is now narrowed to the line La Bassée—Wytschaete, whereas if the relief had taken place yesterday it would have had to extend from La Bassée to the Canal.

The following orders for concentration of troops when relieved from the trenches were issued:

(1) Battalions not in the trenches, viz. 2nd Battalion Grenadiers, Irish Guards, Herts Battalion, will march in the above order under Lieut.-Colonel W. R. A. Smith, Grenadier Guards, on Ypres level crossing J 13 A,

thence by road passing J 12, the south edge of J 11, southern portion of I 15.14, thence through I 13 A, thence to Ouderdomm. Starting-point road junction at Y of Ypres. Time, 4 P.M.

(2) All first-line transport, except pack animals, which will accompany Battalions, will march under Brigade Transport Officer Captain Gough to Ouderdomm, in time to arrive there by 2 P.M. It will be met by Captain R. de Crespigny, who will point out bivouacking areas to units.

(3) Units will arrange to have a meal waiting for them on arrival at Ouderdomm; after eating this they will march independently to Meteren, where they will go into billets. The three battalions under Lieut.-Colonel Smith will march together under his orders. The route from Ouderdomm to Meteren *via* Westoutre—Montnoir—La Manche.

(4) Officers commanding all units will be responsible that the route that they have to follow is reconnoitred by daylight.

Orders were first sent for these battalions to start at 4 P.M., and later the time was altered to 10.45 P.M. The 2nd Battalion Grenadiers arrived at the rendezvous in plenty of time, and as the Hertfordshire Territorials did not turn up, Lieut.-Colonel Smith waited for it till past midnight, and then marched off. It was bitterly cold, and owing to the frozen state of the road extremely slippery. On account of the accumulation of guns and transports, the battalions were forced to march in single file down the side of the road, and to pass miles of wagons before they were able to march in fours. At 3 A.M. they had some tea, and arrived at their destination at 8.30, when they went into billets.

CHAPTER VII.

2nd Batt.
Nov. 1914.

LETTER FROM BRIGADIER-GENERAL THE EARL OF CAVAN TO THE OFFICER COMMANDING THE GRENADIER GUARDS

The 2nd Battalion moves back to-night about 15 miles with the rest of the Brigade to refit, reorganise, and rest. It leaves the line intact, and, in spite of great loss and untold sufferings and hardships, it fought the battle of Nov. 17 with as good a nerve as the battle of the Aisne. It has perhaps had the hardest time of any of the four battalions, as its rest days in Corps Reserve were entirely taken up with marching and making counter-strokes at various parts of the line.

I can never express what I think of the great courage and endurance shown by officers and men during the defence before Ypres, and I should like to put on the regimental records not only my sense of pride at being their Brigadier, but my debt to the Battalion for their great devotion to their duty. The men have all kept up a respectable appearance, which has been an example, considering that it has been absolutely impossible to change an article of clothing for four weeks. It is hoped that some officers and men may be able to get home for a few days' complete rest and change.

(Signed) CAVAN, Brigadier,
Commanding 4th Guards Bgde.

CHAPTER VIII

NOVEMBER 1914 TO MARCH 1915

Diary of the War

IN November 1914 the war of stagnation had already begun. The power of modern weapons in defence had made open warfare an impossibility, and the struggle in France had now assumed the character of siege warfare. Lines of trench some five hundred miles in length stretched from the Belgian coast to the Swiss frontier, and high explosive in every form and shape was fired from monster guns or thrown by hand. Miles of barbed wire covered the ground between the opposing lines of trenches, and sappers and miners continued to mine and to counter-mine. At the time it was thought that this state of things was merely the prelude to a gigantic battle which would decide the issue of the war.

The British Army at the beginning of November was holding a longer line than it well could hold, and in December Sir John French was able to shorten the line to thirty miles in length. In co-operation with the Eighth French Army, under General D'Urbal, the British Army attempted to advance in the direction of Wytschaete, but after several unsuccessful attacks these operations ceased. In January there were three weeks' comparative quiet, and then the enemy commenced an organised attack on Givenchy, but was effectually stopped by the First Division. The Germans made a more successful effort near Guinchy, and some ground was temporarily gained by them, but a determined counter-attack by the 4th (Guards) Brigade restored the line. South of La Bassée Canal the 3rd Battalion Coldstream and 1st Battalion Irish Guards captured a place known as the Brickstacks; on February 14 the 82nd Brigade was driven out of their trenches east of St. Eloi; and two days later the Twenty-eighth Division was forced to retire. In both cases the lost ground was recovered by counter-attacks. On March 10 the battle of Neuve Chapelle was fought, and lasted three days.

In addition to the fighting in the north in co-operation with the British and Belgian armies, the French were engaged practically all along their line. For purely sentimental reasons they continued their attacks on Alsace: although there were local successes, no actual gain of territory was made, and their losses were enormous.

The movements of the Russian Army were at first partly successful. Under the Grand Duke Nicholas it invaded East Prussia, invested the fortress of Königsberg, and reached the Masurian Lake region. The Southern Russian Army entered the north of Austria, cleared Galicia as far as the River San, and invested Przemysl. Its advance was, however, checked by the severe defeat which it suffered at Tannenberg, and it was forced to retire from East Prussia, which it again invaded in October. In the meantime, the Germans assembled a large army in Silesia, and advancing from Posen, forced the Russians to retire into Poland. Soon afterwards the Germans invaded Russia itself, and gained a victory at Grodno. In Austria the Russians were more successful, and after defeating the Austrian Army at Rawazuska, succeeded in capturing the stronghold of Przemysl which had been considered impregnable.

On March 18 an unsuccessful attempt was made by the combined British and French Fleets to force the Dardanelles. This was the beginning of the Gallipoli campaign.

In German South-West Africa General Botha landed at Swakopmund, near Walfish Bay, in February, and advanced to Jackalswater and Riet. A British Expeditionary Force also began operations in the Cameroons, and there was some fighting in German East Africa.

Naval warfare was practically at an end by the beginning of 1915, as all the German ships had been cleared off the high seas. The German Fleet itself had taken refuge in Kiel Harbour, and there was nothing for the British Fleet to do but to wait patiently, in the hope that it would one day emerge and give battle. During March the blockade of Germany began, but the problem of how to deal with neutrals had not been solved, and the Germans were able to get all they wanted through Holland and the three Scandinavian countries.

The 1st Battalion

Chapter VIII.

1st Batt. Nov. 1914.

On the 14th the 20th Brigade marched through Bailleul, Steenwerck, Sailly, Bac-St.-Maur to the trenches in the neighbourhood of Fleurbaix, where it relieved the 19th Brigade. The Grenadiers were on the right, the Scots Guards in the centre, and the Border Regiment on the left. Brigadier-General F. J. Heyworth, D.S.O., arrived from England, to take over the command of the Brigade.

Throughout November the Brigade remained in the same line of trenches. At first there was a great deal of rain, but towards the end of the month it changed to snow and was bitterly cold. The men suffered very much from trench feet, as the ground was in a shocking condition. Goats' skins were issued, and also some white smocks for patrol duty at night, as the dark uniforms showed up so clearly in the snow.

Major C. E. Corkran came from the Staff, to take over the command of the Battalion from the 17th till the 29th, when Lieut.-Colonel L. R. Fisher-Rowe arrived from England to assume command. On the 20th a draft of 100 men arrived with the following officers: Captain J. A. Morrison, Captain the Earl Stanhope, Second Lieutenant Lord Brabourne, Second Lieutenant Lord William Percy, Second Lieutenant Rhys Williams.

The Eighth Division under Major-General Davies arrived from England, and completed the Fourth Corps.

The enemy was constantly busy digging sapheads, and the shelling was continuous. Lieutenant E. S. Ward was wounded on the 15th, but although there were a number of casualties in the Brigade the Battalion did not suffer much. On the 29th Captain Rose commanding the 55th Company R.E. was killed. His loss was keenly felt by the whole Brigade, and especially by the Grenadiers, as he had never spared himself, and had been of the greatest assistance to all the officers. On the 24th Major G. F. Trotter, M.V.O., D.S.O., joined the Battalion.

Chapter VIII.

1st Batt. Nov. 1914.

On December 1 His Majesty the King paid a visit to the Division, accompanied by Lieutenant H.R.H. the Prince of Wales, the President of the French Republic, General Joffre, and Major-General Sir Pertab Singh.

Dec.

Special Order of the Day by His Majesty the King

General Headquarters, *Dec.* 5, 1914.

Officers, Non-Commissioned Officers and Men,

I am very glad to have been able to see my Army in the Field.

I much wished to do so, in order to gain a slight experience of the life you are leading.

I wish I could have spoken to you all, to express my admiration of the splendid manner in which you have fought and are still fighting against a powerful and relentless enemy.

By your discipline, pluck, and endurance, inspired by the indomitable regimental spirit, you have not only upheld the traditions of the British Army, but added fresh lustre to its history.

I was particularly impressed by your soldierly, healthy, cheerful appearance.

CHAPTER VIII.
1st Batt.
Dec. 1914.

I cannot share in your trials, dangers, and successes, but I can assure you of the proud confidence and gratitude of myself and of your fellow-countrymen.

We follow you in our daily thoughts on your certain road to victory.
GEORGE R.I.

The weather all the month of December was very bad, and it was with difficulty that the trenches were kept from falling in. A draft of 66 men under Captain E. O. Stewart arrived on the 3rd, and one of 45 men under Captain the Hon. G. H. Douglas-Pennant on the 12th. On the 15th Second Lieutenant E. H. J. Duberly and Second Lieutenant T. Parker-Jervis joined the Battalion, and on the 17th a draft of 60 men with Lieutenant C. H. Greville and Second Lieutenant C. R. Rowley arrived. On the 21st Second Lieutenant F. O. S. Sitwell, Second Lieutenant C. F. Burnand, and Second Lieutenant C. T. R. S. Guthrie joined the Battalion, and on the 23rd a draft of 41 men under Second Lieutenant G. R. Westmacott arrived. On the 28th Second Lieutenant C. G. Goschen arrived.

There were numerous cases of frostbite, and a certain amount of sickness owing to the cold wet weather, but considering the constant soaking the men received, and the amount of water in the trenches, the health of the Battalion was on the whole good.

The Battalion was constantly engaged in digging and improving the trenches as far as possible, but the water-logged condition of the ground, combined with the vigilance of the German snipers, made the work difficult. The bombing and sniping continued daily, and were accompanied occasionally by high-explosive shells. The latter were, however, generally directed by the Germans against any place that would be likely to harbour generals or staff. On one of the visits which the Prince of Wales paid to the 1st Battalion, he narrowly escaped one of these shells, which exploded outside the house he was in. On the 19th Lieutenant J. Teece, the Quartermaster, was wounded, and Lieutenant Mitchell took over his duties.

On the 18th an organised attack on the German trenches was made by the 22nd Brigade. The 20th Brigade was ordered to assist with two half battalions by attacking the edge of the Sailly—Fromelles road. It was decided to double-man the trenches opposite the point of attack, and the Scots Guards were therefore withdrawn from the right, being relieved by the Grenadiers. The attack was to be undertaken by half a battalion of the Scots Guards and half a battalion of the Border Regiment. Brigade Headquarters were transferred to La Carbonière Farm, so as to be in close touch with the trenches. The guns being short of ammunition, the artillery decided not to open fire till just before the attack was launched. The Grenadiers had to go down, and relieve the Scots Guards in broad daylight, and this unusual activity in our lines, which was far too apparent, gave the enemy ample warning of our intended attack. The Scots Guards launched their attack at the pre-arranged time, but the signal was not understood down the line, with the result that the attacks were by no means simultaneous. The men of the Border

CHAPTER VIII.
1st Batt.
Dec. 1914.

Regiment found great difficulty in getting through their own wire entanglements, which considerably delayed them. The Scots Guards, however, succeeded in rushing the German trenches and bayoneting the occupants, but a machine-gun which they were unable to knock out caused a large number of casualties. The other attacks having failed, the Scots Guards were ordered to return, as the Germans had been able to bring up large reinforcements.

Although little had been accomplished, the enemy had been obliged to keep all their men in the trenches to resist this attack, and had therefore been unable to send reinforcements farther south. This was practically the sole object of our attack.

Christmas came with the whole country deep in mud and slush. Parcels of shirts, socks, etc. were received from Colonel Streatfeild, who succeeded in supplying the wants of the Battalion with the utmost regularity, while luxuries were sent by Major-General Sir Reginald Thynne, an old Grenadier Commanding Officer, who had undertaken to send one surprise packet to every man in each battalion, in addition to the parcels which he sent regularly from the officers' wives to any Grenadier prisoners in Germany.

On the 24th Captain Morrison, on behalf of the King's Company, addressed the following telegram to the King:

The Officers, N.C.O.'s, and men of the King's Company, Grenadier Guards, respectfully offer Your Majesty best wishes for Christmas and the New Year.

His Majesty's answer was as follows:

CHAPTER VIII.

1st Batt. Dec. 1914.

I heartily thank Officers, N.C.O.'s, and men for their message of Christmas and New Year greetings, which I warmly reciprocate. You are all more than ever in my thoughts at this moment.

GEORGE R.I., Colonel-in-Chief.

Christmas Day passed off without a shot being fired by either side in that part of the line. This does not appear to have been the result of any definite agreement, but simply a tacit understanding on the part of both forces to refrain from firing during that day.

Many experiments were made with mortars and bombs at Bac-St.-Maur. Officers who were present afterwards asserted that they infinitely preferred the enemy's shot and shell to the uncertain and erratic explosions during these experiments. The new trench mortar had a way of moving round and facing the wrong way after one or two shots had been fired, which was disconcerting.

Though the art of bomb-throwing was still in its infancy, the importance of this form of trench warfare had already impressed itself on every one in France. The Ordnance at home was confused by the many recommendations that were made, and issued bombs of every pattern, in order to ascertain by practical means which was the best; but as every brigade favoured a different bomb, the selection became a matter of great difficulty. In every brigade a company of 150 bomb-throwers was formed, and the men were thoroughly trained. Second Lieutenant Rhys

Williams was selected to command the company of bomb-throwers in the 20th Brigade.

Towards the end of December the constant heavy rain had played havoc with the trenches. The whole country had become completely water-logged, and as soon as water was pumped out of one portion of a trench it broke through in another. The Germans were in the same plight, and could be observed at pumping operations daily. It was impossible to dig any trench below a depth of two feet, and in some places it became necessary to build breastworks over the ground.

One of the great difficulties the men in the trenches had to contend with was that the rifles during an attack were rendered useless by the mud. Whenever an attack was made the rifles became so clogged with mud that the men had nothing but the bayonet to fight with. To carry 200 or more rounds of small-arms ammunition all through the day, and then find they are merely ornamental when the fighting begins, is rather disheartening, and the Divisional Authorities therefore devised a rough canvas cover to slip over the muzzle of the rifle. This cover could be pulled off instantly when required, but even if the rifle was fired with the cover on no harm was done. A letter found on a German colonel some months later revealed the fact that the enemy had been much struck with the idea of a cover of this sort, and had taken steps to have one made on the British pattern.

The following letter from His Royal Highness the Duke of Connaught, Colonel of the Grenadiers, and at the time Governor-General of Canada, was forwarded for the officers of the Battalion to read:

GOVERNMENT HOUSE, OTTAWA,
January 12, 1915.

MY DEAR STREATFEILD—Most grateful thanks for three letters of the 23rd, 29th, and 30th of December.

I have been deeply interested with all the regimental news you have so kindly sent me, especially with the letters of Colonel Wilfred Smith and Captain Morrison, and the very gratifying order of General Capper. It is really splendid to hear how well both battalions have done under most serious and trying circumstances, which must have tried the nerves and endurance of all ranks to the very utmost.

As I expected, our Officers have set a splendid example of capacity and bravery. It is hard to think what terrible losses all this splendid work has entailed on the Regiment, and how many Officers we have to mourn. May they not have given their precious lives for nothing, but may their names and example be ever preserved in the Regiment in whose honour they have fallen.

I hope that never again will companies have to occupy so large a front as ours have done; with less good troops the risk would appear to me to have been too great to run.

I am glad to hear such good accounts of our 4th Reserve Battalion. I thank you for so kindly sending on my message to the 1st and 2nd Battalions. I was anxious that they should know that although so far away they were in my thoughts.—Believe me, yours very sincerely,

(Signed) ARTHUR.

LIST OF OFFICERS OF THE 1ST BATTALION GRENADIER GUARDS ON JANUARY 1, 1915

Lieut.-Colonel L. R. Fisher-Rowe . Commanding Officer.
Major G. F. Trotter, M.V.O., D.S.O. Second in Command.
Lieut. C. V. Fisher-Rowe . . Adjutant.
2nd Lieut. E. H. J. Duberly . Machine-gun Officer.

198 THE GRENADIER GUARDS

CHAPTER VIII.

1st Batt. Jan. 1915.

Lieut. C. Mitchell	Acting Quartermaster.
Capt. J. A. Morrison	King's Company.
2nd Lieut. C. T. R. S. Guthrie	,, ,,
2nd Lieut. C. G. Goschen	,, ,,
Captain the Hon. G. H. Douglas-Pennant	No. 2 Company.
2nd Lieut. Lord Brabourne	,, ,,
2nd Lieut. C. F. Burnand	,, ,,
Captain the Earl Stanhope	No. 3 Company.
2nd Lieut. Lord William Percy	,, ,,
2nd Lieut. G. R. Westmacott	,, ,,
Captain the Hon. R. Lygon	No. 4 Company.
Lieut. M. A. A. Darby	,, ,,
2nd Lieut. F. O. S. Sitwell	,, ,,
2nd Lieut. J. Parker-Jervis	,, ,,

The following officers from the Artists' Rifles were attached to the Battalion: Second Lieutenant Crisp to the King's Company, and Second Lieutenant A. Moller to No. 2 Company.

Jan.

The Battalion occupied the same trench line all January, and every four days was relieved by the Scots Guards, when it went into Divisional Reserve. On the 11th a draft of 65 men under Captain W. E. Nicol arrived, and on the 26th one of 60 men under Lieutenant H. W. Ethelston. On the 27th Lieutenant A. S. L. St. J. Mildmay joined.

Some officers of the Grenadiers were lent to the Scots Guards, who were very short of officers, and remained away for some time. On the 5th Second Lieutenant Crisp, who had been attached to the Battalion from the Artists' Corps, was coming across an open place, where the trenches had fallen in and had become impassable, when he was shot through the body and died shortly afterwards. Lieut.-Colonel Fisher-Rowe, who was only fifty yards away at the time, came up

Lieutenant-Colonel L. R. Fisher Rowe
Commanding 1st Battalion
Died of wounds received at Neuve Chapelle 10 March 1915

to give him morphia, but found him quite unconscious. He had done so well, and made himself so popular, that his death was much regretted by the Battalion.

With this exception there were no casualties among the officers and very few among the men, although the Germans expended a large amount of ammunition on that part of the line.

The redoubts were finished, and proved a great success. It was curious to note that the Germans were struck with the same idea, and began constructing forts in rear of their inundated trenches. A certain amount of leave was granted to the officers and N.C.O.'s, and those who had been out some time were all given a week at home.

February found the Battalion still in the same trenches, which had by now been very greatly improved. The problem of the water had been partially solved by the efforts of the R.E., and the men were able to take some pride in their trench line. There was a certain amount of sickness, with occasional cases of influenza. A motor ambulance, presented by Captain J. A. Morrison to the Battalion, arrived, and while the officers and men much appreciated the gift, the Medical Authorities were much concerned at the irregularity of the proceeding.

On the 13th Lieutenant R. F. C. Gelderd-Somervell joined the Battalion, and Captain the Earl Stanhope left to take up his duties as A.D.C. to the General Commanding the Fifth Army Corps. He had proved himself such a good officer that the Commanding Officer was sorry to lose him. On the 23rd Captain E. F. F. Sartorius joined the Battalion, and took over command of No. 3 Company.

There had been a certain number of casualties among the men from sniping and shell-fire, but the greater part of the losses were from sickness.

On March 3 the Battalion was relieved by the Canadians, and billeted in the Rue du Bois. It marched the next morning to Neuf Berquin, and on the following day to Estaires. On the 10th it joined the rest of the 20th Brigade, which was on the main Estaires — La Bassée road. Before taking over the trenches, Lieutenant Darby was sent up to go over the ground, so that he might be able to guide the companies when they went up. At luncheon-time he returned with the intelligence that the shelling in the front trench was terrific, and that even as far back as the reserve trenches the noise was deafening, all of which seemed to point to a lively time for the Battalion.

As the Battalion marched up, the men were much impressed by the sight of the Chestnut Battery going into action. This crack battery of the Royal Artillery, manned by splendid men and drawn by picked horses, came thundering down the road, and as it passed the men of the Grenadiers broke into a cheer.

Although the enemy's shells were bursting over the Battalion, only one actually pitched near the men, doing no damage, and in the evening the Battalion went into billets, the King's Company in the Rue du Bacquerot, and Nos. 2, 3, and 4 in Cameren Lane.

CHAPTER IX

NOVEMBER 1914 TO MAY 1915 (2ND BATTALION)

THE Battalion remained in billets at Meteren from November 22 till December 22. The casualties among the officers had been severe, and there only remained Lieut.-Colonel Smith, Major Jeffreys, Captain Ridley, Captain Cavendish, Lieutenant Hughes, Lieutenant and Adjutant the Hon. W. Bailey, Lieutenant Beaumont-Nesbitt, Lieutenant Marshall, Second Lieutenant Cunninghame (Transport Officer), Second Lieutenant Gerard, Lieutenant and Quartermaster Skidmore, and Captain Howell, R.A.M.C. (attached).

The King inspected the 4th Guards Brigade at Meteren, and afterwards presented Distinguished Conduct Medals to a certain number of N.C.O.'s and men.

In the evening the following special order was issued :

The Brigadier is commanded by His Majesty the King, the Colonel - in - Chief, to convey to the four battalions of the Brigade of Guards the following gracious words which His Majesty addressed to the four Commanding Officers : " I am very proud of my Guards, and I am full of admiration for their bravery, endurance, and fine spirit. I wish I could have addressed them all, but that was impossible. So you must tell them what I say to you. You are fighting a brave and determined enemy, but if you go on as you have been doing and show the same spirit, as I am sure you will, there can only be one end, please God, and that is Victory. I wish you all good luck."

Dec. 21. On December 21 the news arrived that the Indian Corps had been heavily attacked, and driven out of its trenches between La Bassée Canal and Richebourg. The First Corps was at once to be moved down to this part of the line, and that evening orders were received by the Second Division to be ready to march at two hours' notice. When a line of trenches stretches some hundreds of miles, the rough must be taken with the smooth, and the 2nd Battalion Grenadiers was soon to find that the site of its trenches was anything but an ideal one. To dig a trench in a water-logged valley outraged all preconceived principles; yet it was in such a locality that the men of the Grenadiers were to find themselves for the following months.

Minor operations, as they were called, consisted in nibbling away a few hundred yards. The casualties which occurred daily from bombing and sniping were hardly taken into account. Yet those who took part in this monotonous underground warfare did as much to win the war as those who were fortunate enough to fight in one of the big battles.

Dec. 22–23. The 4th Brigade marched off early by Merville to Bethune, about nineteen miles, and there billeted fairly comfortably. The next day it marched on, and halted in a field at Essarts, near

Le Touret, in readiness to support the 2nd Brigade. In the evening it moved on again, and took over the line at Rue de Cailloux from the Royal Sussex Regiment after dark. These trenches were very bad, and had been hastily improvised from dykes, when the Germans succeeded in capturing our front-line trenches a few days before. The water was always knee-deep, in some places waist-deep, in mud and water, and as the enemy's trench was within twenty-five yards, his snipers, who were always enterprising, had plenty of opportunities of shooting. The taking over of these trenches was complicated by men getting stuck, and having to be dug out, so that it was nearly six hours before the relief was completed. In some cases it took four hours to dig the men out, during which time many of them fainted several times. No. 1 Company under Captain Sir M. Cholmeley, No. 2 under Captain P. A. Clive, and half No. 3 under Captain Cavendish, were in the firing line, while the other half of No. 3, and No. 4 Company under Captain Ridley were in reserve.

CHAPTER IX.

2nd Batt. Dec. 1914.

The early morning began with considerable sniping and bombardment with trench mortars. It was bitterly cold, and the water in the trenches made communication almost impossible. It seemed madness to attempt to hold such a line of trenches, and yet there was no alternative.

Dec. 24.

Notes of warning arrived from General Headquarters:

It is thought possible that the enemy may be contemplating an attack during Christmas or New Year. Special vigilance will be maintained during these periods.

And again later :

Please note that when the enemy is active with Minenwerfer, it is generally the prelude to an attack.

The enemy had the advantage of the ground, for not only did his trenches drain into ours, but he was able to overlook our whole line. In addition to this he was amply supplied with trench mortars and hand grenades, so that we were fighting under very great difficulties. He mined within ten yards of our trench, and blew in the end of No. 2's trench, after which he attacked in great force, but was unable to do more than just reach our line. Captain Sir M. Cholmeley, Bart., and Second Lieutenant J. H. Neville were killed. Sergeant G. H. Thomas, who had just been awarded the D.C.M., was also killed, while Second Lieutenant G. G. Goschen was wounded and taken prisoner. He had a narrow escape of being drowned in the trench, and was propped up by one of the men just in time. Lieutenant Eyre and Second Lieutenant Mervyn Williams were wounded.

In the evening Lieut.-Colonel Smith came to the conclusion that fighting under such conditions was only courting disaster, and that it would be clearly better to dig a new line of trenches during the night, but it was absolutely necessary to finish the new line before daylight—otherwise it would be useless. Accordingly he gave orders for a new line to be dug, and the men, soaked and stiff with cold as they were, set to work at once. Rockets and fireballs gave the enemy's snipers their opportunity, and the freezing water and hard ground made the work difficult. There was, however, no artillery fire, though the Minenwerfer were nearly as bad, and threw large shells into our trenches. The new line was just completed as dawn broke on Christmas morning.

<small>Chapter IX.
2nd Batt.
Dec.
1914.</small>

The sniping continued steadily the next day with great accuracy, and the slightest movement drew a shot at once. Captain E. G. Spencer Churchill was wounded in the head in this way, the bullet making a groove in his skull. The new trenches, however, threatened to become as wet as the old ones, although in the worst places they were built with a high parapet and a shallow trench. No. 3 Company, under Captain Cavendish, in particular succeeded in erecting an elevated trench of this nature, in spite of the incessant sniping which was carried on during the night.

<small>Dec. 25.</small>

Lord Cavan sent a message :

> Hearty congratulations on good night's work. Thank Captain Cavendish and his Company. Am absolutely satisfied with arrangements. Report when and how you manœuvre the little stream.

It being Christmas Day, plum puddings and other luxuries were distributed, and Princess Mary's present of a box, containing a pipe, tobacco, and cigarettes, was much appreciated.

In the evening the Battalion was relieved by the 3rd Battalion Coldstream, and marched back to Le Touret, where it billeted, and remained for forty-eight hours.

Chapter IX.
2nd Batt. Dec. 1914.

The Battalion was now composed as follows :

Lieut.-Colonel W. R. A. Smith . .	Headquarters.
Major G. D. Jeffreys	,,
Lieutenant and Adjutant the Hon. W. R. Bailey	,,
2nd Lieut. M. Williams (Machine-gun Officer)	,,
Lieutenant and Quartermaster J. H. Skidmore.	,,
Capt. J. S. Hughes	No. 1 Company.
Lieut. A. K. S. Cunninghame (Transport Officer)	,, ,,
2nd Lieut. J. N. Buchanan . . .	,, ,,
2nd Lieut. G. W. V. Hopley . .	,, ,,
Capt. P. A. Clive, M.P. . . .	No. 2 Company.
Lieut. F. G. Marshall	,, ,,
2nd Lieut. J. C. Craigie . . .	,, ,,
2nd Lieut. H. C. L. Rumbold . .	,, ,,
Capt. A. B. R. R. Gosselin . . .	No. 3 Company.
Capt. R. H. V. Cavendish, M.V.O. .	,, ,,
Lieut. C. R. Gerard	,, ,,
2nd Lieut. H. S. E. Bury . . .	,, ,,
Capt. E. D. Ridley	,, ,,
Lieut. F. G. Beaumont-Nesbitt . .	No. 4 Company.
Lieut. C. R. Britten	,, ,,
2nd Lieut. E. G. Williams . . .	,, ,,

Attached—Captain F. D. G. Howell, R.A.M.C.

Dec. 27-28. The Battalion returned to the same line of trenches, and found them as unpleasant as before. The cover had been improved, and the communication trenches were better, but the water stood in them as deep as ever. On the night of the 28th it blew a gale, and the cold was intense. The rain that came down all night not only filled the trenches with more water, but broke down the parapet and loopholes in many places. The men passed a miserable night, soaked to

NOVEMBER 1914 TO MAY 1915

the skin, with no means of keeping warm, and although the constant repairs to the parapet kept them employed, the sniping made all work difficult and dangerous.

A few of the enemy's 6-inch shells fell on the trenches, but not with sufficient accuracy to cause any damage. The trenches were still in a terrible state, communication was impossible, and there were numerous cases of frostbite. In the evening of the 29th the Battalion was again relieved by the 3rd Battalion Coldstream, and went back to Le Touret, where it remained two days.

On the 31st it returned to the flooded trenches again, and was subjected to the usual sniping and bombing. The Germans were using a trench mortar which fired large bombs from some distance into our line, while at that time we had nothing more than hand grenades, which were somewhat primitive and dangerous to the thrower. The water, however, was the greatest difficulty our men had to contend with: it made the communication trenches impassable, and accounted for more men than the enemy's bullets. It ate away the parapet, rotted the men's clothing, rusted and jammed the rifles, retarded the food supply, and generally made the life of the men in the trenches hideous; but in spite of all this discomfort the men remained cheerful and in good spirits.

Lord Cavan, who was much exercised by the water problem, gave orders that all impossible places were to be vacated and watched by pivots, and the R.E. received instructions from

Chapter IX.
2nd Batt.
Dec. 1914.

Dec. 29–30.

Dec. 31– Jan. 2.

him to give their attention to this portion of the line. Our artillery proceeded systematically to flatten out any house on the enemy's side, as it was found that the smallest building usually harboured snipers, while the enemy's artillery kept up a desultory fire; but after what the Battalion had been accustomed to at Ypres, it seemed mere child's play.

Second Lieutenant H. C. Rumbold happened to be engaged in drawing at one of the gunners' observation posts, when a shell struck it; in addition to being wounded, he was struck by the falling masonry, and was consequently sent home. Though the casualties in the 4th Brigade had lately been very heavy, drafts were sent from home with great efficiency, and the 2nd Battalion Grenadiers had a fair supply of officers. The Coldstream was, however, very short, and the Brigadier found it necessary to transfer the following officers from the Grenadiers to the Coldstream: Lieutenants Kingsmill, Abel-Smith, Lang, and Creed.

On January 2 the Battalion was relieved by the South Staffords, and went into reserve at Locon, where it billeted and remained till the 7th of January.

The Prince of Wales, on one of his many visits to the Battalion, brought the men a gramophone, which was much appreciated by every one, and helped to enliven the evenings.

A few days' rest worked wonders with the Battalion, and converted ill-shaved men, in clothes sodden and coated with mud, once more into smart, well-turned-out Guardsmen. The line now taken over was near Rue du Bois, and the Battalion Headquarters were at Rue des Berceaux. Two companies were in the firing line, with two platoons in the front trench and the other two in support; the remainder of the Battalion formed the reserve.

CHAPTER IX.

2nd Batt. Jan. 1915.

The rain continued in torrents, and the trench line became a sort of lake. The companies, not in the front trench, were engaged in digging second-line trenches, and a trench that was dug by Nos. 2 and 4 Companies was known for two years after as the Guards' trench. It was considered a model of what a good trench should be.

The usual routine was to relieve the men in the trenches every twelve hours, and bring them back to be dried, rubbed, and cleaned; and there was not much sickness, although several men were crippled with rheumatism, and would have found great difficulty in marching any distance. The gruesome task of removing the dead was effected by floating the bodies down the communication trenches.

On the 12th the following order was circulated from Brigade Headquarters:

The Brigadier has much pleasure in forwarding a copy of a letter received from General Monro, and desires that it should be read to every man.

"I have this moment heard from an officer of the Indian Corps an account of what he saw at the fight for Givenchy, in which the 1st Brigade was engaged. His position enabled him to see the attack of the Coldstream, and the following are his words : ' They marched forward without the least hesitation under the most terrific fire, just as though they were on parade. The Indian Brigade watched the progress of the Guards with the profoundest admiration. I thought perhaps the officers and privates of the Brigade of Guards might like to know the admiration which their conduct inspires in outsiders. We who have been through much with them know right well that the description I have given merely represents their normal behaviour in action, yet possibly it may please the men to hear what I have written.' "

Lieut.-Colonel Smith in a private letter to Colonel Streatfeild wrote :

I cannot thank you enough for the excellent officers you have sent me out. I have had the sorrow of seeing nearly a whole battalion of first-rate officers go one by one, and yet you have been able to send me a second lot who promise to be almost as good.

The Battalion was relieved by an Indian regiment, and went into billets at Le Touret to rest for two days, after which it returned to the trenches in Rue des Bois near Rue des Berceaux. The water was as bad as ever, and even rose after a snowstorm. The whole country was waterlogged, and there was constant difficulty in keeping up the parapets, which crumbled and fell in great blocks, in spite of the ceaseless labour expended on them. The enemy's snipers took every advantage of the crumbling parapets, and accounted for many of our men. Sergeant Croft was killed by a sniper, and Corporal Parkinson, who, as Lord Bernard Gordon-Lennox's orderly, must have evaded thousands of bullets and shells, was shot dead by a stray bullet.

After another four days in reserve at Les Choqueaux, the 4th Brigade marched to Gorre in support of the First Division, which endeavoured to retake the trenches which had been lost at Givenchy. Having waited about all day, the Brigade returned to its billets at Les Choqueaux in the evening. The same procedure was gone through the following day, but on neither occasion was the Brigade wanted.

Chapter IX.
2nd Batt. Jan. 1915.

Four officers of the Grenadiers had been temporarily attached to the Scots Guards: Second Lieutenant H. S. E. Bury, Second Lieutenant G. Hamilton Fletcher, Second Lieutenant A. H. Lang, Second Lieutenant J. A. Denny. On the 25th they were all four hit by a shell that exploded in the trench. Second Lieutenants Bury, Hamilton Fletcher, and Lang were killed, and Second Lieutenant Denny was severely wounded.

About this time a case of cerebral meningitis, or spotted fever, was discovered at the Guards' Depot at Caterham, Surrey, and orders were given for all drafts from England to be isolated. This caused a certain amount of inconvenience, as it was by no means easy to isolate a draft of 200 men. There were at the time only eight subalterns with the Battalion, which made the duty very heavy for the officers, but some of the other battalions had not even so many.

From the 28th to the 30th the Battalion remained in billets at Les Choqueaux, and on the 30th marched to Bethune. It was only during marches of this length that the whole Battalion assembled together, and saw itself as a Battalion, instead of in isolated companies. It presented an extraordinary appearance. Hung round like a Christmas tree, wearing fur waistcoats, gum-boots, and carrying long French loaves, braziers, charcoal, spades, and sandbags, it looked more like a body of irregular troops from the Balkans than a battalion of Guards.

On February 1 the Battalion marched to Annequin, and No. 1 Company under Lord Henry Seymour went into the trenches at Guinchy, to reinforce the Coldstream Guards who had been heavily engaged. On the 2nd the whole Battalion took over from the Irish Guards the trenches from La Bassée road to the Keep, where it remained till the 5th. Although there was heavy shelling, the casualties were not large, but Second Lieutenant G. W. V. Hopley was badly wounded, and Sergeant Buttle killed.

On February 1 the Germans broke the line in the Guinchy neighbourhood, and Cavan's 4th Brigade was brought up. A company of the 2nd Battalion Coldstream, supported by one company of Irish Guards, was ordered to counterattack, but failed to retake the lost trench. Lord Cavan, having left orders that the ground was to be held at all costs, went off, and arranged a heavy bombardment from the howitzers and siege guns. As soon as this ceased 50 men from the 2nd Battalion Coldstream, followed by 30 men from the Irish Guards, with a company of the 2nd Battalion Grenadiers in support, dashed forward, and succeeded in taking all the lost ground. The attack was so successful that the Grenadiers never came into action.

During the whole of February the 2nd Battalion Grenadiers occupied the trenches at Guinchy. The usual routine was forty-eight hours in the trenches, and forty-eight hours' rest in billets at Beuvry. The weather, which at home is only noticed by people with weak conversational powers, becomes a matter of enormous importance when you have to stand in a ditch for two days and two nights. The wet and cold made the life in the trenches at first very trying, but later, when the spring began, the nights in the trenches became bearable.

Chapter IX.

2nd Batt. Feb. 1915.

Sniping and bombing with intermittent shelling were of constant occurrence. The sad news that some officer, sergeant, or private had been killed was passed down the trenches with wonderful rapidity, and was known at once by the whole Battalion. The line of trenches now occupied by the Battalion was much drier than those it had been accustomed to, and far more intricate. When the trenches were known the relief became easy, although it was always carried out in the dark, but at first, when the officers and N.C.O.'s took over the trenches for the first time, it was long before every one settled down.

The forty-eight hours' rest was spent in comparative comfort in billets at Beuvry, where the inhabitants still lived in spite of the proximity to the trenches. When the moment came to leave the billets and return to the trenches, the Battalion moved up in small parties at a time, in case the road should be shelled. Through endless transport of all kinds the men slowly wound their way. They usually met food going up, empties coming back, ammunition and supplies of all sorts, and as it became darker the road was more difficult. They often passed French troops

CHAPTER IX.
2nd Batt.
Feb. 1915.

on the way, with the secondary French transport, a motley collection of every conceivable sort of vehicle. Yet with all these different streams of men and wagons there was never any confusion or accident. As the platoons neared the trenches, stray bullets usually began to fly, and occasionally shells. Then each company, on reaching its allotted communication trench, disappeared, and so reached the firing line.

The Battalion Headquarters were in the cellar of the ruins of a house, and here the business part of the work was carried on by clerks and orderlies. Sometimes shells fell on the remains of the house, but the cellar was never reached. A motor canteen presented by Lord Derby to his old Battalion now arrived, and proved a great boon. It could provide hot drinks for 300 men at a time.

On the 7th Second Lieutenant H. A. R. Graham was badly wounded, and subsequently had to have his arm amputated. Captain A. B. R. R. Gosselin was bending down trying to dress his wound, when a piece of shell struck him in the neck and killed him instantaneously. On the 8th Second Lieutenant P. L. M. Battye was wounded in the leg, and Lieutenant Britten was sent to hospital with enteric fever.

On the 18th the Germans succeeded in taking a small portion of the French trenches on our right, and that evening the French sent a party to retake it. No report came, however, as to whether they had been successful or not, and considerable doubt existed as to whether this particular trench was in German or in French hands.

In order to decide this point, the French sent a reconnoitring party down our communication trench on the right, and asked Captain P. A. Clive's permission to move down our trench. Captain Clive not only offered to help, but decided to go himself. Accompanied by Major Foulkes, R.E., he led the French reconnoitring party into the trench of doubtful ownership, and there found a dug-out full of German kit, with a lighted candle burning. This evidence of German occupation satisfied the French party, but Captain Clive insisted on making further investigation, and crept on in pitch darkness, followed by Major Foulkes. Suddenly he was challenged in deep guttural German by a sentry, not two yards off. " Français, Français," he replied in a voice to which he was uncertain whether he should give a French or German accent. " Halt, oder Ich schiesse," was the reply, and the nationality of the occupants of the trench was settled beyond dispute. Even Captain Clive was convinced, and as the bullets whistled past him when he retired, the nationality of their makers was forcibly impressed on his mind.

The shelling varied : on some days it was mild, and on others for no apparent reason it became very violent. The difference, however, between the shelling here and that which the Battalion had been accustomed to near Ypres was, that while the German gunners at first had it all their own way, they were now not only answered but received back as many shells as they sent over. A great deal of work was done by the Battalion during the month, and the digging was constant night

CHAPTER IX.
2nd Batt.
Feb.
1915.

and day. The Keep was strengthened, many new communication trenches were dug, all very deep, eight to nine feet, and the right of the line, near the French, was made very strong. Supporting trenches were dug, and eventually the whole line was straightened out and wired. The majority of the men thoroughly understood how to dig, and the newcomers very quickly learnt from the old hands. On February 20 Lieutenant R. D. Lawford and a draft of sixty men joined the Battalion, and on the 23rd Second Lieutenants A. H. Penn, O. Lyttelton, and Viscount Cranborne arrived.

March.

For the first ten days in March the Battalion rested, and remained in billets at Bethune, where it had concerts and boxing competitions. On the 10th it marched to a position of readiness east of Gorre, with the remainder of the 4th Brigade, to form the reserve to the 6th Brigade, which was the pivot on which the whole move at Neuve Chapelle hung, though it did not come into action. The attack made by the 6th Brigade proved a most gallant but disastrous business, and the casualties were very heavy. At 3 P.M. the 4th Brigade was ordered up to support another attempt, which, however, never came off, and it therefore returned to its billets at Bethune. On the 11th the 4th Brigade was again moved up to the same place, but again was not wanted.

Captain Ridley, who held the almost unique record in the 4th Brigade of having taken part in every engagement from the commencement of the war, and who had been constantly fighting for five months, having twice been slightly wounded, went home sick, as the Commanding Officer and the doctor insisted on his taking this opportunity of having a rest.

CHAPTER IX.

2nd Batt. March 1915.

On the 12th the 2nd Battalion Grenadiers relieved the Irish Guards at Givenchy, where the trenches, which were comparatively new, were shallow and the parapet not bullet proof. The village was a complete ruin, the farms were burnt, and remains of wagons and farm implements were scattered on each side of the road. This part of the country had been taken and re-taken several times, and many hundreds of British, Indian, French, and German troops were buried here. The roads were full of shell-holes, bricks, tiles, cart-wheels, and debris of every description. The shelling and sniping went on intermittently, but the habits of the enemy were known, and when the shelling began it was generally easy to estimate how long it would last, and when it would begin again.

On the 16th Major Lord Henry Seymour and Captain J. S. Hughes were transferred to the 1st Battalion in the Seventh Division, and Captain C. de Crespigny joined the Battalion from Brigade Headquarters.

On the 22nd Lieutenant F. G. Marshall, who had been having tea with the doctor at the dressing-station, was returning to the trenches, when a stray bullet killed him. The casualties in the trenches were at that time not great, but occasionally at night a violent shelling would begin, directed towards the rear of the trenches, in the hopes of catching the troops coming up to relieve those in the front line.

CHAPTER IX.
2nd Batt.
March 1915.

The terrible tragedies that went on daily between the two firing lines gave some idea of the barbarous cruelty of the Germans. Men who were wounded in any attack or raid were forced to lie out between the lines, often in great agony, but whenever any of our stretcher-bearers attempted to reach them they were promptly fired at by the Germans. To show the vitality possessed by some human beings, cases occurred of men being left out wounded and without food or drink four or five days, conscious all the time that if they moved the Germans would shoot or throw bombs at them. At night German raiding parties would be sent out to bayonet any of the wounded still living, and would feel these unfortunate men's hands to see if they were stiff and cold. If any doubt existed, the bayonet settled the question. In spite of this, men often managed to crawl back just alive, and were quickly resuscitated by their comrades.

April.

On April 1 Major B. H. Barrington-Kennett, and on April 2 Second Lieutenant Hon. G. S. Bailey and Second Lieutenant P. K. Stephenson, joined the Battalion.

While digging a communication trench, in what had once been the Curé's garden, some men of the Battalion unearthed some silver, and also some presumably valuable papers. It seemed to the men that this was treasure-trove, but Lieut.-Colonel Smith, on hearing of the find, insisted that it should all be carefully packed up, papers, silver, and all, and sent to the French authorities for safe keeping. The owner, some weeks later, wrote a letter of profound gratitude, and enclosed a plan showing where some more of his treasures were buried. Another search was made, and these were all recovered, with the exception of one box which had been blown to bits by a shell.

All throughout April the Battalion remained in the same trenches, and was relieved every forty-eight hours by the Irish Guards, when it went into billets at Preol. A new trench howitzer was produced by the artillery with a range of 520 yards, which put us more on an equality with the enemy, and gave the men confidence. The mining had now become a regular practice, and every one was always listening for any sound that might denote mining operations. The shelling continued regularly, and at times a battalion coming up to take its turn in the trenches would be subjected to an unpleasant shelling.

The Commanding Officer, Lieut.-Colonel W. Smith, was accustomed to what he called "stumble round the trenches" every day, and many visits were paid by Lord Cavan and his staff, who became quite proficient in evading the various missiles which the enemy daily aimed at the trenches. On one of these occasions the Prince of Wales, who was a constant visitor, tried his hand at sniping, and as there was an immediate retaliation, his bullets very probably found their mark. The men were delighted to see His Royal Highness shooting away at the enemy, and when, as sometimes happened, the evening shelling of the Germans—" the evening hate," as it was termed by the men—began while the Prince was in the trenches, the men were always anxious to hear

CHAPTER IX

2nd Batt.
April 1915.

that His Royal Highness had finished his tour in safety.

On April 21 Captain G. L. Derriman and Second Lieutenant C. O. Creed joined the Battalion, with a draft of thirty men. On the 12th Major Lord Henry Seymour returned to the Battalion. On the 13th Second Lieutenant P. K. Stephenson left to join the 1st Battalion, and on the 26th Captain R. H. V. Cavendish was appointed Town Commandant at Bethune.

The weather gradually changed, and instead of the general gloom, the appalling mud, snow, and rain, the days began to be bright and hot, although the nights were still cold.

On the 23rd the Battalion relieved the Post Office Rifles (Territorials), and continued to remain in the trenches, with two companies in the firing line and two in reserve, relieving each other every two hours.

May.

LIST OF OFFICERS OF THE BATTALION
ON MAY 1, 1915

Lieut.-Colonel W. R. A. Smith . .	Headquarters.
Major G. D. Jeffreys	,,
Lieutenant and Acting Adjutant Hon. W. R. Bailey	,,
2nd Lieut. D. Abel-Smith (Machine-gun)	,,
Lieut. and Quartermaster W. E. Acraman	,,
Major Lord Henry Seymour . .	No. 1 Company.
Lieut. A. K. S. Cunninghame (Brigade Transport)	,, ,,
2nd Lieut. J. N. Buchanan . . .	,, ,,
2nd Lieut. A. H. Penn . . .	,, ,,
Capt. P. A. Clive	No. 2 Company.
Capt. G. L. Derriman	,, ,,
2nd Lieut. J. C. Craigie . . .	,, ,,

2nd Lieut. Viscount Cranborne . . No. 2 Company.
2nd Lieut. Hon. P. P. Cary . . . ,, ,,
Major B. Barrington-Kennett . . No. 3 Company.
Lieut. A. F. R. Wiggins . . . ,, ,,
Lieut. A. V. L. Corry . . . . ,, ,,
2nd Lieut. R. D. Lawford . . . ,, ,,
Major C. R. C. de Crespigny . . No. 4 Company.
Capt. I. St. C. Rose . . . . ,, ,,
2nd Lieut. E. G. Williams . . . ,, ,,
2nd Lieut. O. Lyttelton . . . ,, ,,
2nd Lieut. Hon. G. S. Bailey . . ,, ,,
2nd Lieut. C. O. Creed . . . ,, ,,

Attached—Captain F. D. G. Howell, R.A.M.C.

The Battalion remained in the trenches at Givenchy until May 12, when it was relieved by the London Scottish, and went into billets at Le Casan. During the time it had occupied these trenches, it had done a great deal of work, and altered the appearance of the line.

On the 9th the offensive on the Richebourg—Festubert line began. To the 4th Brigade was assigned the task of holding the Givenchy—Cuinchy line, while the First, Eighth, and Indian Divisions were to carry out the attack. A terrific bombardment on both sides opened early in the morning, but no attack developed against that part of the line. The attack by our First Division proved a costly failure, although the French made some progress near Notre Dame de Lorette.

News was received of the German gas attack at Ypres, and precautions had consequently to be taken. The question of respirators became very important, and masks of all sorts and kinds were tried. Here were thousands of men absolutely unprepared, who at any moment might be

Chapter IX.
2nd Batt.
May 1915.

suffocated, but the idea of taking precautions against gas had never occurred to us, any more than precautions against wells being poisoned. Such things had been ruled out of civilised warfare by the Hague Convention. It is hardly to be wondered at that this perfidious treachery on the part of the enemy took the whole Army at first completely by surprise, but an antidote was quickly provided in the shape of gas helmets.

On the night of the 11th Lieutenant A. V. L. Corry, accompanied by Sergeant Skerry, Lance-Corporal Hodgson, and Private Gillet, went out, and commenced cutting the barbed wire in front of the German trenches. While engaged in this they came in contact with a German patrol, one of which was shot by Lieutenant Corry, a second was killed by a bomb thrown by Private Gillet, while a third was killed by Sergeant Skerry. The German officer in command of the patrol drew his revolver and shot Sergeant Skerry and Corporal Hodgson dead, and wounded Private Gillet, who afterwards succumbed to his wounds. Lieutenant Corry, finding the remainder too numerous to tackle single-handed, had perforce to retire to the trenches.

On the 14th we began a systematic bombardment of the German lines opposite Richebourg — L'Avoué — Festubert. This continued for two days, and prepared the line for the second attack, which was to be carried out by the Second and Seventh Divisions and the Indian Corps. There was a distinct salient at this part of the German line, and it was for this reason that it was chosen for attack. The country was flat, although intersected with water-courses, and owing to the barrage of fire from the enemy constant difficulty was experienced in bringing up any supports.

CHAPTER IX.

2nd Batt. May 1915.

CHAPTER X

THE BATTLE OF NEUVE CHAPELLE
(1ST BATTALION)

<small>Chapter X.
1st Batt.
March 1915.</small>
For a long time the question had been discussed whether it was humanly possible to break through a line of trenches. Owing to the great defensive power of modern weapons, the thickness of the barbed-wire obstacles, and the dangers the attacking force would have to run in leaving their trenches and crossing the open, it was generally believed that no attack could possibly succeed. Further, in spite of repeated attempts, the Germans had failed time after time to break through our line.

But there was another consideration which we had to take into account. The French had recently suffered enormous losses, with comparatively small gains to set against them, and they were beginning to think that since Ypres we had not taken our proper share of the fighting. Sir John French determined, therefore, to prepare a regularly organised attack on the enemy's line near Neuve Chapelle. He selected this portion in the hope that, if the enterprise succeeded and the ridge overlooking Lille was reached, the La Bassée—Lille line would be threatened,

THE BATTLE OF NEUVE CHAPELLE

and possibly the enemy might have to abandon Lille. He communicated his plans to Sir Douglas Haig in a secret memorandum, and put him in command of the whole attack.

It was arranged that the assault should be undertaken by the 4th and Indian Corps in the First Army. The guns were to be massed west of Neuve Chapelle, and were to smash the wire entanglements, and break down the enemy's trenches before the infantry attempted to advance. Later they were to concentrate their fire on the enemy's supports and reserves, and prevent any more men from being sent up to the firing line. This was the first time that we used what afterwards became a regular feature of the attack—the *barrage* of fire.

The sorely tried Seventh Division was again given a very difficult task, and the 1st Battalion Grenadiers was once more to bear the brunt of the attack.

The officers of the Battalion at the time were as follows:

Lieut.-Colonel L. R. Fisher-Rowe	Commanding Officer.
Major G. F. Trotter, M.V.O., D.S.O.	Second in Command.
Lieut. C. V. Fisher-Rowe	Adjutant.
Lieut. J. Teece	Quartermaster.
2nd Lieut. E. H. J. Duberly	Machine-gun Officer.
Capt. W. E. Nicol	Bombing Officer.
Captain the Hon. G. H. Douglas-Pennant	King's Company.
Lieut. H. W. Ethelston	,, ,,
2nd Lieut. C. T. R. S. Guthrie	,, ,,
2nd Lieut. C. G. Goschen	,, ,,
Major G. W. Duberly	No. 2 Company.
Lieut. Lord Brabourne	,, ,,
2nd Lieut. C. F. Burnand	,, ,,

CHAPTER X.
1st Batt.
March 1915.

2nd Lieut. A. Foster . . . No. 2 Company.
Capt. E. F. F. Sartorius . . No. 3 Company.
2nd Lieut. Lord William Percy . ,, ,,
2nd Lieut. G. R. Westmacott . ,, ,,
2nd Lieut. R. G. Gelderd-Somervell ,, ,,
Captain the Hon. R. Lygon, M.V.O. No. 4 Company.
Lieut. M. A. A. Darby . . . ,, ,,
Lieut. A. S. L. St. J. Mildmay . ,, ,,
Attached—Captain G. Petit, R.A.M.C.

Mar. 10. It was on the 10th of March that the attack began. At 7.30 A.M. all the troops were in position, and a powerful bombardment from our massed batteries was opened on the trenches protecting Neuve Chapelle, but the enemy made no reply. After thirty-five minutes' bombardment the infantry advanced; the Eighth Division and the Garhwal Brigade from the Anglo-Indian Corps attacked, and captured the village and entrenchments. But the success thus gained was more or less thrown away, owing to the delay that occurred in bringing up the Reserve Brigades. All day our men waited for reinforcements to continue the advance, but by the time they arrived it was dark. So there was nothing to do but wait until next morning, and meanwhile the Germans had had time to bring up more troops.

Mar. 11. Being in the Reserve Brigade, the 1st Battalion Grenadiers did not reach the firing line till the following morning, when the weather was thick and misty. This made artillery observation impossible, and as many of the telephone wires had been cut by the enemy's shells on the previous day, communication between the different Brigades became a matter of great difficulty. The position of affairs now stood thus: the

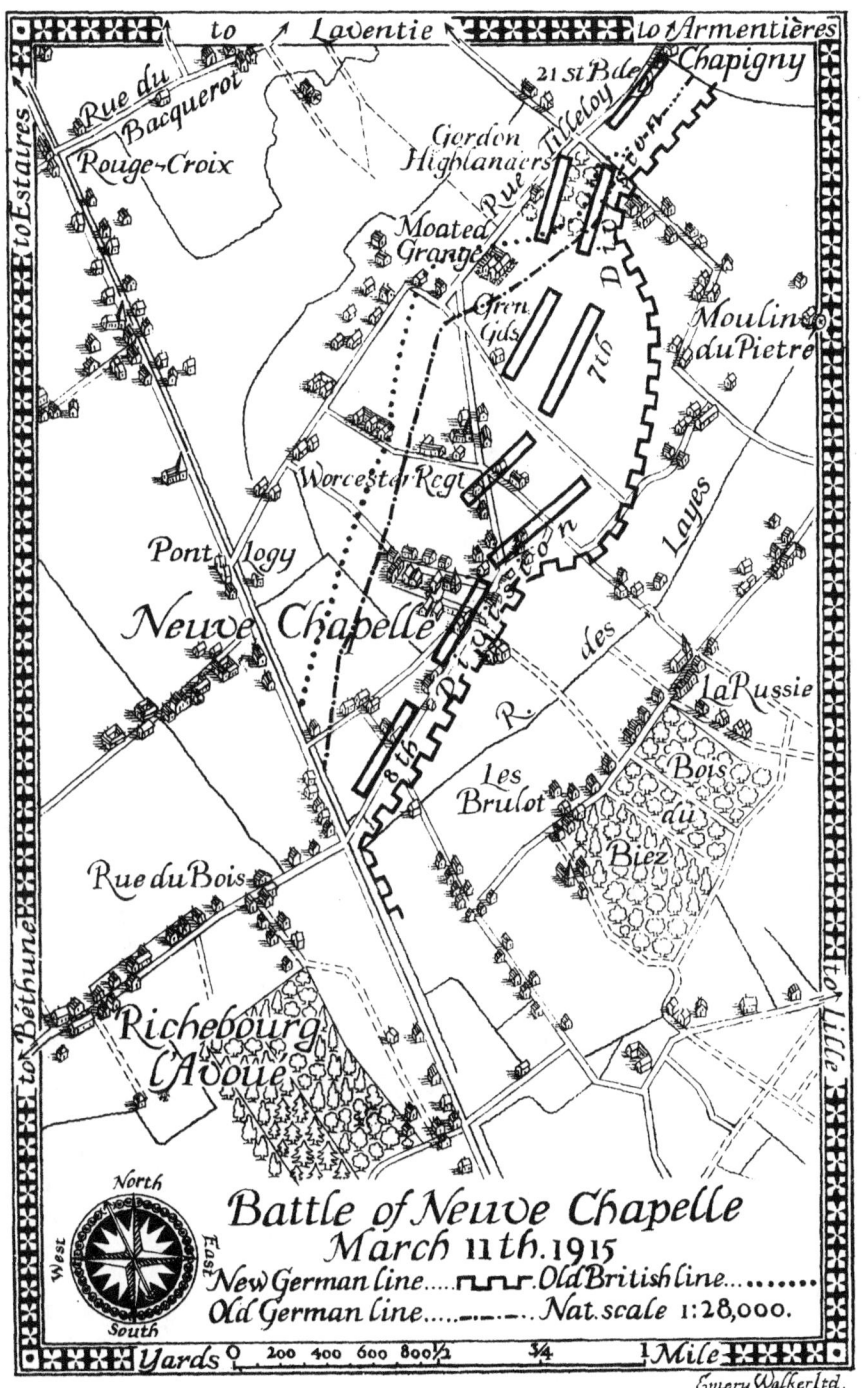

THE BATTLE OF NEUVE CHAPELLE 227

Eighth Division had carried the German trenches north of Neuve Chapelle, but had not succeeded in crossing the River des Layes, and the Garhwal Brigade on their right had also been held up in front of the Bois du Biez. The Seventh Division was on the extreme left, with the 21st and 22nd Brigades in the firing line and the 20th Brigade in support. The 21st Brigade was reported to be holding a position with its right resting on the captured German trenches some two hundred yards east of Moated Grange, and in touch with the Eighth Division, but it was soon discovered that it did not extend so much to its right as it imagined, and the 20th Brigade was therefore sent up to fill the gap. The attack along the whole line was delayed until the leading battalions of the 20th Brigade were ready.

Chapter X.
1st Batt.
March 1915.

The 1st Battalion Grenadiers was now ordered to move up into the old British line of trenches. It started off at 4 A.M., led by Brigadier-General Heyworth, and after passing down the Rue du Bacquerot struck off across the fields, keeping along a trolly line. Dawn was just breaking, and the flashes of the shells lit up the sinister sky. The trolly line ended on a road where, in the uncertain light, glimpses could be caught of trestles, barbed wire, and ammunition boxes, standing near the remains of a house. Now for the first time bullets could be heard striking the trees, and the men realised that they were nearing the front line. The men in front eager to go forward moved rather too fast, which made it difficult for those in the rear to keep touch with them, and the platoon leaders, afraid of losing touch with the rest of the Battalion, had even to urge the men to double. On reaching the Rue Tilleloy, the Battalion followed it for a few hundred yards south, keeping behind a breastwork until it came to a road which led to the left, and apparently ended in a ruined farm. There it received orders to go into some support trenches, and at 7 A.M. Lieut.-Colonel Fisher-Rowe sent for the Company Commanders, and explained their orders to them. The Battalion was to advance in columns of platoons at fifty yards interval in the following order:

No. 2 Company.	The King's Company.
Platoon	Platoon
No. 5. 2nd Lieut. Foster.	No. 1. Lieut. Ethelston.
No. 6. 2nd Lieut. Burnand.	No. 2. 2nd Lieut. Guthrie.
No. 7. Lieut. Lord Brabourne.	No. 3. 2nd Lieut. Goschen.
No. 8. Major Duberly.	No. 4. Capt. Douglas-Pennant. |// 200 yards. //
No. 4 Company.	No. 3 Company.

Leaving the old British line it advanced across the open, over trenches which had been captured from the Germans the day before. Almost immediately after the advance began, Captain Douglas-Pennant was struck by a shell, and mortally wounded just as he had emerged from a trench, and was looking round to see whether his company was going in the right direction.

When the accounts written by the Divisional and Brigade Staffs are compared with those written by the Commanding Officer and individual officers, there can be no doubt that the information, which trickled back during the day's fighting, was often so incorrect, that it led not only General

Capper, but also General Heyworth, to form entirely wrong conclusions as to what was happening in front, and the orders issued were in many instances unintelligible. Communication between the Battalion and the Brigade was maintained by orderlies, and on several occasions when the orderlies were killed the orders never reached the front line, or reached it so long after they had been despatched that the situation in front had completely changed. It hardly seems to have been realised at Divisional Headquarters, how much the artillery bombardments on both sides had obliterated all landmarks. Roads were mentioned of which no trace could be seen, and the four lines of trenches, the old and the new German lines, and the old and the new British lines, no doubt added considerably to the lack of clearness in the orders.

The whole position was most complicated, as the Germans had been only partially driven back on the 10th, and consequently their line in places faced in different directions. Though Neuve Chapelle itself was in our hands, the enemy still occupied part of their old line farther north. In order to attack this position, it was necessary to come down the old British trench, and then advance due west for a quarter of a mile, after which the attacking force had to wheel round, and go in a northerly direction.

Whether such intricate manœuvres could ever have been successfully accomplished in the face of machine-gun fire is very doubtful, but there seems to have been no other way of attacking this part of the enemy's line, which jutted out at right angles, and made any advance by the Eighth Division an impossibility.

To accomplish its difficult task, the 1st Battalion Grenadiers started with the Gordons on their left. It had hardly reached the road when it came in for a murderous enfilade fire from the German machine-guns on its left front, which very much puzzled the men, who imagined the enemy to be straight in front of them. Two platoons under Lieutenant Ethelston and Second Lieutenant A. Foster had pushed on, and were quite one hundred yards ahead of the rest of the line, but No. 2 Company on the left, being nearest to the German machine-guns, lost very heavily. Lieutenant Lord Brabourne and Second Lieutenant C. F. Burnand were killed, in addition to a large number of N.C.O.'s and men. Soon afterwards Second Lieutenant A. Foster was mortally wounded, being hit in five places.

Meanwhile the Gordon Highlanders in the orchard were held up by the enemy, and could make no headway against the machine-guns in front of them. Lieut.-Colonel Fisher-Rowe, after having gone round the front line, saw clearly that unless steps were taken to silence this machine-gun fire on the left his Battalion would soon be annihilated. He accordingly sent back a message to Brigade Headquarters explaining his position. Apparently he was under the impression that the Battalion had reached the River des Layes, but as a matter of fact it was astride a small stream much farther back. General Heyworth ordered him to hold on where he was, in the hope that when the Gordons cleared the orchard the

THE BATTLE OF NEUVE CHAPELLE 231

Grenadiers would be able to press home their attack.

The platoons had naturally telescoped up during this advance, as those in rear were always pushing on to get into the front trenches. Sergeant-Major Hughes, in command of the last platoon of the King's Company, was joined by Lieutenant Westmacott with his platoon, and soon afterwards by Lieutenant Somervell. Lieutenant Goschen also managed to get his platoon up to the front trench, where Lieutenant Duberly with his machine-gun arrived a little later. No. 4 Company under Captain Lygon, having passed through two lines of trenches occupied mostly by the Devonshire Regiment, had come up on the left of No. 2. Lieutenant Darby with No. 13 Platoon managed to cross a ditch full of water by means of a plank bridge, and get touch with the Gordon Highlanders; but when Lieutenant Mildmay attempted to follow with his platoon, he found the enemy had a machine-gun trained on it, and had to wade through the water farther to the left. Captain Sartorius was seriously wounded as he came along at the head of No. 3 Company; his two orderlies attempted to carry him back, but were both shot. Second Lieutenant Lord William Percy, who was close behind, was wounded in the thigh; Lieutenant A. Darby was shot through the heart as he was lighting a cigarette, and Second Lieutenant Mildmay, who was close to him, was badly wounded. The casualties among the other ranks were very heavy.

The 1st Battalion Grenadiers found itself from

Chapter X.

1st Batt. March 1915.

the start in a hopeless situation, and was enfiladed the moment it crossed the road.

But it continued to go forward in spite of the German machine-guns, and stubbornly held on to the position it had gained. Men who had been wounded early in the day had to be left lying where they fell, and many of them were subsequently killed by shrapnel. The King's Company was unfortunate enough to lose two of its best sergeants: Sergeant Russell was killed, as he followed Lieutenant Ethelston into the front trench, and Sergeant Annis fell somewhat later.

Just before dark the Battalion received orders to dig in where it was, and the advanced position to which Lieutenant Ethelston and his platoons clung had to be reached by a communication trench. The darkness made all communication very difficult, and the piteous cries of the wounded and dying, who asked not to be trodden on, added to the troubles of the officers, who were trying to collect their platoons. When orders were subsequently received for the Battalion to retire and get into some reserve trenches, it was found that the casualties had been very heavy. It was disappointing to learn that the British line on the right had been 200 yards ahead of the Battalion, and that all the losses had been incurred in passing over ground captured by the Eighth Division.

The Battalion assembled by degrees, and retired to the place appointed to it, which was not far from the junction of the three roads. During its retirement Second Lieutenant R. G. Somervell was mortally wounded, and was picked up by a

THE BATTLE OF NEUVE CHAPELLE 233

stretcher-bearer of another battalion. Rations were brought up and issued, and the men afterwards got what sleep they could, but they were wet through, and spent a most uncomfortable night.

Chapter X.
1st Batt.
March 1915.

Lieutenant Ethelston was now in command of the King's Company, and Second Lieutenant Westmacott of No. 3, while Major Duberly and Captain Lygon retained command of their companies.

Having grasped the gravity of the situation, the Germans were now hurrying up guns and men to the threatened portion of the line as fast as they could. At an early hour they opened a savage bombardment on the trenches, and almost continuously throughout the morning shells were falling round the men in rapid succession. Only two actually dropped amongst the Grenadiers, but these caused many casualties.

Mar. 12.

In the afternoon the Battalion was ordered to support the Scots Guards, who were to undertake the attack with the Border Regiment. The orders were to advance with the right on the Moulin du Piètre, but although this looked on paper a perfectly clear landmark, it was not so easy to locate from the trenches. In the orders the abbreviation Mn. was used for Moulin, which was new to the majority of platoon commanders, but even those who knew its meaning were quite unable to discover the mill. They could not see much through their periscopes, and nothing at all resembling a mill was to be observed. Presumably, as the Grenadiers were to support the Scots Guards, they should have followed them, and made a considerable détour; but the Staff Officer who directed the initial stages of the advance appears to have told them to go straight for the Moulin du Piètre.

From information obtained from a German prisoner it appeared that the enemy intended to retake Neuve Chapelle that day at all costs, and that reinforcements had been sent up to enable them to do so. Major Trotter with the left half Battalion started off down the road leading past Brigade Headquarters, where he was joined by Captain Palmer, the Brigade Staff Captain. No. 4 Company under Captain Lygon was here ordered to advance in two lines with two platoons of No. 3 under Sergeant Powell and Sergeant Langley in support. After having gone forward for about half a mile it came under enfilade fire from the right, which seemed to indicate that it was not going in the right direction. Captain Lygon decided to bear to the right, and sent word to Lieutenant Westmacott, who was farther back with the remainder of No. 3, to swing round in that direction, as they were all going too far to the left. He himself hit off a communication trench which led to the front line, but after the leading half company had passed through, the Germans trained a machine-gun down this trench, which made it impossible for the remainder to follow. Half of No. 4 Company and the two platoons of No. 3 therefore took refuge in a ruined house. Captain Lygon endeavoured to move down the front trench to the right, but found all farther progress stopped by a deep stream which cut the trench in two. After

THE BATTLE OF NEUVE CHAPELLE 235

several ineffectual attempts to cross this stream, he turned back, but the German machine-gun made all attempts to return by the communication trench an impossibility. His half company was practically caught in a trap, from which it would be impossible to escape in daylight. There

CHAPTER X.
1st Batt.
March 1915.

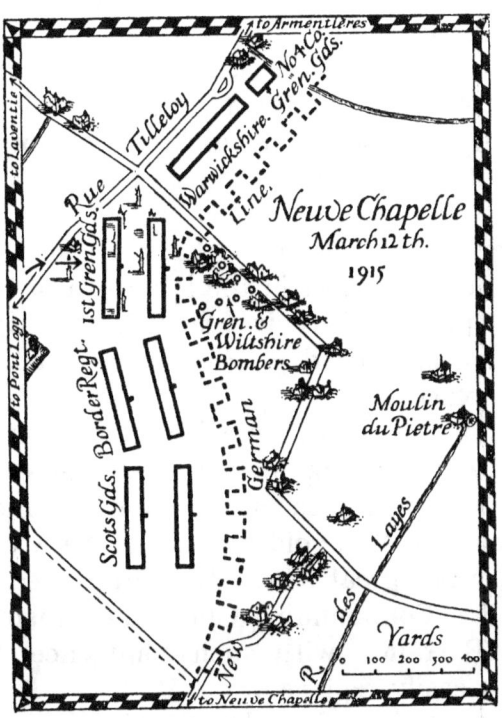

was therefore nothing to do but to wait until it was dark. Eventually, Lieutenant Fisher-Rowe, the Adjutant, who had been sent in search of this lost company, swam the stream, and told Captain Lygon what was happening on the right.

Major G. Trotter had been hit in the head by a

shrapnel bullet, and although the wound was not serious it placed him *hors de combat* for the rest of the day.

Meanwhile, the remainder of the Battalion, after waiting two hours, received orders to advance, but after passing the old British line, instead of keeping straight on, it began to swing to the left, in the same way as No. 4 had done. Lieutenant Westmacott, observing this, ran forward to tell the platoons to swing round to the right, but in the smoke it was not easy for the platoon leaders to make out what exactly was the objective.

There seems no doubt that for some time the Grenadiers were lost in the labyrinth of trenches, but in spite of all their difficulties the right half Battalion succeeded in getting eventually to its proper place.

About the same time Lieut.-Colonel Fisher-Rowe, who came up with the companies in support, was struck in the head by a bullet and killed. The death of " the old friend," as he was always called, was a great loss. He had proved himself so good a Commanding Officer, and inspired the whole Battalion with such confidence, that he was not easily replaced.

The Scots Guards and Border Regiment having made a most gallant assault without any bombardment to aid them, managed to capture some of the German front trenches, and the 1st Battalion Grenadiers which, with the exception of No. 4 Company, had got up to its right place, was now ready to support them. Seeing an opportunity of taking another bit of trench,

THE BATTLE OF NEUVE CHAPELLE 237

Lieutenant Westmacott advanced with some men of his company, who were able to throw their grenades at the retiring Germans. Men of the 1st Batt. Wiltshire and Border Regiments joined in, and soon bombs were flying about in every direction.

CHAPTER X.

1st Batt.
March 1915.

But the event which overshadowed all other trench fighting was the advance of Captain Nicol with his bombers. This was watched with admiration by the whole line, and the Germans could be seen pursued everywhere by the Grenadier bombers, and surrendering in large numbers.

Meanwhile Private Barber advanced by himself down one of the enemy's communication trenches with a bag of bombs : when a bullet from one of the enemy's snipers struck the bombs he was carrying, he threw them away, and they exploded. Gathering up a fresh supply from a dead man, he rushed along, throwing them with such effect that a large number of Germans put up their hands and surrendered. He continued his advance until he was shot by a sniper, and was responsible for taking over one hundred prisoners. For this conspicuous act of bravery he was awarded the Victoria Cross.

Another gallant exploit was also rewarded by the Victoria Cross. Lance-Corporal W. D. Fuller, seeing a party of the enemy trying to escape along a communication trench, ran towards it, and killed the leading man with a bomb. The remainder, finding no means of evading his bombs, surrendered to him, although he was quite alone.

Major Nicol himself was later awarded the D.S.O., and many thought that he should have received the V.C.

Chapter X.

1st Batt. March 1915.

The enemy could be seen streaming away, and the rifle-fire consequently dwindled to nothing. The ground was torn up by shell-fire, so that all landmarks were obliterated, and the dead and dying were lying about in large numbers everywhere. Major-General Capper sent an order to the Battalion to support the Scots Guards by attacking a point in the German line to their right. The order was received by Lieutenant Westmacott, who found that the situation had so altered since the order was written that it would mean having his right flank in the air, and exposed to enfilade fire. He therefore consulted Colonel Wood, commanding the Border Regiment, who also thought the time had passed for an attack of this nature, and advised him to remain where he was in support of the Scots Guards.

Not entirely convinced, Lieutenant Westmacott ran back to consult Major Duberly, and met him as he was coming up with the Adjutant, Lieutenant Fisher-Rowe. All three officers returned to the firing trench to discuss the point again with Colonel Wood, and although Major Duberly was at first strongly in favour of carrying out the order, it was eventually agreed that to take on the attack ordered some hours ago, under entirely different conditions, would mean practical annihilation.

Soon afterwards orders were received for the Battalion to withdraw to the original line fifty yards in rear, where they remained for the night. The only officers left with the Battalion were Major Duberly, in command; Lieutenant Fisher-

THE BATTLE OF NEUVE CHAPELLE 239

Rowe, Adjutant; Lieutenant Ethelston, King's Company; Second Lieutenant C. G. Goschen, No. 2; Lieutenant Westmacott, No. 3; Captain Lygon, No. 4; and Second Lieutenant Duberly with the machine-guns.

CHAPTER X.

1st Batt. March 1915.

During the night Major Duberly and Captain Lygon went up to reconnoitre the Royal Scots Fusiliers' trenches, from which the Battalion was expected to attack the next morning. On their return Major Duberly went to Brigade Headquarters to discuss the situation with General Heyworth, who decided to go round the trenches himself. He accordingly started off, accompanied by Captain Lygon, and having visited the front trench gave orders for the Grenadiers to relieve the Royal Scots Fusiliers on the right of the line, with a view to attacking Moulin du Piètre.

Unfortunately the rations had only just arrived, and were being distributed when the orders were received. As it was essential that this move should be accomplished before daylight it was impossible to see that each man received his rations before the Battalion moved off. They started at 3.30, led by Captain Lygon. Owing to the darkness and the lines of trenches to be crossed, progress was necessarily slow. Though the distance was only 1000 yards, the constant climbing in and out of trenches in the dark, the shell-holes, and the remains of barbed-wire obstacles, made it seem interminable.

Mar. 13.

On the way Lieutenant Westmacott, who was standing on the parapet directing his men where to cross over a trench, was blown up by a bomb thrown by a wounded German who was lying close

Chapter X.
1st Batt.
March 1915.

by. He had a wonderful escape, and although completely stunned, he recovered sufficiently to join his company again later in the day. The Battalion was sadly in need of officers, and he insisted on returning that evening in spite of his dazed condition.

Captain Lygon led the Battalion over a maze of wet trenches and ditches to where the Royal Scots Fusiliers were in front of the Moulin du Piètre, and the companies as they came up were ordered to get into the trenches. But as the day dawned slowly it was found that there was no room in the trenches for the men, as the Royal Scots Fusiliers were still there, and there was not time for them to get away. There were but some mere scratches in the earth, which would hardly hold a quarter of the men. The lighter it got the more obvious became the peril of the Battalion's position. Major Duberly did all he could. Absolutely regardless of danger, he went about shouting to the men to dig themselves in where they were, and endeavouring to establish communication between the groups of men who were making themselves some sort of shelter.

Soon after daybreak the firing became intense, and the whole ground was ploughed up with shells and furrowed with machine-gun bullets. Major Duberly was killed early in the day, and Lieutenant Fisher-Rowe, who came down a communication trench filled with water, was wounded in the leg and unable to move, just as he had nearly reached the trench. His satchel, containing the orders, was passed up by the men to Captain Lygon in the front trench. The

THE BATTLE OF NEUVE CHAPELLE 241

orders were to the effect that the Grenadiers were to attack Moulin du Piètre in co-operation with the Eighth Division on the right after a bombardment, which would last from 9 to 9.30 A.M. The Gordons were to attack on the left.

CHAPTER X.

1st Batt. March 1915.

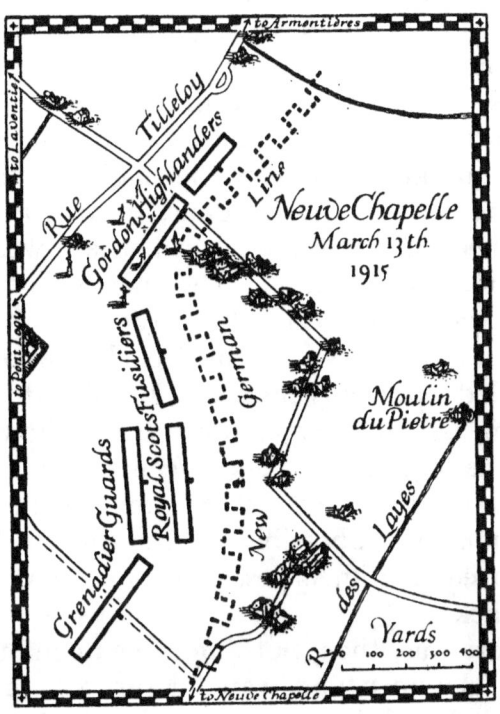

Captain Lygon, on whom the command of the Battalion now devolved, found himself in a position of extreme difficulty. Owing to the distances between the groups he had no means of sending messages to the men on the right and left, and the roar of musketry and bursting shells made all communication by word of mouth out of the

CHAPTER X.

1st Batt.
March
1915.

question, though it was evident that before an attack could be carried out with any prospect of success, the men would have to be formed up and got into some sort of order, in spite of the withering fire.

To make matters worse, some of our own heavy guns were dropping shells on the trenches occupied by the Gordon Highlanders, under the impression that that part of the line was held by the Germans. The Gordons wisely withdrew to their support trenches until the mistake was rectified.

As our attack was to be made at the same time as that of the Gordons, it was more than ever necessary to wait until they were in a position to co-operate. The enemy on the right front was causing most of the casualties, and owing to the curve in the trenches would have enfiladed any advance on Moulin du Piètre. Captain Lygon wriggled down the shallow trench, over the legs of the men, to consult the Gordons, but found that any attack from them was for the moment impossible. The Eighth Division was in equal difficulties, and found it impossible to attack.

There was, then, nothing to be done but to lie out in the open and wait for further orders, and in the infernal din of shell-fire the Battalion went through a terrible ordeal. The shallow scratches they had managed to dig gave little protection, and the casualties were consequently very heavy. One incident may be quoted to give some idea of the way in which the men's nerves were strained. Two men were observed to get up and walk about, and were shouted at, and told to lie down. All

THE BATTLE OF NEUVE CHAPELLE 243

they did was to smile inanely, and very soon, of course, they were shot by the enemy. They had gone clean off their heads.

Twice orderlies were sent back with a report of the position occupied, and when it was dark Captain Lygon sent Lieutenant Westmacott to report the situation to Brigade Headquarters, while the Gordon Highlanders sent a subaltern on the same errand.

Captain Petit with the stretcher-bearers behaved in the most gallant manner, and succoured the wounded oblivious of shells and bullets.

Orders were at last sent to the Grenadiers and Gordon Highlanders to withdraw, and to march to Laventie, but owing partly to a mistake on the part of the guides, partly to the darkness, the Battalion did not reach its billets until 2 A.M. The only three officers left with the Battalion now were Captain Lygon, Lieutenant Goschen, and Lieutenant Duberly; but Major Trotter, who had recovered from his wound, met them on arrival, and took over command.

It was a source of deep disappointment to the men to feel that many lives had been lost, and little accomplished. On each day the Battalion had been given a very difficult and intricate task, and it was entirely owing to the indomitable pluck of the men that, in spite of all their difficulties, they had invariably succeeded in reaching their destination.

The casualties in the Battalion at Neuve Chapelle were 16 officers and 325 N.C.O.'s and men. Lieut.-Colonel L. R. Fisher-Rowe, Major G. W. Duberly, Captain the Hon. G. H. Douglas-

CHAPTER X.

1st Batt.
March
1915.

Pennant, Captain E. F. F. Sartorius, Lieutenant H. W. Ethelston, Lieutenant Lord Brabourne, Lieutenant M. A. A. Darby, Second Lieutenant C. F. Burnand, Second Lieutenant A. C. Foster, Second Lieutenant R. Gelderd-Somervell were killed, and Major G. F. Trotter, D.S.O., Lieutenant C. V. Fisher-Rowe, Second Lieutenant C. T. R. S. Guthrie, Second Lieutenant Lord William Percy, Second Lieutenant G. R. Westmacott, and Second Lieutenant A. L. St. J. Mildmay were wounded.

The total British losses during three days' fighting were : 190 officers and 2337 other ranks killed, 359 officers and 8174 other ranks wounded, and 23 officers and 1728 other ranks missing.

Ten days later Major-General Capper sent the following message to the Battalion :

> The Divisional General has now received the report on the action of Neuve Chapelle on March 10–14. He desires to express his appreciation of the steady conduct of the 1st Battalion Grenadier Guards, which maintained a difficult position in the open under very adverse circumstances. The conduct of Lance-Corporal W. Fuller and Private T. Barber and the grenade-throwers of this Battalion commands the admiration of every one who heard of their exploits, and testifies in the highest degree to the gallant spirit which animates this Battalion.

At the end of the month the Commanding Officer conveyed to the Battalion stretcher-bearers a message received from the G.O.C. Seventh Division, expressing his appreciation of the courage and devotion to duty displayed by them during the recent action.

Moreover, when Sir John French, the Commander-in-Chief, inspected the Battalion with the

THE BATTLE OF NEUVE CHAPELLE 245

rest of the 20th Brigade in April, he made them a short but most impressive speech, in which he praised their conduct at Neuve Chapelle, and referred to the heavy losses they had suffered. He made a special reference to the gallant death of Lieut.-Colonel Fisher-Rowe.

CHAPTER X.

1st Batt. March 1915.

In a private letter written by command of the King to Colonel Streatfeild, Lieut.-Colonel C. Wigram said:

> The King has read your letter of the 17th inst., and is much distressed to hear how terribly the 1st Battalion suffered. It is indeed heart-breaking to see a good Battalion like this decimated in a few hours. His Majesty has heard from the Prince of Wales, who has seen the remnants of the Battalion, and he told His Majesty how splendidly they had taken their losses.

Major G. Trotter, in spite of his wound in the head, insisted on returning, and took command of the Battalion, and Lieutenant Charles Greville, who had rejoined the Battalion on the last day of the battle of Neuve Chapelle, was appointed Adjutant. Captain Nicol and Lieutenant C. Mitchell, who had been employed at Brigade Headquarters, returned to the Battalion.

On the 15th Major Lord Henry Seymour and Captain J. Hughes came from the 2nd Battalion. On the 20th a draft of 350 men arrived with the following officers: Captain M. Maitland, Captain G. C. G. Moss, Lieutenant the Earl of Dalkeith, Lieutenant Lord Stanley, Second Lieutenant the Hon. C. Hope Morley, and Second Lieutenant A. B. Lawford.

On the 21st Lieut.-Colonel C. Corkran arrived and took command of the Battalion, and on the 24th Lieutenant C. Mitchell was appointed Adjutant in the place of Lieutenant C. Greville, who proceeded to Brigade Headquarters for duty with the Grenade Company.

The greater part of the rest of the month was spent in billets, when the Battalion was reorganised, but the usual routine was followed, and the Battalion took its turn in the trenches.

Nothing worth recording happened in April. The days that were spent in the trenches were uneventful, and when in reserve the Battalion went into billets at Estaires. On the 2nd, Lieutenant Corry and Lieutenant St. Aubyn, on the 21st a draft of thirty men under Second Lieutenant C. Dudley Smith, and on the 27th Captain F. L. V. Swaine, Second Lieutenant E. O. R. Wakeman, and Lieutenant L. E. Parker joined the Battalion.

The first few days in May were spent in the trenches, which the enemy's artillery at times shelled very heavily. It was thought at first that this denoted an attack, but although the Battalion stood to arms nothing serious in the way of an attack developed. On the 3rd Captain J. Morrison was wounded, and there was a certain number of casualties. On the 2nd Captain T. Dickinson, 16th Cavalry, Indian Army, was attached to the Battalion, and on the 12th Captain W. S. Pilcher arrived.

On the 9th the 1st Battalion Grenadiers with the remainder of the 20th Brigade moved up to the support trenches in rear of the Eighth Division, but was not called upon to go into action.

CHAPTER XI

THE BATTLE OF FESTUBERT

THE 1ST BATTALION

IN May the French resolved to make a determined attack on the German line in Artois, and in order to prevent the enemy moving up any reinforcements to support that part of the line, Sir John French agreed to attack simultaneously at Festubert, where the German Seventh Corps was posted.

Sir Douglas Haig, who was entrusted with the task, began operations on May 9, when the Eighth Division captured some of the enemy's first-line trenches at Rougebanc, while the First and Indian Divisions attacked south of Neuve Chapelle. But the enemy's positions proved much stronger than had been expected, and little progress was made in either place. During this attack the 1st Battalion Grenadiers was never engaged, but remained in close support. Lieut.-Colonel Corkran himself accompanied the Eighth Division, and remained with it in case the services of the Battalion should be required.

A second attack was made by the Eighth Division east of Festubert on the 10th, preceded

CHAPTER XI.

1st Batt. May 1915.

May 9.

May 10–11.

248   THE GRENADIER GUARDS

CHAPTER XI.

1st Batt.
May 1915.

by a long artillery bombardment, the Seventh Division remaining in reserve. During the interval between the attacks of the 9th and 15th, the Seventh Division was brought up on the right of the First Corps, the Canadian Division being in support, while the Indian Corps still remained on the left.

On the night of the 10th the 1st Battalion marched to Bethune, where it was billeted in a tobacco factory, and on the 11th moved to Hinges. The roll of officers of the Battalion was as follows:

Lieut.-Colonel C. E. Corkran, C.M.G.	Commanding Officer.
Major G. F. Trotter, M.V.O., D.S.O.	Second in Command.
Lieut. C. Mitchell	Adjutant.
2nd Lieut. E. H. J. Duberly .	Machine-gun Officer.
Lieut. J. Teece	Quartermaster.
Capt. M. E. Makgill-Crichton-Maitland	King's Company.
Capt. W. S. Pilcher . . .	,, ,,
Lieut. F. C. St. Aubyn . .	,, ,,
Lieut. Lord Dalkeith . . .	,, ,,
2nd Lieut. C. G. Goschen . .	,, ,,
Capt. F. L. V. Swaine . . .	No. 2 Company.
Lieut. Lord Stanley . . .	,, ,,
Lieut. R. P. de P. Trench . .	,, ,,
2nd Lieut. C. Dudley Smith . .	,, ,,
Capt. J. S. Hughes (attached from 2nd Batt.)	No. 3 Company.
Lieut. O. Wakeman . . .	,, ,,
2nd Lieut. P. K. Stephenson . .	,, ,,
2nd Lieut. L. E. Parker . .	,, ,,
Capt. G. C. G. Moss . . .	No. 4 Company.
2nd Lieut. the Hon. C. Hope Morley	,, ,,
2nd Lieut. A. B. Lawford . .	,, ,,
2nd Lieut. E. O. R. Wakeman .	,, ,,
Capt. W. E. Nicol . . .	Grenade Company.
Capt. C. H. Greville . . .	,, ,,
Capt. G. Petit	R.A.M.C.

Attached—Lieut. F. M. Dickinson.

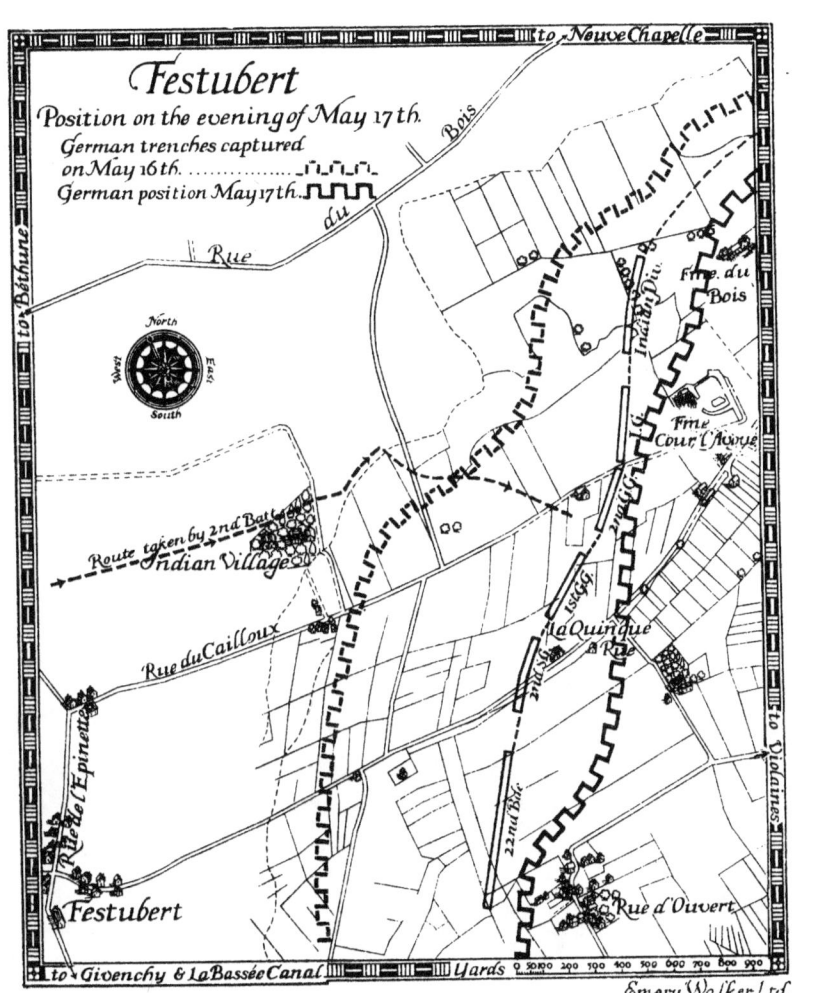

THE BATTLE OF FESTUBERT 249

On the 15th the Seventh Division moved up to the trenches north of Festubert, and the 1st Battalion Grenadiers marched to the assembly trenches in and around Dead Cow Farm. The attack was opened by the 20th Brigade. On the right was the 2nd Battalion Scots Guards, supported by the 2nd Battalion Gordon Highlanders, and on the left the 2nd Battalion Border Regiment, supported by the 1st Battalion Grenadiers, while the 6th Battalion Gordon Highlanders was in reserve. On the right of the 20th Brigade was the 22nd Brigade, and on the left the Second Division.

The attack began at 3.15 A.M. on the 16th. The Scots Guards met with little opposition, and easily secured their objective, but the 2nd Border Regiment had hardly started when it came under a murderous machine-gun fire. It lost a large number of men and most of its officers, including the Commanding Officer, Lieut.-Colonel Wood, but it succeeded nevertheless in reaching the enemy's trenches. In the meantime, however, the 2nd Battalion Scots Guards had pushed on beyond the German support line, so that its left was in the air. Even in the support trenches, which were only thirty yards in rear of the front line, the 1st Battalion Grenadiers came in for a great deal of shelling, and one shell burst in the middle of No. 8 Platoon, killing four men and wounding many others, including Lieutenant Dickinson and Lieutenant St. Aubyn, who was struck in the face by a piece of shrapnel. All the time a stream of wounded from the front trenches was passing by, some walking and some on stretchers.

CHAPTER XI.

1st Batt. May 1915.

May 15.

May 16.

CHAPTER XI.

1st Batt.
May 1915.

The machine-guns under Lieutenant Duberly were sent up to support the Scots Guards, and helped them greatly. With a view to protecting their left flank, the 1st Battalion Grenadiers was now ordered forward. It was about 10 A.M. Lieut.-Colonel Corkran, who saw clearly that his Battalion would share the same fate as the Border Regiment, if they advanced against the machine-guns, which had inflicted such loss, decided to move his Battalion farther to the south, and advance from the original forming-up trench of the 2nd Battalion Scots Guards, where a communication trench was being constructed by the Gordon Highlanders. Down this trench the 1st Battalion rushed, jumping over a mass of wounded men as it went, and when it reached the German front-line trench, the King's Company under Captain Maitland, and No. 3 under Captain Hughes, remained to consolidate it, while No. 4 under Captain Moss, followed by No. 2 under Captain Swaine, pushed on to prolong the left of the Scots Guards.

Lieut.-Colonel Corkran met Lieut.-Colonel Cator, commanding the 2nd Battalion Scots Guards, and discussed the situation, which was very obscure. One and a half companies of the Scots Guards had most gallantly pushed on right through the German lines, and had completely lost touch with the rest of the Battalion. It was afterwards discovered that they had been surrounded, and cut off by the enemy. The left of that Battalion was consequently in the air. It was determined that the Scots Guards

THE BATTLE OF FESTUBERT 251

and No. 2 Company Grenadiers under Captain Swaine should consolidate the line they had reached, namely, the German third line; No. 4 Company under Captain Moss was to advance over the open on the left, and attack a small house still held by the enemy about six hundred yards off; No. 3 Company under Captain Hughes, from the original German front trench, was to make a bombing attack down a German communication trench leading apparently to the small house; and the King's Company under Captain Maitland was to remain where it was in the German front trench in reserve.

Captain Hughes with No. 3 Company made a most successful advance down the German trench, clearing about three hundred yards of it, and killing a number of Germans, while the bombers under Captain Nicol were equally successful down another German communication trench in which they captured a large number of prisoners. But the advance of No. 4 Company was held up almost immediately by machine-gun fire from the small house. The leading platoon under Lieutenant E. O. R. Wakeman was practically annihilated, and its gallant commander, as he pluckily led his men on to this death-trap, was killed. Second Lieutenant C. Hope Morley was struck by a bullet in the eyes and blinded. Finding any farther advance impossible, No. 4 Company received orders to prolong the left of No. 2 Company, and keep in touch with No. 3 Company, which was in the German communication trench.

At 1 P.M. Lieut.-Colonel Corkran went back to

the 22nd Brigade Headquarters, and got into communication by telephone with General Heyworth, who ordered him to push his Battalion as far forward as he could and assist any advance made by the 22nd Brigade on the right.

Rain began to fall at 6 P.M., and grew into a steady downpour. The two companies, which had been moved up on the left of the Scots Guards, found themselves in some old German trenches, which had to be reconstructed, as they faced the wrong way, and would have been lamentably weak if they had been left as they were. In these ill-covered trenches the men were soaked to the skin, and spent a miserable night, which was not improved by the fact that all the time the officers were busy in getting them into their right order, so that they might be ready to attack at daybreak. Everywhere the wounded, both British and Germans, lay about groaning.

Lieut.-Colonel Corkran, having returned to his Battalion, sent Major G. Trotter to the 22nd Brigade Headquarters as liaison officer, so that close touch might be kept with it.

As soon as it was dark, No. 2 Company was ordered to establish itself as close to the small house as possible and to dig itself in, at the same time gaining touch with No. 3 Company in the German communication trench. The King's Company was to fill up the gap in the line created by the advance of No. 2. It was hoped that the small house might be rushed, but when No. 2 pushed forward it came under such a heavy

THE BATTLE OF FESTUBERT 253

machine-gun fire that it had to abandon all idea of seizing the house. It had accordingly to leave one platoon to hold the line, which it had gained, and to return to the main line.

Early next morning the 1st Battalion advanced another 400 yards, and the men began to dig themselves in, but as the rain continued in torrents the trenches were knee-deep in mud, and it was difficult to provide adequate shelter from the enemy's artillery.

It was while the 1st Battalion was lying in this position that the 4th Guards Brigade was observed coming up in artillery formation, under a hail of shells and bullets; and—a memorable incident—the 1st and 2nd Battalions Grenadiers suddenly found themselves fighting side by side.

Although the Seventh Division had carried several lines of trenches, the part of the German line opposite the extreme left of the 20th Brigade was still in the hands of the enemy. In certain sections of the line the attack had been most successful, while in others the enemy had offered a stubborn resistance. Thus the advance had not been uniform, and there were consequently several places where the German machine-guns were able to enfilade our men. But, in spite of the constant counter-attacks, the enemy had not been able to retake any considerable portion of the ground they had lost on a front of over two miles.

On the evening of the 17th the 21st Brigade received orders to relieve the 20th Brigade, and the 1st Battalion Grenadiers consequently with-

CHAPTER XI.

1st Batt.
May 1915.
May 19.

drew to the second line, where it remained throughout the 18th.

The attack continued next day with varying results. As the weather was heavy, artillery observation was difficult, and the guns were unable to support the infantry attacks. The 1st Battalion Grenadiers was ordered back to Brigade Headquarters in the Rue du Bois, where it bivouacked in a field, and presently moved back to Hinges.

Thus ended the first phase of the battle of Festubert. The Second and Seventh Divisions had succeeded in cutting two gaps in the German line, but unfortunately between the two gaps there lay an untouched and strongly held line, stretching for nearly three-quarters of a mile, which made any farther advance a matter of great difficulty.

On the 20th of May the attack was renewed by the Canadian Division, and on the 24th the Forty-seventh London Territorial Division joined in, but although considerable progress was made, and a large number of Germans accounted for, our defective ammunition supply did not at that time allow us to compete with the Germans on even terms. The net result of the battle was that we pierced the enemy's lines on a total front of four miles. The whole first-line system of trenches was captured on a front of 3200 yards. The total number of prisoners taken was 8 officers and 777 of other ranks, and a number of machine-guns were captured and destroyed.

THE BATTLE OF FESTUBERT

THE 2ND BATTALION

The following is the list of officers of the 2nd Battalion at the battle of Festubert:

Lieut.-Colonel W. R. A. Smith, C.M.G.	Commanding Officer.
Major G. D. Jeffreys	Second in Command.
Lieutenant the Hon. W. R. Bailey	Adjutant.
2nd Lieut. D. Abel-Smith	Machine-gun Officer.
Lieut. W. E. Acraman	Quartermaster.
Major Lord Henry Seymour	No. 1 Company.
Lieut. A. K. S. Cunninghame (Brigade Transport Officer).	,, ,,
2nd Lieut. J. N. Buchanan	,, ,,
2nd Lieut. A. H. Penn	,, ,,
Capt. P. A. Clive	No. 2 Company.
Capt. G. L. Derriman	,, ,,
2nd Lieut. J. C. Craigie	,, ,,
2nd Lieut. Viscount Cranborne	,, ,,
2nd Lieut. the Hon. P. P. Cary	,, ,,
Major B. H. Barrington Kennett	No. 3 Company.
Lieut. A. V. L. Corry	,, ,,
2nd Lieut. C. O. Creed	,, ,,
2nd Lieut. R. S. Corkran	,, ,,
Major C. R. C. de Crespigny	No. 4 Company.
Capt. I. St. C. Rose (Divisional Observation Officer)	,, ,,
2nd Lieut. E. G. Williams	,, ,,
2nd Lieut. O. Lyttelton	,, ,,
2nd Lieut. the Hon. G. S. Bailey	,, ,,

Attached—Captain F. G. Howell, R.A.M.C.

CHAPTER XI.

2nd Batt. May 1915.

The 4th Brigade did not take part in the first phase of the battle, and on the 16th it was moved up to the old line of breastworks at Rue du Bois, to support the 6th Brigade. The 2nd Battalion Grenadiers and Irish Guards were placed immediately behind the 6th Brigade,

May 16.

CHAPTER XI.
2nd Batt.
May 1915.

while the two battalions of Coldstream remained still farther back. The attack of the 5th and 6th Brigades was successful, and the first German line of trenches was taken, but the Indian Division was held up, and could not advance as the barbed wire had not been destroyed.

The 2nd Battalion Grenadiers was not called on to do anything that day, and remained behind the breastworks, where it was subjected to a heavy shelling. Although there were few casualties, the noise was terrific, for not only were the enemy's shells dropping all round, but our own artillery was firing just over the men's heads. It stood by all day, and withdrew in the evening to Lacouture.

May 17.

Next day the 4th Brigade was sent up into the front line. The men had breakfast at 3.30 A.M., an unusually early hour even for those about to take part in the fighting, and after standing by all the morning marched at 1 P.M. to Le Touret, where they received orders to make good the line of La Quinque Rue. This involved not only getting up to the front line, but also attacking La Quinque Rue, which ran about five hundred yards east of it. The Germans were systematically shelling all the roads leading to the trenches, and it was therefore some time before the 2nd Battalion Grenadiers could be moved up in artillery formation across the open *via* Cense du Raux Farm, Rue de l'Epinette, and the hamlet known as " Indian Village."

When it reached the supports of the front line, it was by no means easy to ascertain precisely what line the Battalion was expected

THE BATTLE OF FESTUBERT

to occupy. Units had become mixed as the inevitable result of the previous attack, and it was impossible to say for certain what battalion occupied a trench, or to locate the exact front. An artillery observation officer helped, however, by pointing out the positions on the map.

It was not till late in the afternoon that the 2nd Battalion began to move up into the front line. Progress was necessarily slow, as after the heavy rain the ground was deep in mud, and the shell-holes were full of water. It advanced gradually through a maze of old British and German trenches, much knocked about and obstructed with troops' material and a great many wounded, and passed through the Scots Fusiliers, the Border Regiment, and the Yorkshire Regiment. Its orders were to pass over what had originally been the German front line, and to establish itself about five hundred yards from the German trench at La Quinque Rue. The 5th and 6th Brigades had in the meantime been sent back in reserve, while the Canadian Division had been ordered to come up on the right and take the place of the 20th and 22nd Brigades.

It was dark before the 2nd Battalion Grenadiers reached the line it was ordered to occupy. The men had stumbled over obstacles of every sort, wrecked trenches and shell-holes, and had finally wriggled themselves into the front line. The enemy's trenches over which they passed were a mass of dead men, both German and British, with heads, legs, and other gruesome objects lying about amid bits of wire obstacles and remains of accoutrements. Lieut.-Colonel Smith had originally intended to launch the attack on La Quinque Rue at once, but decided to wait until dawn. Brought up in the dark to an entirely strange bit of country, without any landmarks to guide him, or any means of reconnaissance, and not even certain as to what troops were on each flank, the Commanding Officer was faced with many anxious problems.

The 4th Brigade, however, was no novice at this type of fighting, and it was astonishing to see how quickly the men settled down. The 2nd Battalion Grenadiers was on the right, the Irish Guards on the left, while the 1st and 2nd Battalions Coldstream were in reserve some way back. Lieut.-Colonel Smith ordered Major Jeffreys to take charge of the front line, while he remained in the proper place assigned to the Commanding Officer, which was with the supports. No. 2 Company under Captain P. Clive on the right, and No. 3 under Major Barrington Kennett on the left were in the firing line, and No. 1 under Lord Henry Seymour, and No. 4 under Major C. de Crespigny were in reserve, in some old German breastworks. As No. 1 Company moved up, Second Lieutenant A. H. Penn was shot by a sniper through both legs.

By a curious coincidence the 1st Battalion Grenadiers in the Seventh Division was immediately on the right, so that for the first time in the war the 1st and 2nd Battalions were side by side in the line. Second Lieutenant C. J. Dudley-Smith came over from the 1st Battalion to get touch, and to his surprise found himself amongst brother officers.

THE BATTLE OF FESTUBERT 259

The men had only their little entrenching tools, and with these they dug frantically, and managed to scrape up some sort of protection before the morning. The Germans fired a good deal at first, but finding it difficult to locate exactly the position of the line they determined later to save their shells, and as the morning went on did not molest the Battalion much. The Battalion Headquarters and Reserve Companies came in for a lot of shelling, but owing to the soft ground many shells failed to explode. Sleep in such an advanced position was out of the question, more especially as every moment was precious.

The 4th Brigade was ordered to attack a point marked P 14 and Cour l'Avoué at 9.30 A.M., but owing to the mist and bad weather the attack was indefinitely postponed, and the 2nd Battalion had to remain all day in its hastily made trench, which really offered very little resistance to artillery fire. The weather cleared about 10 A.M. and the enemy began a terrific bombardment, which made things very unpleasant, although it did very little actual damage. It was not till 3.45 P.M. that the 2nd Battalion received orders to attack at 4.30 P.M., which gave no time for adequate preparation. Soon afterwards a second message arrived to the effect that, if the Canadians were late in relieving the 20th Brigade on the right, the attack was not to be delayed, although there would necessarily be a gap on that flank.

The front of the Canadian attack was to extend to the left, so that it overlapped No. 2 Company. The attack was therefore to be made by No. 3 Company alone, although a platoon from

Chapter XI.
2nd Batt. May 1915.

May 18.

CHAPTER XI.
2nd Batt.
May 1915.

No. 2 was to be pushed forward as far as the barricade.

Our guns began their preparation about forty minutes before the attack was ordered, and although they undoubtedly did a good deal of damage, they never succeeded in knocking out the enemy's machine-guns, which remained hidden during the bombardment. The advance was made by No. 3 Company in short quick rushes by platoons, but as the ground was very flat, with no possible cover from the machine-guns, the men never had any real chance of reaching the German trenches. The distance was about 600 yards, and the ground was intersected with ditches full of water. The first platoon was mown down before it had covered a hundred yards, the second melted away before it reached even as far, and the third shared the same fate. The Irish Guards on the right attacked on a much wider front, but were also held up by the machine-guns which swept the whole ground. It was magnificent to see the gallant manner in which they brought up reinforcements on reinforcements, unfortunately with no success.

In the first rush of the Grenadiers Major Barrington Kennett was killed, and Second Lieutenant the Hon. P. Cary was hit soon afterwards. Second Lieutenant Creed was mortally wounded as he rushed on to the attack, and died of his wounds some days later. The only officer left in the Company was Lieutenant Corry, who behaved with great gallantry when the enemy's machine-guns opened fire with a storm of bullets.

Lieutenant Lord Cranborne who commanded

THE BATTLE OF FESTUBERT 261

the platoon from No. 2 Company, which had been pushed up as far as the barricade, was completely deafened by the shells which burst incessantly round his platoon during the attack. Lieut.-Colonel Smith was struck in the head by a bullet as he watched the attack from behind a mound of earth, and though he was carried by Major Jeffreys and Major Lord Henry Seymour into a place of safety, and eventually taken to the dressing-station, he never recovered consciousness, and died the following day. He was buried in the British Soldiers' Cemetery near Le Touret, and his funeral was attended by Lord Cavan and many officers and non-commissioned officers of his battalion. Never was a Commanding Officer more mourned by his men; he had endeared himself to them by his soldier-like qualities and constant care for their welfare. He was a gallant and distinguished soldier, imperturbable in action, never flurried or disconcerted in perilous situations, a strict disciplinarian, but the kindest and best of friends, and his loss was keenly felt by all ranks of the regiment.

Major Jeffreys, now in command of the Battalion, ordered No. 2 Company to reinforce No. 3 and continue the attack, but Captain Clive represented that it would be practically impossible for his Company to cross over the exposed ground under so heavy a fire. The enemy's machine-guns were absolutely undamaged, and commanded the ground over which it would be necessary to pass, and Major Jeffreys was forced to the conclusion that it would be merely throwing men's lives away to ask them to advance.

Chapter XI.
2nd Batt.
May 1915.

At this moment Captain Lord Gort (Brigade-Major) came up to investigate the situation, and Major Jeffreys told him that he did not propose to renew the attack until darkness gave the Battalion some chance of reaching the objective.

Lord Cavan, on hearing from Lord Gort how matters stood, sent orders to the 2nd Battalion to dig in where it was. It had gained 300 yards, and before it could possibly advance any farther it would be necessary to wait until the Canadians came up on the right. Soon after dark the Canadians arrived, and, true to their reputation, carried out their attack in a very dashing manner. They met with very little opposition at first, and got on very well until they were stopped by machine-gun fire. In all probability, if the two attacks had taken place simultaneously, there would have been a far greater prospect of success, but, as things happened, first the 4th Brigade and then in turn the Canadians drew on themselves the attention of all the German troops in that part of the line.

Major Jeffreys contemplated a combined attack all down the line by night, but the Corps Commander sent instructions that the 4th Brigade was to remain where it was, and join up with the Canadians. So another gruesome night had to be spent amongst the dead and dying, and the men had to work hard to make the trench fit to remain in.

May 19. All the next day the 2nd Battalion held this line, and came in for a great deal of shell-fire, but the trenches that had been dug during the night proved sufficient protection, and there were not many casualties. That night the 2nd Battalion Grenadiers was relieved by the 3rd Battalion Coldstream, and went into reserve with the rest of the Second Division.

Chapter XI.

*2nd Batt.
May 1915.*

CHAPTER XII

MAY TO SEPTEMBER 1915

Diary of the War

CHAPTER XII

1915.
April,
May,
June.

At the end of April, Hill 60 near Ypres was taken by the Second Corps under Lieut.-General Sir Charles Fergusson, and was lost again early in May when the enemy used gas. The second battle of Ypres began on May 10, and will always be notorious for the treacherous use of poisonous gas by the Germans. The British Army was totally unprepared for this treachery, and had no gas helmets of any kind, yet such was the tenacious courage displayed by it that the Germans were unable to do more than drive the line back a certain distance. It was in this battle that the Canadians greatly distinguished themselves. The battle of Festubert was the principal offensive at the end of May, although there was continual fighting in other parts of the line.

On May 22 Italy joined the Allies, and declared war on the Central Powers. This was a great blow to the Germans, who had fondly hoped that Italy would remain at least neutral, and it completely altered the situation in Central Europe.

The Gallipoli Campaign commenced, and the British and French troops effected a landing at the extremity of the Peninsula near Krithia in April. In Mesopotamia operations against the Turks were carried forward under great difficulties, while a Turkish Army under the command of German officers made an unsuccessful attempt to cross the desert and attack Egypt. In German South-West Africa General Botha succeeded in pushing his way into the enemy's country, and in capturing a large number of prisoners.

The Zeppelin raids on London and the East Coast began, and as there were practically no defences at the time the Germans were able to carry them out with impunity.

In April the Russian Army continued its advance in Austria, but was gradually driven back by General von Mackensen's German Army. In the extreme north the Germans, supported by their Baltic Squadron, captured the Russian port of Libau. The Austrian Army was now being reorganised by the German General Staff, and by the end of June the combined Austrian and German Armies had recaptured Przemysl and Lemberg, and driven the Russians back over the frontier.

With the exception of continual fighting round Ypres no serious operation was undertaken by the British Army until September, when the battle of Loos was fought.

The Russians were slowly driven out of Poland by the Germans, but had some successes in Galicia.

A second landing on the Gallipoli Peninsula was effected at Suvla Bay, and some farther advance was made later.

The conquest of German South-West Africa was completed by General Botha.

THE 1st BATTALION

<small>CHAPTER XII.

1st Batt.
May
1915.</small>

For the remainder of May the Battalion remained in billets at Robecq. On the 22nd a draft of sixty men arrived, and on the 29th Second Lieutenant Viscount Lascelles, and on the 30th Second Lieutenant F. E. H. Paget joined the Battalion.

On the 23rd, after Divine Service, Major-General Gough, commanding the Seventh Division, after going round the billets made a short speech to each Company, and afterwards talked to a large number of men, which greatly pleased them.

On the 27th the Division was inspected by General Joffre, the French Commander-in-Chief. The three brigades were drawn up in one field in mass, the artillery being in an adjoining field. General Joffre was received with the general salute, and walked down the front of the line. After giving three cheers the whole of the infantry marched past in fours, being played past by the massed pipers of the Division.

On the 31st the sad news of the death of Brigadier-General G. C. Nugent was received. He had served for many years in the Grenadiers before he was transferred to the Irish Guards, and his unrivalled wit and literary talents had long delighted the readers of the *Guards Magazine*. He was a man of exceptional ability, and there is small doubt that had he lived he would have risen to high distinction.

<small>June.</small> The Battalion went into a new line of trenches in front of Festubert and Givenchy, which it took

over from the 6th and 18th Battalions of the London Regiment. On June 3 these trenches were very heavily shelled, as the 6th Battalion Gordon Highlanders was making an attack farther to the right, and there were 3 men killed and 45 wounded. On the 5th the Battalion went into billets at Hingette, and on the 8th moved to Robecq, thence to Essars, where it remained until it relieved the Border Regiment in the trenches on the 14th.

CHAPTER XII.
1st Batt. June 1915.

On the 15th an attack was made by the Seventh Division over some flat ground between two rises at Givenchy. The portion allotted to the Battalion was on the flat ground, where an advance was not a matter of great difficulty, but until the rises on each side had been made good it was useless to attempt to press the attack home in the centre. After going a short distance, the Battalion was forced to wait until the situation on each flank developed. Owing to the nature of the ground the artillery was unable to dispose of the wire entanglements behind these rises, and therefore the Battalions on each side were held up. During this engagement Second Lieutenant Dudley-Smith was killed, Lieut.-Colonel Corkran slightly wounded, and Second Lieutenant Viscount Lascelles wounded in the head. There were sixty-three casualties among the N.C.O.'s and men. The Battalion hung on all day under heavy shell-fire to the line it had gained, but it was found impossible to advance farther on the flanks, and the whole force withdrew to its original line.

Lord Cavan wrote in a private letter: " I am

proud to say that the old 1st Battalion stuck it out last night and to-day in glorious isolation. Pray God they are fed, watered, and replenished to-night. I wrote to Heyworth to pass them a word of encouragement from me if he could."

On the 19th the Battalion was relieved by the Royal Welsh Fusiliers, and went into the reserve trenches in front of Gorre, and on the 21st into billets at Les Choqueaux. On the 24th it returned to the trenches between Givenchy and La Bassée Canal, and on the 27th was relieved by the Border Regiment, and went into billets at Le Preol.

On the 20th Lieutenant Sir A. Napier joined, and on the 23rd a draft of sixty-seven men arrived under Lieutenant R. Wolrige-Gordon and Second Lieutenant G. J. T. H. Villiers.

Lieut.-Colonel Corkran wrote to Colonel Streatfeild, and asked that some drums and fifes might be sent out, and Lord Derby, who paid a visit to the Battalion, promised to procure them and send them out. In the meantime eight men with some musical skill came forward, and offered to form a drum and fife band. The instruments arrived at the end of the month, and were a great success. The band now consisted of six drums and twelve fifes, and marched at the head of the Battalion for the first time on the 30th, when it moved to billets at Busnes.

July.

The Battalion had a good rest, and remained in billets till the 17th of July, when it relieved the Yorkshire Regiment in the trenches at Quinque Rue.

On the 13th Lieut.-Colonel Corkran was promoted to the rank of Brigadier-General, and given command of the 5th Infantry Brigade. His departure was much regretted by the whole Battalion, which had the greatest confidence in him. Major G. Trotter then assumed command, and his appointment as Commanding Officer was confirmed about a week later, and gave universal satisfaction.

The Battalion remained in the trenches from the 17th till the 26th, when it withdrew into billets at Calonne. During the time it was in the trenches there were but few casualties, among them Lieutenant C. G. Goschen, who was wounded in the thigh.

While the Brigade was in billets the officers of the 1st Battalion entertained the officers of the 2nd Battalion at dinner. The Prince of Wales and Captain Lord Claud Hamilton also attended. A few days later the coming of age of Lord Stanley gave another opportunity for a gastronomic triumph composed mainly of bully beef and Maconochie rations. The flies in these hot days became unbearable, and fly-traps and fly-papers were sent out in some measure to mitigate this plague.

On August 3 the Battalion received orders to join the newly formed Guards Division. It was not without regret that it left the Gordon Highlanders and Border Regiment, alongside of whom it had fought for nearly a year, and with whom it had shared the glorious reputation which had been earned by the Division. All the battalions of the Division prepared entertainments to bid them farewell, but the notice was so short that these invitations could not be accepted.

1st Batt. Aug. 1915.

On the 4th the Battalion was inspected by General Gough, the Corps Commander, who wished it God-speed in a short speech, after which it marched to Molinghem. The remainder of the 20th Brigade turned out, and lined the streets of Robecq, through which it passed, while the band of the Seventh Division and the pipers of the 2nd Gordon Highlanders played it out of the divisional area. On the 5th the Battalion marched to Nizernes, and was met by the drums and fifes of the 3rd Battalion Grenadiers.

Lieutenant Lord Stanley, who was suffering from sciatica, refused to go sick, and in order to keep him Colonel Trotter appointed him temporarily Transport Officer.

On the 6th Major-General Capper, commanding the Seventh Division, inspected the Battalion, and took leave of it in the following words :

> Colonel Trotter and all the ranks of the 1st Battalion Grenadier Guards—This is a very sad moment for me to have to say good-bye to you. You have been with us nearly a year, and I feel that with you leaving the heart of the Division is being taken away.
>
> You have seen some very hard fighting, notably at Kruiseik and again at Ypres, when you covered the retirement.
>
> I must congratulate you on the way you have upheld the traditions of your famous regiment. You have always done what has been asked of you. It did not matter whether it was fighting a battle, holding a line, or digging a trench ; you have done well, as a Grenadier always does.

Although you are leaving the Division, yet on some future occasion we hope to have you fighting side by side with us. I can only say again that it is indeed a very sad moment for me, and it only remains for me to say Good-bye.

CHAPTER XII.

1st Batt. Aug. 1915.

CHAPTER XIII

MAY TO SEPTEMBER 1915 (2ND BATTALION)

Chapter XIII.
2nd Batt.
May 1915.

DURING the remainder of May the Battalion remained in billets at La Pugnoy and later at Vendin. On the 24th it was inspected by General Horne, and turned out looking very smart. At the conclusion of the inspection the General addressed it, and said that he wished to convey to it the hearty thanks of the Corps Commander, Lieut.-General Sir C. Monro, as well as his own, for all the good work done by the Battalion during the past five months. Whether it was in billets, where its discipline, good behaviour, and smartness had been an example to the Army, or in the trenches, where it had endured hardships such as few troops had been called upon to bear, or in action against the enemy, the conduct of the Battalion had been all that could be desired. More than that he could not say. They had to deplore the death of their gallant Commanding Officer, whose loss was mourned by all who knew him, but no losses must deter them, and it was their duty to prosecute the war with the utmost energy, until the German Empire lay at the feet of England and her Allies.

On the 31st the Battalion marched with the Irish Guards and the 11th Field Company, R.E., under Major Jeffreys to Nœux les Mines *via* Bethune. The Prince of Wales and Lord Claud Hamilton marched with it most of the way. Some shelling took place *en route*, and it turned out that the enemy's fire, which seemed unaccountably accurate, was being directed by an observation balloon which could be seen behind his lines. As the Battalion moved into its billets the enemy commenced to shell the town, and succeeded in destroying some houses and wounding a few civilians.

On the 25th a draft of 120 men under Second Lieutenant H. A. Clive arrived, and on the 31st Second Lieutenant E. R. M. Fryer joined the Battalion.

During June the Battalion spent alternately two days in the trenches and two days in billets. The billets were at Sailly-la-Bourse, and the trenches at first near Auchy and afterwards at Vermelles.

Every precaution against gas attacks was taken, and an order was issued to the effect that a G on the bugle was to be the signal to prepare for gas. As the Battalion at that time had only two buglers owing to the casualties and the boys who had been sent home sick, the order was difficult to carry out, but men were found who, without being musicians, were at least able to produce the desired note on the bugle.

The trenches at Auchy were indifferent, and required a great deal of attention, but those at Vermelles were much better. The great

CHAPTER XIII.
2nd Batt.
June 1915.

difficulty the men had to contend with at both places was the high crops and long grass which had grown up quite close to the line, and which not only impeded the view, but also provided cover which might be used by the enemy. During the day it was an absolute impossibility for the men to go out and cope with this difficulty, but at night parties were sent out to cut down the crops. The men after working for an hour or so at this work seemed to lose all sense of direction, and when an alarm was given they had no idea in which direction their own trenches lay. It often happened that men would wander off towards the German lines under the impression they were going home. On several occasions when the enemy became aware of any large numbers of men working out in front they would open a heavy rifle-fire on them. All the men in the working party would then at once lie down and wait until the fire subsided; but on one occasion the Germans showed no inclination to cease firing, and the party had to be withdrawn. They crawled back slowly, being guided by Captain Cavendish, who held up his luminous watch to show them the right direction. Every night there were a few casualties, and on the 7th Lieutenant R. S. Corkran who had just gone out with one of these parties was severely wounded by a rifle bullet in the thigh, and died a few days later.

On the 29th Brigadier-General the Earl of Cavan was promoted, and left to take over command of the Fiftieth Division. He was succeeded by Brigadier-General G. P. T. Feilding, who had commanded the 2nd Battalion Coldstream Guards since the commencement of the war, and who had gained a great reputation during the last twelve months' fighting.

On the 28th the Battalion changed its billets from Sailly-la-Bourse to Oblingham, and on July 1 to Annezin. On the 5th it went into the trenches at Annequin in precisely the same part of the line it had occupied in January and February, when hundreds of men had been killed. The trenches were in a hollow, which was generally known as the Valley of Death, and were in a very bad condition. Little seemed to have been done to them since the Battalion was last there, and in many places the parapet was too high and not bulletproof. The Battalion therefore set to work to improve them, and a company of the Queen's Regiment from the Corps troops was sent up to help. This seemed the height of luxury to the men, who were unaccustomed to having other people digging their trenches.

On July 2 Second Lieutenant H. F. C. Crookshank arrived, and on the 5th Second Lieutenant E. H. Noble, Second Lieutenant M. A. Knatchbull-Hugessen, and Second Lieutenant E. W. M. Grigg joined the Battalion.

On the 15th the Battalion took over the trenches at Guinchy, spending alternately two days in the trenches and two days in billets at Bethune. On the 21st it went into Brigade Reserve, and remained for a week at Bethune, and on the 28th moved into billets at Le Preol, and acted as reserve Battalion to the troops in the trenches at Givenchy.

CHAPTER XIII.
2nd Batt.
July 1915.

At Cuinchy, in addition to the regular shelling, the Germans employed their new type of Minenwerfer, from which they fired large bombs, but their effect was local, and as the men were able to see them coming, they did little damage. Once a large wooden bomb landed in a trench without exploding, and was carried off as a souvenir by two stretcher-bearers, who happened to be passing. On the 18th the enemy began shelling Bethune, and continued for nearly a week, which made the men's two days' rest in billets a farce. The shells came screaming and roaring into the town, and terrific explosions followed. The enemy of course had no difficulty in hitting the town and shelling the houses, but it was merely a matter of chance how many men were hit. The shells were at first directed on the railway station, but beyond causing a complete suspension of traffic they did little harm, and there were few casualties. On the 22nd the bombardments became more searching, and many men were killed. The Inniskilling Fusiliers alone lost seventy men that day. The Grenadiers were more lucky, and at first escaped with little loss, but on the 24th some men were wounded and nineteen horses were killed.

On the 20th Captain Derriman who had been appointed Staff Captain to the 4th Brigade was very seriously wounded, and although he was moved down to the base, he never recovered, and died some time afterwards. The pluck he had shown in coming out in spite of a stiff knee which made him lame, and the dogged manner in which he had persisted in serving with the Battalion

OFFICERS OF THE SECOND BATTALION GRENADIER GUARDS.

in the trenches until he was placed on the Staff aroused the admiration of every one.

On the 18th Lieut.-General Gough, the new Commander of the First Corps, Major-General Horne commanding the Second Division, and Brigadier-General G. Feilding commanding the 4th Brigade paid a visit to the Battalion, and went round the trenches at Cuinchy.

During the first fortnight in August the Battalion followed the same routine, spending two days in the trenches at Givenchy followed by two days in billets at Le Preol. Mining operations were begun on a large scale by both sides. It was assumed that as an advance above ground in the face of machine-gun fire was too costly, the only other alternative was to advance under ground and blow up the enemy's parapet. In the craters made by the explosion of the mines men were then pushed, and the position was consolidated. The advantage of this subterranean method of warfare was that the men were safe from rifle- and shell-fire while they were working, but there was always the danger of a counter-mine which meant being buried alive.

On the 2nd the Battalion exploded three mines successfully near Sunken Road, and in doing this blew in some of the enemy's galleries, and that night the Irish Guards exploded three more mines. In each case the positions were consolidated after much bomb-throwing, but the occupation of the craters was always difficult, on account of the bombs from the enemy's Minenwerfer.

CHAPTER XIII.

2nd Batt. July 1915.

Aug.

Chapter XIII.
2nd Batt.
Aug. 1915.

On the 5th Brigadier-General Feilding and the Prince of Wales came round the trenches, and inspected the sap-heads and craters.

On the 6th in the early morning the enemy exploded two mines in the orchard near the shrine. At the time Captain Clive and Second Lieutenant Crookshank were taking out a working party, and had they gone a little farther, all the men must inevitably have been killed, but fortunately they were just short of where the mine exploded. The whole ground moved up in one great convulsion, and when it settled down several men were completely buried. Captain Clive himself was severely cut and bruised by the mass of debris that was blown past him, and after being shot up in the air he came down so doubled up that his teeth were nearly knocked out by his knees. Second Lieutenant Crookshank was completely buried in about four feet of earth, and would inevitably have died had not Captain Clive remembered where he stood before the explosion, and directed the men to search for him. When he was finally dug out it was found that beyond a few bruises and the inevitable shock from the explosion he was not hurt. He was sent back to the dressing-station, but pluckily insisted on returning to his Company in the evening. One N.C.O. was killed by the explosion, and eighteen men who had been buried were sent back suffering from shock and contusions. The work of digging out these men was much retarded by the constant rifle-fire from the enemy's trenches, and the enemy's guns also commenced shelling the neighbourhood of the craters, but were not accurate enough to prevent our consolidating the position.

These two mines wrecked the trench connecting our sap-heads and filled in parts of the saps with debris. The Battalion received orders at once to reoccupy the sap-heads and dig out the saps again. On the 5th Lieutenant D. Abel-Smith was slightly wounded.

On the 7th a draft of drummers arrived, and proved a great acquisition. When the Battalion was in billets at Le Preol, they played "Retreat" in the village street, much to the delight of the remaining inhabitants. On the 10th the enemy again exploded two mines near the Sunken Road, destroying some of their own wire, and the explosion formed a new crater on the northern side of a crater known as "Bluff." Second Lieutenant Hon. G. S. Bailey was killed by a bomb, and Lieutenant A. V. L. Corry was badly wounded. The casualties from mining and bombing in addition to those from rifle-fire and shells were very heavy while the Battalion was at Givenchy, and the digging was most unpleasant on account of the bodies thrown up by mine explosions. On the 12th Lieutenant E. G. Williams was accidentally killed in the Trench Mortar School at St. Venant, where he was undergoing a course of instruction.

Some ten days later the following order was published:

> The Commander-in-Chief has intimated that he has read with great interest and satisfaction the report of the mining operations and crater fighting which have taken place in the Second Division area during the last

two months. He desires that his high appreciation of the good work performed be conveyed to the troops, especially to the 170th and 176th Tunnelling Companies, R.E., the 2nd Battalion Grenadier Guards, the 1st Battalion Irish Guards, the 1st Battalion King's Royal Rifles, 2nd Battalion South Staffordshire Regiment.

The 4th Brigade now received orders to join the newly formed Guards Division.

On the 18th, before their departure, the officers of the 2nd Battalion Grenadiers entertained General Horne, Brigadier-General Feilding, the Commanding Officers of the other regiments in the 4th Brigade, and the principal Staff Officers of the Second Division at dinner in the house of Madame Richepin, who placed all her plate, china, and glass at the disposal of the officers' mess.

The following order was published by Major-General H. S. Horne, C.B., commanding the Second Division :

The 4th Guards Brigade leaves the Second Division to-morrow. The G.O.C. speaks not only for himself but for every officer, non-commissioned officer, and man of the Division when he expresses sorrow that certain changes in organisation have rendered necessary the severance of ties of comradeship commenced in peace and cemented in war.

For the past year by gallantry, devotion to duty, and sacrifice in battle and in the trenches, the Brigade has maintained the high tradition of His Majesty's Guards, and equally by thorough performance of duties, strict discipline, and the exhibition of many soldier-like qualities has set an example for smartness which has tended to raise the standard and elevate the moral of all with whom it has been associated.

Major-General Horne parts from Brigadier-General

Feilding, the officers, non-commissioned officers, and men of the 4th Guards Brigade with lively regret. He thanks them for their loyal support, and he wishes them good fortune in the future.

On the 19th the 4th Brigade, including the 2nd Battalion Grenadiers, left the Second Division to join the newly formed Guards Division, and marched about ten miles to Ham-en-Artois. It was a sort of triumphal progress, and Major-General Horne and the other two Brigadiers came to see them off while detachments from every unit in the Division lined the road. The Divisional Band played them as far as Lillers, and on the way they were joined by Major-General Lord Cavan accompanied by Major Darrell and Lieutenant Oliver Lyttelton.

On the 20th the Brigade proceeded to Renescure, and as it passed by the south of Aire it marched past General Sir Douglas Haig commanding the First Army. In the evening the following order was published by Sir Douglas Haig:

The 4th Guards Brigade leaves my command to-day after over a year of active service in the field. During that time the Brigade has taken part in military operations of the most diverse kinds and under very varied conditions of country and weather, and throughout have displayed the greatest fortitude, tenacity, and resolution. I desire to place on record my high appreciation of the services rendered by the Brigade and my grateful thanks for the devoted assistance which one and all have given me during a year of strenuous work.

(Signed) D. HAIG,
Commanding First Army.

Chapter XIII.
2nd Batt. Aug. 1915.

On the 21st the Brigade marched past Field-Marshal Sir John French in the big square at St. Omer, and presented a very fine appearance. So smart did it look that many of the onlookers were under the impression that it had just come out from England, and one man in the crowd was heard to say as the Grenadiers went past: " Wait till you've been in the trenches a bit, then you won't look so clean and smart, my boys."

In the evening the 4th Brigade received the following message :

The Commander-in-Chief wishes to thank all ranks for the splendid services they have rendered. He is much impressed by their soldier-like bearing, and very much regrets that owing to pressure of work he is unable himself to come and visit all units and speak to them himself.

After marching for several days the Battalion arrived at Campagne les Boulonnais, where it joined the rest of the Guards Division, and remained until September 22.

On August 21 Second Lieutenant the Hon. W. A. D. Parnell, and on the 24th Second Lieutenant H. G. W. Sandeman joined the Battalion.

CHAPTER XIV

FORMATION OF THE GUARDS DIVISION

THE creation of a Guards Division was not regarded without misapprehension by some of the older officers of the Guards. The reputation that had been so dearly won by the original officers, non-commissioned officers, and men of the regiments of Guards, at the expense of thousands of lives, might possibly be thrown away by their successors. The flooding of the army with new recruits might produce an entirely new stamp of man. Was the system alone good enough, were the traditions alone strong enough, to produce the fighting man who had hitherto, rightly or wrongly, been associated with the regiments of Guards? At the time there was no thought of conscription, and therefore it might be necessary to take any men who were willing to join. Would there be a sufficient nucleus of old Guardsmen to ensure that the traditions carefully preserved through many generations were strictly maintained?

The mill through which men of the Guards have to pass, however, is so severe, and the discipline so stern, that no one need have doubted that the new recruits would prove equal to their predecessors.

Chapter XIV.
The Guards Division.
Sept. 1915.

CHAPTER XIV.

The Guards Division. Sept. 1915.

The Guards Division was formed in September 1915, and Major-General the Earl of Cavan, who had commanded the 4th Guards Brigade in every engagement almost since the commencement of the war, was naturally given the command.

He had proved himself a great soldier, and his exceptional ability as a commander of men had rendered him eminently fitted for this command. Thoroughly acquainted with the methods of the enemy, he had shown himself to be resourceful in strategy and bold of decision in action. Upon several occasions he had extricated his Brigade from situations of the utmost peril, and had turned a half-anticipated failure into hard-won victory. In the darkest hour at Ypres he never lost heart: the more hopeless the situation, the greater the opportunity for a gallant fight and great achievement. His perfect confidence in his men was equalled only by their whole-hearted trust in him. His appointment, therefore, was hailed with enthusiasm by all ranks of the Brigade of Guards.

The Guards Division was composed as follows:

The 1st Guards Brigade. Brigadier-General G. P. T. FEILDING.

    The 2nd Batt. Grenadier Guards.
    The 2nd Batt. Coldstream Guards.
    The 3rd Batt. Coldstream Guards.
    The 1st Batt. Irish Guards.

The 2nd Guards Brigade. Brigadier-General J. PONSONBY.

    The 3rd Batt. Grenadier Guards.
    The 1st Batt. Coldstream Guards.
    The 1st Batt. Scots Guards.
    The 2nd Batt. Irish Guards.

FORMATION OF GUARDS DIVISION 285

The 3rd Guards Brigade. Brigadier-General F. J. HEYWORTH.
The 1st Batt. Grenadier Guards.
The 4th Batt. Grenadier Guards.
The 2nd Batt. Scots Guards.
The 1st Batt. Welsh Guards.

CHAPTER XIV.
The Guards Division. Sept. 1915.

Thus there were four battalions of Grenadier Guards, three battalions of Coldstream Guards, two battalions of Scots Guards, two battalions of Irish Guards, and one battalion of Welsh Guards. The 4th Battalion Coldstream Guards formed the Divisional Pioneer Battalion.

The Guards Division formed part of the Eleventh Corps under General Haking, and were placed in the First Army.

ARRIVAL OF THE 3RD BATTALION GRENADIER GUARDS

The 3rd Battalion Grenadiers was the only regular battalion at home. For months it had fretted at being left behind when all the other battalions had left, for they had a history second to none in the British Army, and had taken part in all the great campaigns during the last two hundred years.

3rd Batt. 1915.

Whether it was part of that mysterious thing called the British Constitution, or whether the idea of keeping one regular battalion in London emanated from the brain of some timid member of the Cabinet, is not clear, but the 3rd Battalion remained at home after all the rest of the regular army had gone. At first it was said that two regular battalions would have to remain behind in London, one for the King,

Chapter XIV.
3rd Batt.
1915.

the other for the Houses of Parliament, but His Majesty, having at once disposed of the idea that he needed the services of any regular battalion, Lord Kitchener decided to retain only one battalion, and that happened to be the 3rd Battalion Grenadiers.

The only exceptional event during the time it remained at home that deserves to be chronicled is the fact that for the first time in history this Battalion found the duties in London in service dress. On the 27th of August 1914 the King's Guard, under Captain de Crespigny, mounted for the first time in khaki.

Although the 3rd Battalion was unable to go as a unit, the terrible casualties the 1st and 2nd Battalions had suffered during the first months of the war made it very difficult to find the large draft required, and so it happened that most of the officers and non-commissioned officers made their way to the front in the other battalions.

When the Guards Division was formed it was decided to send out not only the 3rd Battalion but also the 4th Battalion, and to form another reserve battalion. On July 26 the Battalion paraded at Chelsea Barracks, and Colonel Streatfeild read to them a message from Field-Marshal His Royal Highness the Duke of Connaught, who was still Governor-General of Canada:

On hearing our 3rd Battalion has been placed under Orders to leave for the front, I ask you to give them a personal message from myself, wishing them God-speed and success, and assuring them of the great confidence I repose in them nobly to continue their splendid record of the past, and to assist our brave battalions at the

FORMATION OF GUARDS DIVISION 287

front, who have so gloriously maintained the traditions of the First Regiment of Guards. May every blessing rest upon the Regiment, of which I am so proud to be the Colonel.

ARTHUR,
Colonel, Grenadier Guards.

CHAPTER XIV.
3rd Batt. 1915.

The Battalion crossed over *via* Southampton to Havre in the steamboat *Queen Alexandra*, accompanied by a destroyer, and curiously enough was disembarked by one old Grenadier, Captain Sir F. E. W. Harvey-Bathurst, Bt., and entrained by another, Major G. C. W. Heneage. It proceeded by train to Wizernes, where it detrained, and marched into billets at Esquerdes. On July 31 the Battalion was inspected by General Stopford, who said it was the finest Battalion he had seen. On August 18 it took part in a review held on the aviation ground at St. Omer, when M. Millerand, the French War Minister, Lord Kitchener, and Sir John French inspected those battalions of the Guards Division which had arrived.

The 2nd Guards Brigade was complete on August 23, and was placed under the command of Brigadier-General J. Ponsonby, as Brigadier-General Lowther had been appointed Military Secretary to the Commander-in-Chief. On August 26 the officers of the four battalions of Grenadier Guards dined together at Wisques.

During the two months spent at Esquerdes the Battalion was busily engaged in training. Officers and non-commissioned officers went through several courses, and were initiated into the mysteries of bombing and the mechanism of the new Lewis gun.

CHAPTER XIV.

3rd Batt. 1915.

On August 30 Lieutenant A. T. A. Ritchie arrived, and on September 22 Lieutenant Sir Robert Filmer, Bt., was appointed Brigade Transport Officer.

Arrival of the 4th Battalion

4th Batt. 1915.

It was in July that the King on the advice of the military authorities decided to form another Battalion of Grenadier Guards, since the Reserve Battalion had swollen to enormous proportions, in spite of the standard of height being raised. Colonel H. Streatfeild received instructions to this effect, and at once summoned a conference of the commanding officers and adjutants of the two Battalions of the Regiment in London (the 3rd and Reserve Battalions). The part of Chelsea Barracks occupied by the School of Instruction was vacated to make room for the new Battalion, which was to become the 4th Battalion, while the Reserve Battalion was in future to be known as the 5th (Reserve) Battalion.

Major G. C. Hamilton, D.S.O., was appointed Commanding Officer, and Sergeant-Major E. Ludlow, Quartermaster. By July 16 the 4th Battalion completed its establishment, and on the 20th proceeded to Bovingdon Camp. Captain T. F. J. N. Thorne was appointed Adjutant, and the 3rd Battalion lent their Sergeant-Major and Orderly-Room Sergeant to assist the Staff of the 4th Battalion.

On August 15 the 4th Battalion left Bovingdon Camp, and embarked at Southampton for Havre. The King, through Lieut.-Colonel Wigram, sent the following message to Colonel Streatfeild :

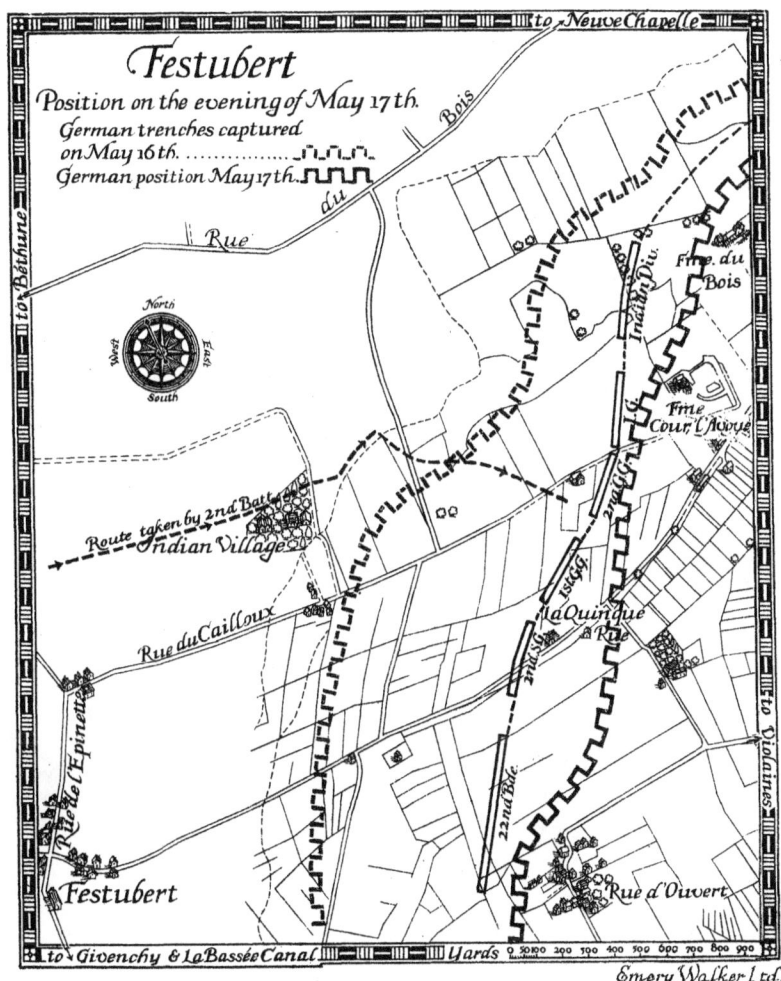

Colonel Sir Henry Streatfeild, K.C.V.O., C.B., C.M.G.
The Lieutenant-Colonel commanding the Regiment

FORMATION OF GUARDS DIVISION 289

His Majesty heartily congratulates the Regiment on being able to place four Battalions in the field, thereby creating a record which will always be cherished in the annals of the Regiment. His Majesty desires you to tell all ranks of the 4th Battalion that they will constantly be in the thoughts of their Colonel-in-Chief, who wishes them every success.

CHAPTER XIV.
4th Batt. 1915.

Field-Marshal His Royal Highness the Duke of Connaught sent the following message from Canada :

My best wishes accompany the 4th Battalion on their first tour of active service. I am confident they will do their duty and emulate their comrades of the older battalions.

ARTHUR,
Colonel, Grenadier Guards.

The Battalion crossed over in the *Empress Queen*, accompanied by a destroyer, and on arrival at Havre proceeded by train to St. Omer, where it detrained and marched to Blendecques. There it remained until the Guards Division was formed in September. On August 21 it was inspected by Brigadier-General Heyworth, who expressed himself pleased with its smart appearance. On September 17, during the inspection of the 3rd Guards Brigade, Major-General the Earl of Cavan complimented Major Hamilton on the way his Battalion had turned out.

CHAPTER XV

BATTLE OF LOOS, 1915

<small>Chapter XV.
Sept. 1915.</small>
In September General Joffre and Sir John French agreed that a determined attempt should be made to break the strong German line. Thousands of guns were to be massed, and after an action by which, it was hoped, the German trenches would be destroyed, twelve infantry divisions were to be launched upon the enemy. Then Sir Douglas Haig, with the First British Army, would attack between La Bassée Canal and Lens, while the French were to force their way through the lines south of Lens.

Sir John French in his despatch thus described the character of the front to be attacked by the British Army:

> Opposite the front of the main line of attack the distance between the enemy's trenches and our own varied from about 100 to 500 yards.
>
> The country over which the advance took place is open and overgrown with long grass and self-sown crops.
>
> From the canal southward our trenches and those of the enemy ran, roughly, parallel up an almost imperceptible rise to the south-west.
>
> From the Vermelles—Hulluch road southward the advantage of height is on the enemy's side as far as the Bethune—Lens road. There the two lines of trenches

cross a spur in which the rise culminates, and thence the command lies on the side of the British trenches.

Due east of the intersection of spur and trenches, and a short mile away, stands Loos. Less than a mile farther south-east is Hill 70, which is the summit of the gentle rise in the ground.

Other notable tactical points in our front were:

"*Fosse 8*" (a thousand yards south of Auchy), which is a coal-mine with a high and strongly defended slag heap.

"*The Hohenzollern Redoubt.*"—A strong work thrust out nearly 500 yards in front of the German lines and close to our own. It is connected with their front line by three communication trenches abutting into the defences of Fosse 8.

Cité St. Elie.—A strongly defended mining village lying 1500 yards south of Haisnes.

"*The Quarries.*"—Lying half-way to the German trenches west of Cité St. Elie.

Hulluch.—A village strung out along a small stream, lying less than half a mile south-east of Cité St. Elie and 3000 yards north-east of Loos.

Half a mile north of Hill 70 is "*Puits 14 bis,*" another coal-mine, possessing great possibilities for defence when taken in conjunction with a strong redoubt situated on the north-east side of Hill 70.

It was arranged that the First Corps, consisting of the Second, Seventh, and Ninth Divisions, under Lieut.-General Hubert Gough, should attack the line between La Bassée Canal and Vermelles, while the Fourth Corps (First, Fifteenth, and Forty-seventh Divisions), under Lieut.-General Sir H. Rawlinson, attacked from Vermelles to Grenay, the Hulluch—Vermelles road forming the boundary between the two Corps.

The attack began at 6.30 A.M. on September 25, after four days' continuous bombardment by our massed guns. Gas was employed, but unfortunately the wind was unfavourable, and it moved so slowly that it retarded the advance. Further, the wire in some places had hardly been touched, and consequently the Second Division was held up from the start. Meanwhile the Ninth Division started well, and even managed to reach the northern end of "Little Willie," but was unable to maintain its advanced position on account of the check to the Second Division. The Seventh Division captured the first line of the trenches and cleared the quarries half-way between the front line and Cité St. Elie, while the leading troops even penetrated as far as Cité St. Elie itself.

By mid-day the First Corps had secured the whole of the German front from the Hohenzollern Redoubt southwards and had pushed forward to the second line at three points. But in this achievement it suffered heavy casualties, and was left too weak to do more than hold on to the position it had gained.

In the Fourth Corps the First Division swept forward, carried the first two lines of German trenches, and reached the outskirts of Hulluch, where it waited for reinforcements, but as these did not arrive it had to fall back on the Lens— La Bassée road. As for the Fifteenth Division, whose objective was Cité St. Augusté, it pushed through not only to Loos, but even over Hill 70, and the 44th Brigade in this division actually reached the outskirts of Cité St. Laurent.

BATTLE OF LOOS, 1915

On the afternoon of the 26th the Eleventh Corps was placed at the disposal of Sir Douglas Haig; it consisted of the Guards Division and the Twenty-first and Twenty-fourth Divisions. The two latter were at once hurried up into the firing line, the Twenty-first Division sending two brigades to Loos while the Twenty-fourth went to the Lens—La Bassée road.

Throughout that Sunday the fighting was very severe, and it was only with the greatest difficulty that we held on to Loos. The First Corps was also being strongly counter-attacked, and the quarries changed hands several times. All day the Crown Prince of Bavaria, who was in command of the army facing the British divisions, was engaged in bringing up reserves from other parts, and by next day he had strengthened his whole line. The German line ran from Auchy—La Bassée over comparatively flat country to the Vermelles—Hulluch road, where the ground became undulating and culminated in Hill 70.

Early on Monday the advance was renewed, but the Germans had started counter-attacking, and a confused struggle went on, with varying success. Several times our line gave way, only to be rallied and go forward again. We managed to maintain our ground on the right and centre of Hill 70, but on the extreme left the enemy pressed the line back towards Loos. In the meantime the 64th Brigade of the Twenty-fourth Division was being driven back and subjected to withering enfilade fire. The line from the Chalk Pit to the northern end of Hill 70 had to

CHAPTER XV.
Sept. 1915.

be abandoned, and Loos was thus left exposed to an attack from the north-east. A brigade of the Third Cavalry Division was then brought up to reinforce the hard-pressed troops who were holding Loos.

THE GUARDS DIVISION

The Guards Division.

The Guards Division arrived early on Sunday morning at Haillicourt, more than ten miles off, and marched through Nœux-les-Mines and Sailly-la-Bourse to Vermelles. For the first time since its creation the Guards Division was to go into action, and naturally, after the fame individual battalions had won in the earlier part of the war, a great deal was expected of it. All the troops were cheered by the news that the Division had arrived and was going in, but the situation had altered a good deal since the attack was first launched. All element of surprise had disappeared, and the Germans had had time to recover from the effects of the first blow and to collect reinforcements. It is doubtful whether the Guards Division ever had any real chance of succeeding in its attack. It had to start from old German trenches, the range of which the German artillery knew to an inch, while the effect of our own original artillery bombardment had died away.

However, there was no alternative but to put in the Guards Division and try and regain as much of the lost ground as possible. Major-General Lord Cavan sent round on the 25th a stirring message to the men, reminding them that great things were expected of the Division, and they were full of confidence as they went into action.

The easiest task fell to the lot of the 1st Guards Brigade, under Brigadier-General Feilding, on the left. It was to advance in the direction of the Bois Hugo and straighten the line, so that it would run parallel to the Lens—La Bassée road. The 2nd Brigade, under Brigadier-General Ponsonby, was to take and hold the Chalk Pit and Puits 14 bis, and the 3rd Brigade, under Brigadier-General Heyworth, to advance against Hill 70. But to a large extent the movements of the 1st and 3rd Brigades depended on the success of the attack of the 2nd Brigade.

Accomplishing their work at once, Feilding's Brigade secured a good position on the ground over which the Twenty-fourth Division had retired. General Feilding, who understood that he was to assist the other brigades by fire as far as possible, at once collected as many smoke-bombs and smoke-candles as he could, and at zero hour formed a most effective smoke-screen, which drew off the fire of a great many German guns from the other attackers.

Success at first also attended the attack of Ponsonby's Brigade. It took the Chalk Pit and Puits 14 bis, but then a tremendous fire from machine-guns in Bois Hugo swept it down, and it was unable to keep its hold on these positions. This made it very difficult for the other brigades to move forward. But on learning that Ponsonby's Brigade was fighting furiously for the possession of the Chalk Pit, Lord Cavan decided

CHAPTER XV.

The Guards Division. Sept. 1915.

that the only way to relieve the strain on them was to order Heyworth's Brigade to advance. It did so, and this course proved successful in enabling Ponsonby's Brigade to retain possession of the Chalk Pit. Going forward, Heyworth's Brigade took Hill 70, but it too found it impossible to keep what it had won. The enemy's trenches were marked on the map as being on the crest of the hill, but in reality they were on the reverse slope, and had never been touched by shell-fire.

The net result of the attack of the Guards Division was the establishment of the British front along a line running, roughly, northward from the south-eastern end of Loos and parallel to the Lens—La Bassée road. Another attempt to gain Puits 14 was made by the 1st Battalion Coldstream on the 28th, but was no more successful than the first. As before, a small party reached the Puits, but was driven out again by enfilade fire.

Measured by the length of the advance made during the battle and the extent of ground taken from the enemy, the results of the battle of Loos would seem distinctly disappointing, more especially when the casualty list of 45,000 men is considered. But to estimate these operations in terms of geography is a mistake. The smallness of the theatre of operations and the comparatively narrow depth of our advance give a totally misleading impression of the success of the battle. It is obviously more valuable to put out of action 50,000 Germans and gain half a mile than to gain five miles and only inflict a loss of 10,000. When it is realised that we drove the enemy from positions which they considered impregnable to the assaults of modern weapons, that their casualties must have been as heavy as, if not heavier than, our own, and that we took 3000 prisoners (including 50 officers), 26 field-guns, and 40 machine-guns,—it will be seen that Lord Kitchener's description of the battle as a substantial success was not very far wide of the mark.

THE 2ND BATTALION

The following were the officers of the 2nd Battalion Grenadier Guards who took part in the battle:

Lieut.-Colonel G. D. Jeffreys .	Commanding Officer.
Major Lord Henry Seymour .	Second in Command.
Capt. the Hon. W. R. Bailey .	Adjutant.
Lieut. W. E. Acraman .	Quartermaster.
Lieut. D. Abel-Smith .	Machine-gun Officer.
2nd Lieut. the Hon. A. V. Agar-Robartes .	,, ,,
Lieut. A. K. S. Cunninghame (Transport Officer) .	No. 1 Company.
Lieut. J. N. Buchanan .	,, ,,
Lieut. E. W. M. Grigg .	,, ,,
2nd Lieut. L. St. L. Hermon Hodge	,, ,,
2nd Lieut. H. G. W. Sandeman .	,, ,,
Capt. A. F. R. Wiggins .	No. 2 Company.
Lieut. F. O. S. Sitwell .	,, ,,
Lieut. E. H. Noble .	,, ,,
Lieut. H. A. Clive .	,, ,,
2nd Lieut. H. F. C. Crookshank .	,, ,,
Capt. R. H. V. Cavendish, M.V.O. .	No. 3 Company.
2nd Lieut. W. H. Beaumont-Nesbitt	,, ,,
2nd Lieut. I. H. Ingleby .	,, ,,

Chapter XV.	2nd Lieutenant the Hon. B. B. Ponsonby	No. 3 Company.
2nd Batt. Sept. 1915.	2nd Lieut. E. R. M. Fryer . .	,, ,,
	Capt. A. de P. Kingsmill . .	No. 4 Company.
	2nd Lieutenant the Hon. W. A. D. Parnell	,, ,,
	2nd Lieut. M. A. Knatchbull-Hugessen	,, ,,
	2nd Lieut. C. Crosland . . .	,, ,,
	Capt. E. A. Aldridge, R.A.M.C. .	Medical Officer.

Sept. 26. The 1st Guards Brigade, under Brigadier-General Feilding, reached Vermelles early on the Sunday morning, and at 1 P.M. on the same day it was ordered forward to the old British trenches near Le Rutoire, where the two Coldstream battalions were placed in the firing line, and the 2nd Battalion Grenadiers and 1st Battalion Irish Guards in support. The orders General Feilding received from Major-General Lord Cavan were to advance and hold a line running parallel to the Lens—La Bassée road. The two Coldstream battalions found no difficulty in doing this, and having straightened the line, they occupied what had formerly been the German first-line trench.

The 2nd Battalion Grenadiers was not brought into action, as the 1st Guards Brigade could not advance until the Germans had been driven from the Chalk Pit Wood and Puits 14. The enemy, however, shelled the reserve trenches intermittently, and caused a few casualties. Second Lieutenant C. Crosland and five N.C.O.'s and men were wounded.

Sept. 27. On the 27th the 2nd Battalion Grenadiers was ordered to move up to the old German first-line trenches, which it did about 9 P.M., eventually settling down in the new position

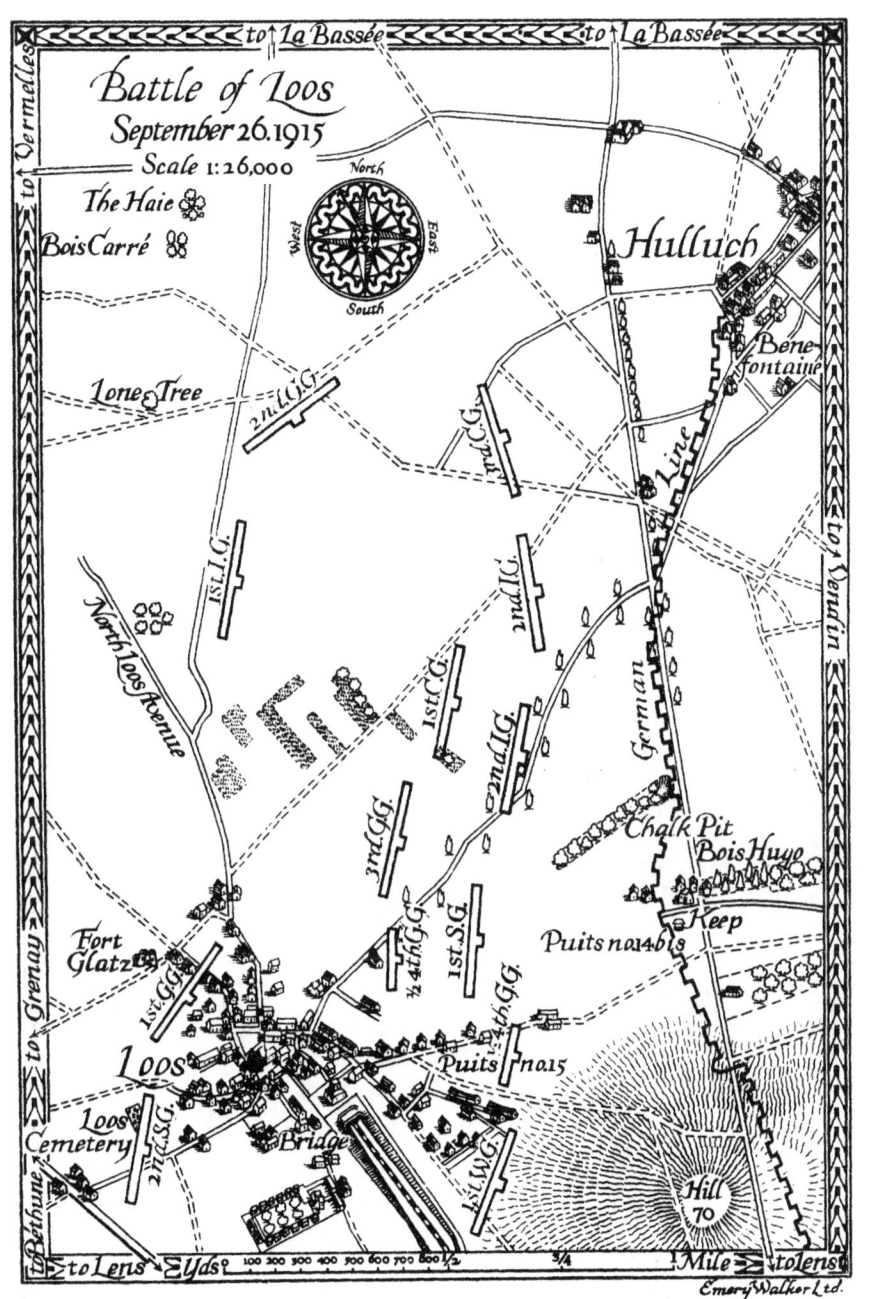

BATTLE OF LOOS, 1915

about midnight. No. 3 and No. 4 Companies were placed in the old German second line, while the Battalion Headquarters and No. 1 and No. 2 Companies were in rear of the old German first line. Two men were killed and five wounded during this operation.

2nd Batt.
Sept.
1915.

In this position it remained until the 30th, when it was relieved by the 9th Battalion Royal Fusiliers, and retired to billets at Mazingarbe.

THE 3RD BATTALION

The 2nd Guards Brigade reached Vermelles about 7 P.M. on Saturday, September 25, having marched *via* Ligny-les-Aire, Burbure, and Houchin. The officers of the 3rd Battalion Grenadiers were:

3rd Batt.

Colonel N. A. L. Corry, D.S.O.	Commanding Officer.
Major G. F. Molyneux-Montgomerie	Second in Command.
Lieut. G. G. B. Nugent	Adjutant.
Lieut. G. H. Wall	Quartermaster.
Capt. G. N. Vivian	No. 1 Company.
Lieut. G. G. Gunnis	,, ,,
Lieut. E. H. J. Wynne (Transport Officer)	,, ,,
2nd Lieut. C. T. E. Crabbe	,, ,,
2nd Lieut. A. T. Ayres Ritchie	,, ,,
Capt. C. F. A. Walker	No. 2 Company.
Lieut. C. S. Rowley	,, ,,
Lieut. A. Anson	,, ,,
2nd Lieut. F. D. Lycett-Green	,, ,,
2nd Lieut. R. Williams (Machine-gun Officer)	,, ,,
Lieutenant the Hon. F. O. H. Eaton	No. 3 Company.
Lieut. G. P. Bowes Lyon	,, ,,
2nd Lieutenant the Hon. A. G. Agar-Robartes	,, ,,

2nd Lieut. H. D. Vernon	. .	No. 3 Company.
Capt. E. G. H. Powell .	. .	No. 4 Company.
Capt. W. R. C. Murray (Bombing Officer)	. . . .	,, ,,
Lieut. C. M. C. Dowling	. .	,, ,,
Lieut. G. F. R. Hirst .	. .	,, ,,
Lieut. F. Anson .	. .	,, ,,
2nd Lieut. T. C. Higginson	. .	,, ,,

Attached—Lieut. A. T. Logan, R.A.M.C.

Sept. 25. It was bitterly cold on the night of the 25th, which was spent by the 3rd Battalion Grenadiers in the old British front trench north-west of Loos. Some of the platoons got into an old remnant of a trench, and some had to lie down outside. So chilly was it that sleep was difficult, and the men had constantly to get up and run about to warm themselves, and then try to snatch a little more rest.

Sept. 26. At 3.30 next morning the 3rd Battalion started off in the direction of Loos. At first it marched in fours, but on coming into the shell area assumed artillery formation, and went across the open. While ascending the slope it was not fired upon, but when it came down the hill towards Loos shrapnel burst all round it. When the Battalion arrived at the bottom of the hill, which it lost no time in doing, it relieved the Scots Guards, and got into what had formerly been the German third-line trenches. Both officers and men were filled with admiration at the intricate dug-outs they found, twenty to thirty feet down in the chalk; evidently great trouble had been expended on this part of the line, and the German officers had been accustomed to live almost in luxury.

As soon as the 3rd Battalion reached the trench, it was ordered to dig communication trenches and repair the parapet. Soon the men were soaked to the skin by pouring rain, and an icy cold wind added to their discomfort, as they had no prospect that night of getting either dry or warm.

CHAPTER XV.

3rd Batt. Sept. 1915.

Colonel Corry, being the senior Commanding Officer of the Brigade, was sent to serve temporarily on the Divisional Staff, so that he might be able to assume command of the Brigade in the event of the Brigadier being killed. The command of the 3rd Battalion Grenadiers therefore devolved on Major Molyneux-Montgomerie.

Next day this was the position. The 3rd Battalion Grenadiers was still in the line of trenches in front of Le Rutoire farm, with its right on the Loos Redoubt. In front of it was the 1st Battalion Scots Guards, with its right on the village of Loos. The 2nd Battalion Irish Guards was on the left of the Scots Guards, with the 1st Battalion Coldstream in support. At 2 P.M. Brigadier-General J. Ponsonby collected the commanding officers near the Loos Redoubt, and informed them that an attack was to be made that evening on Chalk Pit Wood by the 2nd Battalion Irish Guards, supported by the 1st Battalion Coldstream, and on Puits 14 (a large colliery) by the 1st Battalion Scots Guards, supported by the 3rd Battalion Grenadiers. A heavy bombardment was to start at 3 P.M. The Irish Guards were to advance at 4 P.M., but the Scots Guards were to wait until the wood was captured before they began their assault on the

Sept. 27.

Puits. The enemy was known to be strongly entrenched along Hill 70 to Puits 14.

3rd Batt.
Sept.
1915.

Instructions were given for the 3rd Battalion Grenadiers to follow the 1st Battalion Scots Guards and occupy its trench as soon as it was quitted. Major Montgomerie, now in command of the Battalion, immediately went forward with Captain Powell to find a way down the old German communication trenches between the Scots Guards' and Grenadiers' lines. On his return he sent orders to all company commanders to come to the right of the Battalion line near the Loos Redoubt, and there explained the situation. He ordered them to go back and bring their companies one after another to the communication trench he had found.

This operation necessarily took a long time, and the whole Battalion began to file down through a maze of communication trenches towards the line held by the Scots Guards. The intervening ground was being searchingly shelled, but at 4 P.M. the Grenadiers reached the trench from which the Scots Guards were to advance. This trench had become much broken down during the last days' fighting, and there were many wounded lying about, some of whom had been there for two days. When he arrived Major Montgomerie found that the attack had already begun, and that the Scots Guards were well away over the open, making for Puits 14. He therefore ordered No. 1 and No. 2 Companies, as they emerged from the communication trenches, to follow on at once in support of the Scots Guards. No. 3 and No. 4 Companies,

BATTLE OF LOOS, 1915

under Lieutenant Eaton and Captain Powell, were kept in reserve under the immediate orders of the Brigadier, who had now established his headquarters in that trench.

CHAPTER XV.

3rd Batt. Sept. 1915.

The Irish Guards, supported by the Coldstream, succeeded in gaining Chalk Pit Wood, but the Scots Guards had a more difficult task with Puits 14. After they had passed the Hulluch—Loos road they were not only shelled, but came in for heavy machine-gun fire from Hill 70 and Bois Hugo. The fire came almost entirely from the right flank. The two Grenadier companies under Captain Vivian and Captain Walker pushed on under terrific shell-fire, and came up with the Scots Guards just outside Puits 14, stubbornly defended by the Germans. Regardless of the machine-guns which were mowing down our men, the Scots Guards and two companies of Grenadiers pressed on, and endeavoured to reach Puits 14, but very few of the Scots Guards and not more than a dozen Grenadiers, under Lieutenant Ritchie, actually got into the Puits, where they threw bombs into a house occupied by the enemy.

But the enemy had not occupied this position for a year without thinking out every possible event, and machine-guns were soon turned on the attackers from every direction. Finding it impossible to retain possession of the Puits, the Scots Guards retired with the two companies of Grenadiers to just in front of Chalk Pit Wood, making it equally impossible for the enemy to hold his position. Lieutenant Ritchie and Second Lieutenant Crabbe, not knowing of this retirement, remained with six men among the buildings in the Puits, until they found themselves almost surrounded by Germans who had come from the Bois Hugo. At first they tried to drive the enemy back, but, finding themselves outnumbered and in danger of being captured, they decided to retire. The majority of the party got back to Chalk Pit Wood, but Second Lieutenant Crabbe was last seen standing on a wall throwing bombs at the enemy when he was killed. Captain Vivian, Lieutenant Ritchie, Lieutenant Dowling, and Lieutenant Lycett-Green were wounded. The last afterwards had his leg amputated. Lieutenant Rowley, also wounded, was too badly hurt to be moved, and so was left behind and taken prisoner. Lieutenant Ritchie, finding himself alone and wounded, walked slowly back to Chalk Pit Wood, where he collected all the men he could, and told them to dig themselves in for the night. He then came back and reported to General Ponsonby the result of the attack. Captain Walker was left behind in the retirement, but was able to get back after dark.

Lieutenant Ritchie, who commanded No. 1 Company after Captain Vivian was wounded, was specially recommended for "exceptional courage and ability." In spite of his injuries he continued to fight on with his company for six hours, and even when the retirement was ordered he made a valuable reconnaissance. Captain Walker was also specially mentioned for the splendid way he led his company into action.

Meanwhile the Irish and Coldstream Guards on the left had established themselves in the

Chalk Pit and adjoining wood, where they dug themselves in.

When darkness fell, Brigadier-General Ponsonby ordered another company from the Grenadiers to support the Scots Guards. Major Molyneux-Montgomerie, on receiving the order, went out with Lieutenant Ritchie to find the exact position of the two companies, and having done this he sent back a guide to bring up another company. No. 4, under Lieutenant Hirst, started off, but was held up by machine-gun fire, and it was two hours before it was able to reach the other two companies, who had suffered very much during the attack. The 3rd Battalion Grenadiers was now prolonging the line of the Scots Guards to the right, and holding from the south-west corner of Chalk Pit Wood to the corner of Loos, facing Puits 14.

The positions remained unchanged during the night and following morning, with shelling at intervals by the enemy, who knew the range of the trench precisely. In the afternoon the 1st Battalion Coldstream made a very gallant attempt to take Puits 14 from the Chalk Pit, but the attack failed. During the night two platoons of No. 3, under Lieutenant Eaton, were sent to make a line across the Loos—Hulluch road facing north, and to establish communication with the 1st Battalion Coldstream towards the Chalk Pit. Lieutenant F. Anson in No. 4 was wounded early that morning, and Captain Murray, in charge of the 3rd Battalion bombers, was very severely wounded while making a plucky raid on the Puits buildings.

Chapter XV.
3rd Batt.
Sept. 1915.
Sept. 29–30.

Until the night of the 30th the Battalion remained in the same trenches. It was very wet and cold, and the constant shelling greatly interfered with the work of bringing up supplies. The remnant of No. 2 Company, under Captain Walker, was moved to the left, and was used, together with No. 3 Company, to continue the line facing north, thus completing the junction between the 2nd and 1st Guards Brigades.

When the Brigade was relieved on the night of the 30th, the Berkshire Regiment came up to take the place of the Grenadiers. The relief did not finish till past 2 A.M., when the Battalion, much exhausted after its three days' fighting, marched slowly back through Noyelles and Sailly-la-Bourse to Verquigneul, which was reached about 6 A.M.

Among the officers the casualties were: Second Lieutenant Crabbe, killed; Captain Vivian, Captain Murray, Lieutenant Ritchie, Lieutenant Lycett-Green, Lieutenant F. Anson, and Lieutenant Dowling, wounded; Lieutenant Rowley, missing. The total casualties—killed, wounded, and missing—amounted to 229.

The following message was sent from the Brigadier to Colonel Corry:

To the Commanding Officer 3rd Battalion Grenadier Guards.

I wish to express to the 3rd Battalion Grenadier Guards my appreciation and admiration at their steady advance under very deadly fire to the attack on September 27. Lord Cavan, commanding the Guards Division, a former Grenadier Guardsman, has expressed

BATTLE OF LOOS, 1915   307

to me the sincere pride with which he watched his old regiment advance to the assault.

CHAPTER XV.

J. PONSONBY, Brigadier-General,
Commanding the 2nd Guards Brigade.

3rd Batt.
Sept.
1915.

THE 4TH BATTALION

The 3rd Guards Brigade, under Brigadier-General Heyworth, marched *via* Lambres, Lières, and Marles-les-Mines to Haillicourt, where it arrived on Sunday morning the 26th. At Marles-les-Mines it had to halt for six hours to allow a cavalry corps to pass, and as the men never knew when their turn would come to advance, they had to sit down on a muddy road and wait. The battalions were crowded into billets for a short time at Haillicourt, where the violent bombardment of the French attack at Souchez could be distinctly heard. In the afternoon the Brigade moved off, and marched to Vermelles, where it remained for the night.

4th Batt.
Sept. 26.

The officers of the 4th Battalion Grenadier Guards were:

Lieut.-Colonel G. C. Hamilton, D.S.O.	Commanding Officer.
Major the Hon. C. M. B. Ponsonby, M.V.O.	Second in Command.
Capt. T. F. J. N. Thorne	Adjutant.
Lieut. M. G. Williams	Machine-gun Officer.
Lieut. C. E. M. Ellison	,, ,,
2nd Lieut. E. Ludlow	Quartermaster.
Capt. J. A. Morrison	No. 1 Company.
Lieut. G. E. Shelley	,, ,,
2nd Lieut. G. A. Ponsonby	,, ,,
Captain Sir G. Houstoun-Boswall, Bart.	No. 2 Company.

308 THE GRENADIER GUARDS

Chapter XV.
4th Batt.
Sept. 1915.

Lieut. E. F. Penn	No. 2 Company.
Lieut. P. Malcolm	,, ,,
Capt. E. D. Ridley	No. 3 Company.
2nd Lieut. M. A. T. Ridley	,, ,,
2nd Lieut. A. H. Tompson	,, ,,
Capt. H. L. Aubrey Fletcher, M.V.O.	No. 4 Company.
Lieut. E. R. D. Hoare	,, ,,
2nd Lieut. B. C. Layton	,, ,,
2nd Lieut. M. H. Macmillan	,, ,,
Lieut. E. Brunton, R.A.M.C.	Medical Officer.

Lieutenant Blundell, Lieutenant Britten, Lieutenant R. Leigh Pemberton, and Lieutenant Tennant were left at Vermelles with the transport.

On the 27th Brigadier-General Heyworth received orders to attack Hill 70. The movements of the 3rd Guards Brigade more or less depended on the success of the 2nd Brigade. Originally it had been decided not to go through Loos, but to leave it on the right and to rendezvous close in rear of the Loos—Hulluch road, but these orders were afterwards cancelled.

Lieutenant-Colonel Hamilton explained to the company officers the general plan of attack, with some more detailed particulars about the part the 4th Battalion was to play, but on being ordered at once to accompany General Heyworth, who was going into Loos, he handed the command of the Battalion to Major Ponsonby, and told him to bring it to a position of deployment in Loos, where he himself would meet them. At the same time Captain Aubrey Fletcher was sent forward to reconnoitre the best route into Loos, and Lieutenant Blundell was ordered to bring up the Brigade S.A.A. and tool limbers to Fort Galatz.

BATTLE OF LOOS, 1915

At 2.30 the 4th Battalion moved off in fours down the Vermelles—Douai road, with No. 1 Company, under Captain Morrison, leading, and on reaching the top of the ridge assumed artillery formation. The order of march was: 4th Battalion Grenadiers, Welsh Guards, 2nd Battalion Scots Guards, and 1st Battalion Grenadiers. For one and a half miles, under heavy artillery fire—not shrapnel, but percussion H.E.—and in full view of the Germans, the 3rd Guards Brigade advanced in artillery formation. Perfect order was maintained in spite of the shells, which burst all round, and there was not a man out of his place. Nothing more splendid has ever been recorded in the annals of the Guards than the manner in which every battalion in the Brigade faced this trying ordeal. The 4th Battalion Grenadiers was all the time under machine-gun fire from the right, and during this stage of the attack Lieutenant Hoare was wounded.

On nearing Loos the 4th Battalion Grenadiers was ordered to double down the slope and get into a trench which ran through some ruined houses. The German artillery was now directing its attention to Loos, and using a great many gas shells. Major Ponsonby, guided by Captain Aubrey Fletcher, led the Battalion down an old German communication trench immediately north of Fort Galatz. It had already gone some distance along the trench when General Heyworth arrived at full gallop down the road, and ordered Captain Ridley and the men in rear of him who had not yet entered the communication trench to follow him at once. It would seem that

CHAPTER XV.

4th Batt. Sept. 1915.

CHAPTER XV.
4th Batt.
Sept. 1915.

the Battalion had either advanced too far or was going in the wrong direction. In any case from that moment it was divided into two parts.

Captain E. Ridley took with him Nos. 6, 7, and 8 platoons from No. 2 Company under Captain Sir George Houstoun-Boswall, No. 10 platoon from No. 3 Company under Lieutenant M. Ridley, with a few men from No. 4 Company, and worked down a trench towards the outskirts of Loos. Here they were again met by General Heyworth, who told them to go through the town and await Lieut.-Colonel Hamilton. Passing through the ruins at a rapid pace, Captain Ridley and his party reached the corner of the church which was being heavily shelled. The noise was deafening; shells were bursting in every direction and houses were falling in. The enemy's snipers were shooting at every place which might shelter a man. Through this hideous pandemonium the platoons came, not yet taking any part in the battle, but simply on their way to the place from which the attack was to start.

It was then found that Lieut.-Colonel Hamilton had been gassed and so placed *hors de combat*. Captain E. Ridley was told to take his platoons to the south-east corner of the town, but at that moment Major Ponsonby, accompanied by the Adjutant, Captain Thorne, and also Captain Fletcher, arrived and guided them to their destination. Major Ponsonby had been hastily sent for and told by the Brigadier to take command of the Battalion in Colonel Hamilton's place. Finding the Battalion split in two, he at once sent back for what really was the main portion, but the orderly who took the message was killed, and the order never reached Captain Morrison. Meanwhile the men were placed in a shallow trench just outside the town and facing Hill 70.

Chapter XV.
4th Batt.
Sept. 1915.

Here they were joined by Lieutenant M. Williams and Second Lieutenant Ellison with the machine-guns, who had made their way across country while the limbers went by road. Corporal C. Gould, who brought up the limbers under continual shell-fire, met on the way a runaway horse racing down the road at full gallop with a bomber's wagon behind him, fully loaded with bombs. The driver had been killed, and the horse, terrified by the shells, was making for home. Corporal Gould succeeded in stopping the horse, and put one of his men on the wagon. On arrival at Loos the machine-guns were carried on by hand.

The Welsh Guards now came up under Lieut.-Colonel Murray Threipland, who said that General Heyworth wished the attack to begin at once. Major Ponsonby, however, realised that to attempt an attack with the small force at his disposal was merely to court failure, and sent back word to General Heyworth stating what had happened to his battalion, and adding that he hardly considered the few platoons under his command sufficient to carry out the attack with any prospect of success. Messages, however, take some time to deliver, and every moment might be precious. He therefore consulted Colonel Murray Threipland, who undertook the attack, giving him instructions to join in on the left.

CHAPTER XV.
4th Batt.
Sept.
1915.

The firing line was composed of the Prince of Wales's Company of the Welsh Guards on the right, and Nos. 6 and 7 platoons of the 4th Battalion Grenadiers, under Sir George Houstoun-Boswall, on the left. Nos. 2 and 3 Companies of the Welsh Guards and Nos. 8 and 10 platoons of the Grenadiers were in support, while Colonel Murray Threipland kept his 4th Company as a reserve, and to it were added the remaining Grenadiers, including the men of the Battalion Headquarters. As soon as the men were formed up Major Ponsonby decided to take command himself, and sent Captain Ridley back to find the remainder of the Battalion.

Colonel Murray Threipland sent a message to General Heyworth to warn him that the attack had been launched, but the news had just arrived that the 2nd Guards Brigade had been unable to retain their hold on Puits 14. At this General Heyworth appears at first to have contemplated cancelling the attack, but on receiving orders from Lord Cavan to relieve the pressure on the 2nd Brigade by launching the attack on Hill 70, he destroyed the cancelling order.

So the attack started. Steadily the 4th Battalion Grenadiers and 1st Battalion Welsh Guards advanced towards Hill 70. At first they met nothing but rifle-fire, but on reaching the crest of the hill they were greeted by a murderous machine-gun fire, which caused great havoc among the front line. Staggered for a moment, the men hesitated, but Major Ponsonby urged them on, and they got to within twenty-five yards of the German trenches. There had

BATTLE OF LOOS, 1915   313

been no attempt at any surprise in this attack, which was not supported by artillery, although the cavalry machine-guns rendered all assistance they could. The enemy's machine-guns were cleverly placed and were most effective, especially in the neighbourhood of Puits 14 bis, which was now again in the hands of the Germans.

CHAPTER XV.
4th Batt.
Sept. 1915.

Explicit orders had been given by General Heyworth to the commanding officers on no account to advance over the crest of the hill; when a line on the reverse slope of the hill had been occupied it was to be consolidated. Owing to Lieut.-Colonel Hamilton having been gassed, the Grenadiers knew nothing of this order, and pushed on, while the Welsh Guards remained just under the crest of the hill. But the Grenadiers' position was quite untenable on account of the machine-guns which were enfilading them, and they withdrew to behind the crest.

Darkness now came down, and the exact position of the front line was not clear to those in rear. It was known that Hill 70 had been taken, and that somewhere on this hill were the Welsh Guards and a portion of the Grenadiers, with isolated parties in front of them. The 2nd Battalion Scots Guards, under Colonel Cator, was being sent up to relieve the front line, while the 1st Battalion Grenadiers remained in reserve in Loos.

During the last part of the advance Major Myles Ponsonby was hit while advancing with his men. Captain Thorne, the Adjutant, remained with him, although they were only twenty-five yards from the Germans, tied up his wounds, and, seeing how badly he was wounded, gave him morphia tablets. Early next morning Major Ponsonby died. No more glorious end could have been than his. He died, as Lord Cavan afterwards put it in a private letter, a great and lionhearted Grenadier fighting to the last, within a few yards of the Germans.

Captain Thorne was himself wounded in the head, and after leaving Major Ponsonby he tried to get back when it was dark. On the way he came upon two drummers who had been acting as orderlies; one had been killed and the other wounded through the leg. Knowing that if he left the boy where he was, he would probably be killed, he determined to carry him back. He put him on his shoulders and started off, but must have made some noise, for the Germans at once put up a flare and fired at him with machine-guns. He fell forward at once with the drummer—both killed.

Captain Sir George Houstoun-Boswall, who was in command of the first line of Grenadiers during this attack, behaved with great gallantry, and was killed as they were nearing the German trenches. Captain Fletcher was badly wounded earlier in the attack, as was Lieutenant M. Ridley: thus all the officers who took part in the attack were either killed or wounded.

When the attack started Lieutenant Mervyn Williams was ordered by Major Ponsonby to follow with his machine-guns in case of a counter-attack, and to leave Lieutenant Ellison behind in Loos with the reserve guns. The machine-gun party therefore followed on till it got to the top of Hill 70, where a large number of Grenadiers who had been killed were found. Crawling on, the men suddenly realised that they had gone too far and that there were Germans firing behind them, so they wheeled round, and came across Captain W. Berkley with some Welsh Guards and a small number of Grenadiers under Lieutenant M. Ridley, who was badly wounded. The fire was very heavy and there seemed no prospect of being able to advance. Uncertain where the remainder of the force was, the party hesitated to fire for fear of killing its own men. It was pouring with rain, and as darkness came on Lieutenant Williams decided to dig in where he was on Hill 70.

It is necessary now to return and follow the movements of the other half of the Battalion. It was moving down the German communication trench quite unconscious that General Heyworth had diverted the two last companies to Loos. When Captain Morrison arrived at the spot appointed as a rendezvous, he waited. The attack had clearly begun, as the shelling was very violent, but no orders of any sort came to him, nor did he know what had become of Major Ponsonby, Captain Fletcher, and Captain Thorne, any one of whom might have been able to explain to him the situation. He accordingly sent off an orderly to the Brigade Headquarters asking for instructions. But it was far from easy to find the Brigadier in the middle of a battle, and as the first orderly did not return he sent a second, and repeated this process until four orderlies had gone. He had with him No. 1

Company (his own), one platoon of No. 2 Company under Lieutenant Penn, two platoons of No. 3 Company under Lieutenant Tompson, and the greater part of No. 4 Company under Second Lieutenant Layton and Second Lieutenant Macmillan.

As no orders came, he formed up the men and determined to take part in the fighting. He had been told that the 3rd Guards Brigade were to attack Hill 70, and that the 4th Battalion Grenadiers were to form part of the attacking force. It was clearly wrong, therefore, for these companies to be doing nothing. But he could see no sign of the rest of his battalion, and efforts to obtain instructions had proved fruitless. At this moment he observed the 2nd Brigade attacking Puits 14, and thereupon decided to take on himself the responsibility of joining in, feeling sure that if he was wanted by the 3rd Brigade to attack Hill 70 he would be in the best position to assist them; rather than remain inactive he thought it best to throw his forces in anywhere.

Captain Morrison's men now extended for attack, and came up on the right of the 1st Battalion Scots Guards just as they were attacking Puits 14. The ground in this part of the line was being fiercely contested, and they found themselves under very severe machine-gun fire. When the Scots Guards retired from Puits 14, this portion of the 4th Battalion Grenadiers found themselves completely isolated. They lay down where they were under heavy fire, and when it was realised that the 2nd Guards Brigade

BATTLE OF LOOS, 1915

could make no farther advance, Captain Morrison gave his men orders to crawl back and dig themselves in on the Hulluch—Loos road. During this movement Second Lieutenant Macmillan was wounded in the head. Captain Morrison then went back and reported his position to General Heyworth, who told him to go up with the 2nd Battalion Scots Guards, under Colonel Cator, and dig in a line on Hill 70.

That evening the 2nd Battalion Scots Guards was sent up to relieve the 4th Battalion Grenadiers, but fifty men of No. 3 Company, who had originally formed part of the attacking force and were now without an officer, finding how thinly this line was held, insisted on staying where they were in order to strengthen the line.

Early in the morning the 4th Battalion went to the Loos—Hulluch road, and remained there till the night of the 29th, but it was found that there were still the fifty men of the Battalion already mentioned on Hill 70, in addition to some thirty who had joined the 3rd Battalion in the 2nd Brigade. The machine-gun section, under Lieutenant Williams, also remained out on Hill 70, hoping that the attack would be renewed, when it could join in. Some Engineers had got out to them and erected barbed-wire entanglements partially across their front. Wounded men were continually crawling back to this little oasis in the desert of shell-holes. Painfully and slowly, inch by inch, these maimed men would arrive, often being sniped by the enemy. It was such an exposed spot that,

Chapter XV.

4th Batt. Sept. 1915.

Sept. 28.

beyond helping them into the shallow trench, the men in this party could do little.

About 8.30 that night Lieutenant Williams saw a party of Germans crawl out and advance toward some of our wounded who were unable to move. They appeared to be quite unaware of the handful of men in this trench. Feeling sure they intended to take the wounded prisoners, when their injuries would, no doubt, be dressed, he gave orders that no one was to fire. The Germans crept on slowly, but on reaching the wounded, to Lieutenant Williams' horror, they proceeded to bayonet them. It was hardly necessary for Lieutenant Williams to give the order to fire, as the men with the machine-guns had seen this dastardly act, and the two machine-guns soon wiped out the whole party of Germans. Our wounded men were finally rescued by the Scots Guards when they came up, and Lieutenant Williams retired with the machine-guns to Loos.

Meanwhile, Captain Morrison had succeeded in collecting the men who had been scattered in various parts of the line. They had all joined in the attack somewhere, although they received no instructions to do so. That night the Battalion marched back to Vermelles, and went into billets.

The casualties among the officers were : Lieut.-Colonel G. Hamilton and Lieutenant Shelley, gassed; Major the Hon. M. Ponsonby, Captain Thorne, Captain Sir George Houstoun-Boswall, Second Lieutenant A. Tompson, killed; Captain Aubrey Fletcher, Lieutenant P. Malcolm, Second Lieutenant M. Ridley, Lieutenant E. R. D.

BATTLE OF LOOS, 1915

Hoare, Second Lieutenant Macmillan, wounded. The total casualties in other ranks amounted to 342.

THE 1ST BATTALION

The officers of the 1st Battalion Grenadier Guards at this time were:

Lieut.-Colonel G. F. Trotter, M.V.O., D.S.O.	Commanding Officer.
Major C. R. C. de Crespigny	Second in Command.
Lieut. E. H. Duberly	Adjutant.
2nd Lieut. P. K. Stephenson	Machine-gun Officer.
Capt. M. E. Makgill-Crichton-Maitland	King's Company.
Lieutenant Sir A. L. M. Napier, Bt.	,, ,,
Lieutenant Lord Stanley	,, ,,
2nd Lieut. G. J. T. H. Villiers	,, ,,
2nd Lieut. A. G. Bonham-Carter	,, ,,
Capt. F. L. V. Swaine	No. 2 Company.
Lieut. R. P. le P. Trench	,, ,,
2nd Lieut. F. E. H. Paget	,, ,,
2nd Lieut. C. Leeke	,, ,,
2nd Lieutenant the Hon. I. A. Charteris	,, ,,
Major W. E. Nicol, D.S.O.	No. 3 Company.
Lieut. O. Wakeman	,, ,,
2nd Lieut. E. Heneage	,, ,,
Capt. W. S. Pilcher	No. 4 Company.
Lieutenant Viscount Lascelles	,, ,,
Lieutenant the Earl of Dalkeith	,, ,,
Lieut. A. A. Moller	,, ,,
Capt. G. Petit, R.A.M.C.	Medical Officer.

The 1st Battalion reached Vermelles on the Sunday with the rest of the 3rd Guards Brigade. On Monday it advanced towards Loos, and was placed in reserve, which meant being heavily shelled, without taking any active part in the fighting. It received orders to occupy the old

CHAPTER XV.

1st Batt.
Sept.
1915.

German second-line trench on the outskirts of Loos, and Lieut.-Colonel G. Trotter left it there under Major de Crespigny while he went forward to Brigade Headquarters. The advance of the 3rd Guards Brigade into Loos under heavy shell-fire already referred to was described afterwards by a General as one of the most splendid and inspiring sights he had ever seen.

Major de Crespigny led the 1st Battalion to an old German trench just outside Loos, and ordered the men to put on gas helmets. Lieut.-Colonel Trotter, having been told to keep his battalion well under cover and to wait for further orders, returned to find that they had already carried out these instructions. The attack by the 4th Battalion Grenadiers and Welsh Guards started, but when General Heyworth found they could not capture and hold Hill 70 he decided to take up a line a little short of the crest of the hill and not to throw in the reserves. The 1st Battalion Grenadiers therefore remained just outside Loos, and in the evening sent up digging parties to assist the Royal Engineers.

Sept. 28.

All next day the 1st Battalion Grenadiers remained in this trench, where it was heavily shelled. The Germans of course knew the exact range of this trench, and were able to hit it with monotonous regularity, but the dug-outs were so craftily constructed that little damage was done. The danger lay in entering and coming out of these caves, and a certain number of men were killed in this way. All night digging parties were sent out to work on the lines in front. Marching in the dark through Loos was a hazardous proceeding, as the roads were a mass of shellholes into which men frequently fell, and since the parties had to work in the open with the German trenches not very far off, their task was a perilous one. Flares were sent up, and if a man moved the Germans started firing at once. Nevertheless the Battalion got through a great deal of work, and barbed wire and sand-bags were taken up to the Scots Guards, who were now holding the line on Hill 70.

The 1st Battalion stayed in the same trenches next day, but the front line was by no means straight. This enabled the Germans to bring up a field-gun, with which they enfiladed the whole trench. When the shells first arrived down the trench from no one knew where, there were a great many men outside the dug-outs, and consequently many casualties. Major W. E. Nicol was hit in the head by a fragment of a shell, and died soon afterwards; Second Lieutenant Villiers had his jaw broken in two places, and Lieutenant Sir A. Napier was wounded in the thigh. The total casualties among other ranks were 45.

On the 30th the Battalion was relieved by a battalion of the 37th Brigade, and retired into billets at Sailly-la-Bourse.

CHAPTER XVI

OCTOBER, NOVEMBER, DECEMBER 1915

Diary of the War

CHAPTER XVI.
1915.

THE marshy condition of the ground and the bad weather made operations on any large scale impossible, and, with the exception of raids in various parts of the line, no serious offensive movement was attempted. In December Field-Marshal Sir John French resigned command of the British Army in France, and took over command of the Forces in the United Kingdom. He was succeeded by General Sir Douglas Haig.

In October the Bulgarians, under the impression that the Central Powers were winning the war, decided to join them, and declared war on the Allies.

In Mesopotamia the British Forces reached Kut-el-Amara with a view to the capture of Bagdad.

The campaign in Gallipoli having reached a deadlock, it was decided to withdraw the British Forces and abandon the attempt to reach Constantinople by that route. The whole of the Forces were successfully withdrawn with only three casualties.

OCTOBER TO DECEMBER 1915

THE 1ST BATTALION
ROLL OF OFFICERS

Lieut.-Colonel G. F. Trotter, M.V.O., D.S.O.	Commanding Officer.	
Major C. R. C. de Crespigny	Second in Command.	
Lieut. E. H. J. Duberly	Adjutant.	
Lieut. P. K. Stephenson	Machine Gun Section.	
Lieut. the Earl of Dalkeith	Bombing Officer.	
Lieut. Lord Stanley	Transport Officer.	
Lieut. J. Teece	Quartermaster.	
Capt. M. E. Makgill-Crichton-Maitland	King's Company.	
2nd Lieut. F. G. Bonham-Carter	,, ,,	
Capt. F. L. V. Swaine	No. 2 Company.	
Lieut. R. P. le P. Trench	,, ,,	
2nd Lieut. F. E. H. Paget	,, ,,	
2nd Lieut. C. Leeke	,, ,,	
2nd Lieut. the Hon. I. A. Charteris	,, ,,	
Capt. C. H. Greville	No. 3 Company.	
Lieut. O. Wakeman	,, ,,	
2nd Lieut. E. Heneage	,, ,,	
Capt. W. S. Pilcher	No. 4 Company.	
Lieut. Viscount Lascelles	,, ,,	
2nd Lieut. A. A. Moller	,, ,,	
Capt. G. Petit, R.A.M.C.	Medical Officer.	

CHAPTER XVI.

1st Batt. Oct. 1915.

During October the 1st Battalion remained either in or just behind the trenches until the 26th. The casualties in the other battalions necessitated a certain redistribution of the officers, and Captain R. Wolrige-Gordon, who had returned from sick leave, was transferred to the 3rd Battalion, while Captain Greville and Second Lieutenant F. G. Bonham-Carter went to the 4th Battalion. On October 3 the 1st Battalion relieved the Oxfordshire and Buckinghamshire Light Infantry in the trenches, and came in for a good deal of shelling, during which it had twenty-six casualties. On the 6th it was relieved by the 6th Buffs, and went into billets at Vermelles, where it lived in cellars. From Vermelles to the trenches was a march of one and a half hours through communication trenches practically the whole way, and fatigue parties sometimes amounting to over 150 men were constantly sent up to the front line. Lieutenant O. Wakeman and Lieutenant Lord Lascelles were recommended for the rank of temporary Captain on account of their gallant conduct, and the efficient manner in which they handled their platoons under fire.

On the 7th Second Lieutenant R. W. Phillipps and a draft of 50 men arrived, and on the 9th Second Lieutenant F. C. St. Aubyn and Second Lieutenant H. Alexander joined the Battalion.

On the 14th the Battalion moved up into the trenches near the Hohenzollern Redoubt and occupied the front line south-east of "Big Willie," the name given by the men to the largest of the two German trenches connecting the Hohenzollern Redoubt with the main line of the German trenches.

On the 17th Lieut.-Colonel G. Trotter received orders to direct a bombing attack against the German line towards Slag Alley. The attack was to be undertaken by No. 3 Company under Lieutenant O. Wakeman, and the men went out over the top with the expert bombers leading, but on arrival they found two German machine-guns enfilading the front of the German block. Second Lieutenant the Hon. I. Charteris and Second Lieutenant H. Alexander, two very promising officers, were killed at once, and a large number of men were killed and wounded. Lieutenant O. Wakeman behaved with great gallantry, and went forward to see whether anything could be done. He found that to attempt an advance was impossible, and was just sending back for more reinforcements when he was shot through the top of the skull and was completely paralysed in both legs. Colonel Trotter now sent up Lieutenant Lord Lascelles to take command of the Company, telling him, if possible, to keep all that had been gained, but to use his discretion as to what should be done in the circumstances. Lord Lascelles, on coming up, quickly grasped the whole situation. He saw that while the two German machine-guns were in position, it was a practical impossibility to take the trench, and he very wisely withdrew what remained of that Company to our trenches. It was well that he did so, for soon afterwards the Germans commenced a heavy bombardment, which lasted till noon. The casualties were 2 officers killed and 3 wounded, with 125 of other ranks killed and wounded.

Lieutenant Trench had asked the Commanding Officer the night before whether he might lead the bombers, but his request was refused, as his business was to remain in our trenches and see that every bomb was properly fused before it was passed along to the front. When Lieutenant Charteris, however, was killed, his men, not knowing what was expected of them, started to come back. Lieutenant Trench rallied them, and took them up again, when he was knocked down with a bit of a bomb through his right arm. On the previous day only he had had a nasty blow from a piece of shell on the shoulder, but had refused to take any notice of it. Lieutenant St. Aubyn was also wounded during this bombing attack, but not seriously. In the evening the body of Lieutenant Charteris was recovered, and buried at Sailly-la-Bourse, Lord Stanley superintending the funeral.

On the 10th the Battalion was relieved by the 3rd Battalion Coldstream, and went into billets at Sailly-la-Bourse, but returned to the trenches on the 26th, when Second Lieutenant R. Phillipps, who had only joined the Battalion a fortnight before, was killed. On the 20th Lieutenant G. Inglis and a draft of sixty-eight men arrived. On the 26th the Battalion marched about fifteen miles to Allouagne, where it remained in billets for a fortnight. The King, who was in France, had expressed his intention of inspecting the Guards Division on the 28th, and all the battalions were actually marching to the ground when the news arrived that, owing to an accident to His Majesty, the inspection would not take place. It was known afterwards that while the King was inspecting some troops his horse, frightened by the cheering, had reared up, falling back on His Majesty, and crushing him severely. Before he left France, the following was published in orders :

Special Order of the Day by His Majesty the King

I am happy to have found myself once more with my armies.

It is especially gratifying to me to have been able to see some of those that have been newly created. For I have watched with interest the growth of these troops from the first days of recruit drill and through the different stages of training until their final inspection on the eve of departure for the Front as organised divisions. Already they have justified the general conviction then formed of their splendid fighting worth.

Since I was last among you, you have fought many strenuous battles. In all you have reaped renown and proved yourselves at least equal to the highest traditions of the British Army.

In company with our noble Allies you have baffled the infamous conspiracy against the law and liberty of Europe, so long and insidiously prepared.

These achievements have involved vast sacrifices. But your countrymen who watch your campaign with sympathetic admiration will, I am well assured, spare no effort to fill your ranks and afford you all supplies.

I have decorated many of you. But had I decorated all who deserve recognition for conspicuous valour, there would have been no limit, for the whole Army is illustrious.

It is a matter of sincere regret to me that my accident should have prevented my seeing all the troops I had intended, but during my stay amongst you I have seen enough to fill my heart with admiration of your patient cheerful endurance of life in the trenches; a life either of weary monotony or of terrible tumult. It is the dogged determination evinced by all ranks which will at last bring you to victory. Keep the goal in sight, and remember it is the final lap that wins.

GEORGE, R.I.

November 1, 1915.

On October 31 Major M. Maitland was transferred to the 3rd Battalion.

On November 1 the 1st Battalion went into

CHAPTER XVI.
1st Batt.
Nov. 1915.

Brigade Reserve, and moved into billets on the La Bassée road. On the 10th Lieutenant G. Wilson joined from the Yorkshire Light Infantry, and on the 18th Lieutenant the Hon. P. P. Cary and Second Lieutenant H. V. Cholmeley arrived. On the 16th it went into the trenches at Chapigny with two Companies in the front line, one in support and one in reserve in Rue Bacquerot, where the Germans were very quiet, but the inevitable sniping made it dangerous to any one who exposed himself. A great deal of work had to be done improving and draining the trenches, but the men were wonderfully well equipped during the cold weather, for they had high waders, leather waistcoats, mackintosh caps, and good gloves.

Dec.

On the 26th the Battalion retired into billets at La Gorgue, and went up into the trenches, relieving the 4th Battalion every two days, until December 20, when it went into Brigade Reserve at Laventie. On the 21st the 1st and 4th Battalions Grenadiers dined together, the dinner being arranged by Captain Morrison. On the 23rd Second Lieutenant C. Wilkinson joined the Battalion. On the 22nd the Battalion returned to the front line, again taking turns with the 4th Battalion, and as the trenches were ill suited for Christmas festivities, it was unanimously agreed to postpone the Christmas dinners until January. Captain G. Petit, R.A.M.C., who had been attached to the 1st Battalion for over a year, left to take up another appointment. He had followed the fortunes of the Battalion, and had fought with it in all the battles in which it had taken part during the last twelve months. His departure was therefore much regretted by the officers and men, with whom he was very popular.

The 2nd Battalion

Roll of Officers

Lieut.-Colonel G. D. Jeffreys	Commanding Officer.
Major Lord Henry Seymour	Second in Command.
Capt. the Hon. W. R. Bailey	Adjutant.
Lieut. D. Abel-Smith	Machine-Gun Officer.
2nd Lieut. the Hon. A. V. Agar-Robartes	,, ,,
Lieut. W. E. Acraman	Quartermaster.
Lieut. J. N. Buchanan	No. 1 Company.
Lieut. E. W. M. Grigg	,, ,,
2nd Lieut. L. St. L. Hermon-Hodge	,, ,,
2nd Lieut. H. G. W. Sandeman	,, ,,
Capt. A. F. R. Wiggins	No. 2 Company.
Lieut. F. O. S. Sitwell	,, ,,
Lieut. E. H. Noble	,, ,,
Lieut. H. A. Clive	,, ,,
2nd Lieut. H. F. C. Crookshank	,, ,,
Capt. R. H. V. Cavendish, M.V.O.	No. 3 Company.
2nd Lieut. W. H. Beaumont-Nesbitt	,, ,,
2nd Lieut. I. H. Ingleby	,, ,,
2nd Lieut. the Hon. B. B. Ponsonby	,, ,,
2nd Lieut. E. R. M. Fryer	,, ,,
Capt. A. de P. Kingsmill	No. 4 Company.
Lieut. J. C. Craigie	,, ,,
2nd Lieut. the Hon. W. A. D. Parnell	,, ,,
2nd Lieut. M. A. Knatchbull-Hugessen	,, ,,
Capt. E. A. Aldridge, R.A.M.C.	Medical Officer.

In the redistribution of officers after the battle of Loos, Lieutenant F. O. S. Sitwell and Second Lieutenant I. H. Ingleby were transferred to the 4th Battalion, and Second Lieutenant

CHAPTER XVI.

2nd Batt.
Oct.
1915.

E. R. M. Fryer and Lieutenant L. St. L. Hermon-Hodge to the 3rd Battalion.

On the 3rd the 2nd Battalion returned to the trenches, and took over the section of old British trenches east of Vermelles, where it remained in support of the 2nd and 3rd Battalions Coldstream, who were in the old German trenches south of the Hohenzollern Redoubt. It was hardly in position when the Germans shelled the whole line heavily, and caused some casualties. Two high-explosive shells landed in the trench occupied by No. 1 Company, killing two and wounding five men. Second Lieutenant Sandeman was knocked down, but not seriously hurt, and Lieutenant Craigie was wounded.

This activity on the part of the German artillery was the prelude to a counter-attack, by which the enemy retook the Hohenzollern Redoubt. On the 4th the East Yorkshire Regiment tried to retake this Redoubt, but failed. The 2nd Battalion Grenadiers, still in support, was engaged in digging communication trenches towards the old German trenches which were now our front line. It was an intricate piece of trench line, with the Germans not thirty yards off, and required a great deal of work to make it tenable. On the 5th the 2nd Battalion Grenadiers moved up in the front line, and there was a certain amount of bombing on both sides. For two days the Battalion remained in its trenches, and sniping was reduced to a fine art, as hyposcopic rifles had been provided. On the 7th the Battalion was relieved by the 3rd Battalion Coldstream, and retired to billets at Vermelles, but even here the shells followed it, and fell in and about the village.

On the 8th the Battalion returned to the trenches, and that night the enemy attacked, but were easily driven off. On the 10th Lieut.-Colonel Jeffreys determined to take the enemy's bombing post by surprise, and to bomb up his trench as far as possible. No. 1 Company under Lieutenant H. A. Clive was selected for the task, and the whole scheme of attack was carefully planned and explained to every officer, N.C.O., and man who took part in it. Second Lieutenant Sandeman was ordered to command the party, but Lieutenant J. C. Craigie, the bombing officer, went first. It was a pitch-dark night and very quiet, so that every man had to be careful not to make any noise, more especially as every few minutes a light went up silently. Slowly thirty crawling figures went out, and made their way through the grass. A quarter of an hour went by in silence, and Colonel Jeffreys, fearing that there was some mistake, telephoned to Lieutenant Clive to ask why the attack had not begun, but at that moment the first bombs exploded. Lieutenant Craigie reached the German bombing post in safety, and as soon as the bomb-throwing began in earnest, whistled back, which was the signal for Lieutenant Grigg to come out with a chain of men carrying bombs.

The Germans, surprised by this shower of bombs, hastily retired, and were followed by Lieutenant Craigie and Lieutenant Sandeman up the trench. Having got 150 yards up the German trench, Lieutenant Craigie sent back for reinforcements, and Lieutenant Clive came up himself with another platoon carrying picks and shovels to consolidate the position. Meanwhile in front the Germans were making a stand, and soon a message came back for stretcher-bearers, but the narrowness of the trench made stretchers dangerous, as they might possibly block the trench, so the wounded were carried back over the top. A message had just been received that barbed wire was wanted in front, when the telephone wire was cut by a shell. With a narrow trench full of men filling sand-bags and making fire positions, barbed wire is an awkward thing to carry up, and Lieutenant Clive therefore gave orders that it was to come up over the top. Now carrying the wounded back over the top has a certain sentimental attraction, for anything connected with the wounded is associated in men's minds with the V.C., but carrying barbed wire up, although every bit as dangerous, is mere coolie work. Nevertheless the barbed wire arrived at its destination, and the farthest point taken was consolidated. One thousand five hundred bombs had been thrown, and there were no more available; so when Major Lord Henry Seymour came along, and ordered a second attack to begin at 1 A.M., he found there were no more bombs, and there was nothing else to do but to build up the trench. It was hardly to be expected that Lieutenant Craigie, who had been in front all the way, should escape unscathed, but he got off very cheaply with a piece of a bomb in his leg. Lieutenant Sandeman was untouched. No. 3 Company under Captain Cavendish had remained in support, feeding No. 1 Company with reinforcements as the situation developed. Almost immediately after the attack started, Captain Cavendish sent Lieutenant B. Ponsonby up with one and a half platoons to help No. 1, and soon after Lieutenant Beaumont-Nesbitt was ordered off to look after the Lewis gun. The remaining three platoons were therefore without officers, and were gradually sent up in small parties for various duties. Captain Cavendish himself was ordered not to go up, as he would have been senior to Lieutenant Clive, and would therefore have had to take command in the middle of these operations. Moreover, owing to the telephone wire to No. 1 Company being cut, he became the connecting link between the Commanding Officer and the bombing party. When, therefore, he was ordered at 4.30 to relieve No. 1, he had some difficulty in finding where all his Company had got to, but eventually collected it, and carried out the relief.

The Germans made a further counter-attack early next morning, but failed to regain any of their lost trench. They contented themselves with a heavy bombardment of our line.

The next day the Battalion received orders to cut the wire near the front line, to prepare the way for our attack, which was to take place two days later, but the men had not started when the Germans suddenly began to shell that particular portion of wire with shrapnel. There was something almost uncanny in their accuracy as regards time and place, and it conclusively proved that they must have tapped our tele-

CHAPTER XVI.
2nd Batt.
Oct. 1915.

phone wires. After waiting until the Germans had finished, a party went forth, and carried out the orders.

On the 12th the 2nd Battalion remained in the same trench, and although in the morning there was only intermittent shelling the bombardment increased in intensity during the afternoon. The Germans made a severe bombing attack on the trench which had been taken from them, but were easily beaten off. Although at one time there was some anxiety on our part as to whether the supply of bombs would hold out, the enemy was not only driven off but our bombers succeeded in throwing bombs into his bomb stores, causing two violent explosions. During the whole attack our line was heavily bombed by aerial torpedoes, a particularly accurate and powerful form of trench mortar, but when it got dark the enemy's attack died gradually away. The new Mills grenades proved a great success, as they could be thrown farther than those of the enemy. The Battalion was to have been relieved at 6.45 P.M., but owing to this attack the relieving Battalions did not arrive until nearly midnight, and the relief was not completed until 3 A.M.

On the 13th Major Lord Henry Seymour left to take command of the 4th Battalion, and the same day Lieutenant T. A. Combe arrived. The casualties during the two days in the trenches were 150 killed and wounded.

In a private letter dated October 13, Major-General Lord Cavan wrote to Lieut.-Colonel Jeffreys :

OCTOBER TO DECEMBER 1915

I should like to come and thank all your Battalion for its splendid and glorious work of the past week, but I cannot leave Headquarters till the fight is ended, and I do not want to bother you and your officers and men, but simply wish them rest. In case I cannot manage to come, and we are wanted again quickly, I hope you will accept this letter of my profound gratitude for, and intense admiration of your splendid services. To the men who have repulsed attack after attack on the trench they took so gallantly, I simply could not say enough, and I hope you have already put in names for due reward of those who actually win our battles for us. My heartiest congratulations and undying thanks.

The Battalion went back into billets at Verquin on the 13th, and then to Sailly-la-Bourse. On the 19th it returned to the trenches opposite Big Willie, and owing to some mistake Nos. 1 and 2 Companies were crowded into a trench capable only of holding one Company, with the result that quite an unnecessarily large number of men were hit. On the 19th Second Lieutenant F. A. M. Browning arrived, and on the 21st Major A. St. L. Glyn joined the Battalion as second in command.

On the 22nd the shelling became so violent that a message was sent down the whole British line to the effect that at any moment an attack might be expected. On the 23rd the German artillery turned its attention to a communication trench called "King's Head," which it blew in in several places. Second Lieutenant H. Crookshank was wounded, and there was a certain number of casualties among other ranks.

On the 26th Lieut.-Colonel Jeffreys was sent for to take command of the 35th Brigade, much

CHAPTER XVI.
2nd Batt.
Oct.
1915.

to the regret of the whole Battalion. The Battalion was formed up in mass near Fosse 8, and Lieut.-Colonel Jeffreys thanked it for the splendid manner in which they had supported him during the time he had been in command. He made touching references to his predecessor Lieut.-Colonel W. Smith, and ended by congratulating it on all it had done since the beginning of the war.

Thus the command of the Battalion devolved on Major A. Glyn, who had only just arrived, and who wrote diffidently to General Feilding, pointing out the difficulty in which he was placed by being in command of a Battalion so soon after his arrival. On the 23rd Lieutenant Irvine and on the 31st Second Lieutenant F. J. V. Hopley joined.

Nov.

The Battalion remained in billets at Lapugnoy until November 10, when it marched to Chocques, where it stayed till the 14th, and then marched to La Gorgue. On the 18th Lieut.-Colonel Jeffreys returned to the Battalion, as his appointment to the 35th Brigade had only been temporary, and it was not till some two months later that he was given command of the 58th Brigade. On the 20th Major the Right Hon. Winston Churchill was attached to the 2nd Battalion Grenadiers for instruction. The 1st Guards Brigade took over the line of trenches opposite Pietre, all in a very bad condition—communication trenches flooded, and front-line breastworks crumbling and not bullet-proof. There was consequently a great deal of work to be done, which the incessant shelling retarded, while the weather, being cold and raw, with snow at intervals, made things generally unpleasant. For the rest of the month the Battalion remained in this part of the line, retiring occasionally as far as Merville in reserve.

The suspected presence of a German mine had for some time caused anxiety, and it was therefore decided to send out a party to find and destroy the shaft in the German trenches. Lieutenant the Hon. W. A. D. Parnell, Sergeant Lyon, and eleven men volunteered for the expedition. As soon as the moon had gone down the party started off over the parapet, and advanced cautiously through the long grass which covered the ground between the two lines. They had to cross a stream which was composed of water pumped from the enemy's trenches, but fortunately found a shallow place through which they were able to wade. On arrival at the German trenches they cut the wire, and silently one by one dropped down in the trench, but not a soul was to be seen. They moved slowly forward until they reached the communication trench, where they left two men to look out, and then went down the communication trench, but after going on for about forty yards they heard voices. Their mission was not to alarm the enemy, but to find out if there was an entrance in the German trench to a shaft of any description; so having satisfied themselves that none existed, they returned by the same route they had come, and reported all they had seen to Lieut.-Colonel Jeffreys.

On the night of the 17th two patrols were sent out to explore the enemy's front trench.

Chapter XVI.
2nd Batt.
Dec. 1915.

Lieutenant the Hon. W. Parnell, accompanied by Sergeant Lyon, again started off with eight men. No rifles were carried, but each man was armed with a bludgeon about eighteen inches long, with an iron ring round the head. Two men carried six bombs each. A second party was sent off by the 2nd Battalion Coldstream, and left at the same time. On arrival in the German trench, which they again reached without opposition, the Grenadiers went to the left and the Coldstream to the right.

The party of Grenadiers advanced slowly down the German trench. They had not gone far before they observed a faint ray of light from a dug-out. Lieutenant Parnell halted the party, and directed Sergeant Lyon to go on ahead and see whether there was any sign of a sentry. Sergeant Lyon crept on, and saw that not only was there a sentry, but that on each side of the trench there was a small place hollowed out large enough to hold a man, and, what was more, there was a man in each hollow. Having located the exact position of these Germans, Sergeant Lyon returned, and reported what he had seen.

The whole party then advanced, and Sergeant Lyon flung himself on the sentry, who made no attempt to alarm the others, and did not offer any resistance. The man was accordingly bound and gagged. One of the other Germans in the hollow managed to get out and fire off his rifle before he was bludgeoned. The other made a similar attempt, but was killed before he could manage to fire.

This one shot, however, was sufficient to alarm

the whole German line, and soon the whole trench was in an uproar. Parties were seen to be advancing from all directions. Lieutenant Parnell therefore decided that no farther reconnaissance was possible, and that the only thing to do was to take his party back. So they returned the way they had come as quickly as they could, with the loss of one man, who was killed when the alarm was given.

Lieutenant Parnell was awarded the Military Cross, and Sergeant Lyon the D.C.M. The Coldstream patrol reported it had gone some way down the German trench, but had seen nothing.

For the remainder of the month the Battalion remained in billets at Merville, and afterwards at Riez Bailleul. The Christmas dinner took place at Merville. On the 30th Second Lieutenant T. W. Minchin, Second Lieutenant H. G. Carter, and Second Lieutenant N. McK. Jesper joined the Battalion.

THE 3RD BATTALION

ROLL OF OFFICERS

Colonel N. A. L. Corry, D.S.O.	Commanding Officer.
Major G. F. Molyneux-Montgomerie	Second in Command.
Lieut. G. G. B. Nugent	Adjutant.
Lieut. E. H. J. Wynne	Transport Officer.
Lieut. G. H. Wall	Quartermaster.
Lieut. G. G. Gunnis	No. 1 Company.
Capt. C. F. A. Walker	No. 2 Company.
Lieut. A. Anson	,, ,,
Lieut. the Hon. F. O. H. Eaton	No. 3 Company.
Lieut. G. P. Bowes-Lyon	,, ,,
2nd Lieut. the Hon. A. G. Agar-Robartes	,, ,,

340   THE GRENADIER GUARDS

<small>CHAPTER
XVI.

3rd Batt.
Oct.
1915.</small>

Capt. E. G. H. Powell . . . No. 4 Company.
Lieut. C. M. C. Dowling . . ,,   ,,
Lieut. G. F. R. Hirst . . . ,,   ,,
Lieut. A. T. Logan, R.A.M.C. . Medical Officer.

After the battle of Loos Colonel Corry returned, and resumed command of the 3rd Battalion. Captain Wolrige-Gordon was transferred from the 1st Battalion, and Second Lieutenant L. St. L. Hermon-Hodge and Second Lieutenant E. R. M. Fryer from the 2nd Battalion to the 3rd Battalion, while Captain Sir R. Filmer, Bt., went from the 3rd Battalion to the 4th Battalion.

The 3rd Battalion remained in billets till the 4th, when it took over from the 5th Liverpool Regiment a line of trenches resting on the Hohenzollern Redoubt, and there it remained until the 10th. The Germans were now in possession of the Hohenzollern Redoubt, and the position thus perilously close to them was anything but pleasant. On the 8th the enemy made a determined attack on this line, and surprised our bombers, killing most of them. Lieutenant A. Anson, who was with the bombers, stoutly refused to give way, and was killed with all his party. The bombs with which our men were armed proved useless, as they got very damp and refused to detonate. It therefore became a very one-sided contest, but a machine-gun under Lieutenant R. Williams barred the way to the Germans, and this had to be disposed of before they could advance. Bombs and shells rained down on this machine-gun, and Lieutenant R. Williams was killed. He was replaced by three sergeants in succession, who fought on as gamely

OCTOBER TO DECEMBER 1915

as he had done, and who met with the same fate. The gun was soon afterwards put out of action.

The situation now looked ugly. The enemy was bombing down the trench, and Nos. 2 and 3 Companies had retired somewhat precipitately before the advancing Germans. The 3rd Battalion Coldstream on the right grasped how serious this attack might become, and sent off some bombers who managed to stop the rush. Later on Lieutenant Eaton and Lieutenant Gunnis reorganised the men, and went forward to support the 3rd Battalion Coldstream after they had succeeded in regaining the trench. The Germans fought well, but were forced to retire, when they lost many men. The total casualties in the 3rd Battalion were 137 all ranks, including Lieutenant A. Anson and Lieutenant R. Williams killed, and Captain C. Walker and Lieutenant the Hon. A. G. Agar-Robartes wounded.

On the 10th the Battalion retired into billets at Vermelles, and on the 12th to Vaudricourt, where it remained in reserve until the 14th. On the 9th Captain E. O. Stewart, Lieutenant the Hon. R. P. Stanhope, and Lieutenant P. M. Walker; on the 10th, Second Lieutenant R. W. Parker; and on the 15th Captain Lord F. Blackwood and Lieutenant O. Lyttelton joined the Battalion. The last was appointed Adjutant.

The Battalion returned to the line opposite Big Willie on the 15th, and at once set to work to improve the trenches, but the continual bombing and shelling rather hampered its movements. On the 17th the enemy's shelling became unpleasantly accurate, and the Battalion had 11 men killed and 32 wounded. Lord F. Blackwood was blown up by a shell, and was badly wounded. Captain Dowling and Lieutenant Hirst were buried in their dug-out by a high-explosive shell, and were extricated just in time. That night Major Montgomerie went out with a rifle and fixed bayonet, and tried to ascertain exactly where the sap joined the Coldstream trench. Having gained this information he took out a party and finished the sap.

During the time in the trenches the casualties had been constant and often very heavy: the Battalion lost all four Company Sergeant-Majors. Company Sergeant-Major Tyson was killed, and Company Sergeant-Majors Eason, Aston, and Day wounded. On the 21st the Battalion suffered a very severe loss in the death of Major Molyneux-Montgomerie, who was shot through the head whilst superintending work on Kaiserin Trench under heavy fire.

The constant sniping and bombing caused many casualties, and the total number of killed and wounded since the Battalion came to Loos was 19 officers and 500 non-commissioned officers and men, which proved how dangerous the trenches in the neighbourhood of the Hohenzollern Redoubt were.

On the 25th the Battalion left the front line and marched to Bethune, where it entrained for Lillers, and on arrival went into billets at Norrent Fontes. On the 28th the whole Guards Division was to have been inspected by the King, but this had to be cancelled owing to an unfortunate accident to His Majesty.

OCTOBER TO DECEMBER 1915 343

On the 25th Captain E. N. E. M. Vaughan and Lieutenant Raymond Asquith; on the 29th Lieutenant the Hon. H. E. Eaton, Second Lieutenant B. E. Yorke, and Second Lieutenant E. G. Worsley; and on the 31st Major M. Maitland joined the Battalion.

On November 8 the Battalion marched to La Gorgue, a very long and tiring march of twenty-six kilometres, and went into billets. There it remained until the 14th, and then marched to the trenches just north of Neuve Chapelle. The line here seemed very quiet after the perilous trenches opposite the Hohenzollern; but if the shells were less, the water difficulty was greater than ever. Men had again to stand knee-deep in water, and in the cold weather many felt that the constant bombing and shelling was preferable. Two days in the trenches and two days out was the routine until the 20th, when the whole Brigade moved back again into billets at La Gorgue, and remained there until the end of the month.

In December the Battalion occupied the trenches from Sion Post Lane to Moated Grange North, and continued alternately two days in the trenches and two days out. This portion of the line was in itself comparatively quiet, but the relief was not altogether pleasant, since it was necessary for the relieving companies to go over the top of the ground to get into the front trench. The enemy was, however, singularly inactive in the neighbourhood, and very few casualties occurred. The patrols sent out by the Battalion encountered no opposition, although they boldly went close to the German trenches

344   THE GRENADIER GUARDS

Chapter XVI.
3rd Batt.
Dec. 1915.

and explored the craters. The men of the Battalion were mostly employed in extensive draining operations, carried out under the supervision of Colonel Corry himself, and many improvements were thus effected.

On the 24th a new artillery commander seems to have taken over the German guns, for the front trenches were subjected to a sound and perfectly accurate fire, which contrasted strangely with the previous desultory and usually ill-directed fire. The Battalion spent Christmas Day in the trenches, and a plum-pudding and a pint of beer were given to each man. On the 26th it left the trenches and marched to Merville.

The 4th Battalion
Roll of Officers

4th Batt.

Capt. J. A. Morrison	Commanding Officer.
Lieut. R. S. Lambert	Acting Adjutant.
Lieut. M. G. Williams	Machine-Gun Officer.
Lieut. C. E. M. Ellison	,, ,,
2nd Lieut. E. Ludlow	Quartermaster.
Capt. C. L. Blundell-Hollinshead-Blundell	No. 1 Company.
2nd Lieut. G. A. Ponsonby	,, ,,
Lieut. C. R. Britten	No. 2 Company.
Lieut. E. F. Penn	,, ,,
Capt. E. D. Ridley	No. 3 Company.
Lieut. B. C. Layton	,, ,,
Lieut. the Hon. E. W. Tennant	No. 4 Company.
Lieut. R. D. Leigh-Pemberton	,, ,,
Lieut. E. R. Brunton, R.A.M.C.	Medical Officer.

Oct.

After the heavy casualties it had suffered at Loos, the 4th Battalion had to be reorganised; and Captain Morrison, now in command, redistributed the officers and non-commissioned officers, and as far as possible made up the deficiencies. The Battalion remained in billets at La Bourse until the 3rd, when it was ordered to occupy the trenches on the left of the Hulluch — Vermelles road. Here there was a certain amount of shelling. The system of trenches was highly complicated, and extensive works were being undertaken. The Battalion was ordered to prepare communicating trenches running parallel to Hulluch—Vermelles road, and this work kept the men fully employed for two days.

On the 5th the 2nd Battalion Scots Guards was in trouble, and sent for assistance, as it had had a portion of its trench blown in, and was harassed by the enemy's bombs. Captain E. Penn was sent off at once by Captain Morrison, with 100 men of No. 2 Company and 20 bombers, and told to report himself to Lieut.-Colonel Cator. Lieutenant Sitwell, with No. 4 Company, was ordered to be ready to follow, but no real attack on the 2nd Battalion Scots Guards developed, and neither company, therefore, was wanted. That evening the Battalion retired into billets at Vermelles, but were not free from the shells there, and three high-explosive shells pitched quite close to its billets. Lieutenant E. R. Brunton, R.A.M.C., who had come out with the Battalion, and been with them through the battle of Loos, was killed by a shell on the 8th as he was going round the billets.

On the 9th the Battalion returned to the trenches, and relieved the 1st and 2nd Battalions Scots Guards. Second Lieutenant M. Chapman,

Second Lieutenant G. C. Sloane-Stanley, Second Lieutenant E. W. Nairne, and Second Lieutenant H. H. Sloane-Stanley joined the Battalion that day, and on the 10th Captain Parry, R.A.M.C., arrived. On the 12th Major Lord Henry Seymour came to take over temporary command of the Battalion.

On the 17th bombing attacks by the 1st Battalion Grenadiers and 2nd Battalion Scots Guards began, and the 4th Battalion Grenadiers was ordered to form a continuous chain of men to pass up bombs, sand-bags, ammunition, and tools, and to hold all positions vacated by the Scots Guards as they advanced. Lieut.-Colonel Cator sent back for assistance as his bombers had been knocked out. The 4th Battalion Grenadiers bombers accordingly went up, followed later by 100 volunteers, many of whom had never seen a bomb before. Lieutenant C. Britten on his own initiative took charge of a party of Grenadiers and Scots Guards, after the two Scots Guards officers had been shot, and with great gallantry and coolness successfully drove off the enemy.

The next day Lieut.-Colonel Cator expressed his indebtedness to the 4th Battalion Grenadiers for its timely assistance; and the manner in which the bombers of the Battalion had behaved on this occasion was specially referred to by the Brigadier.

On the 18th the 4th Battalion mourned the loss of a brave and popular officer. Captain Eric Penn was in his dug-out when a shell struck it. He was completely buried, and although still alive when he was extricated, he died a few minutes later.

OCTOBER TO DECEMBER 1915

The continual casualties and the strenuous digging were beginning to tell on the Battalion, and although every two alternate days were spent resting in billets, the high-explosive shells which reached it prevented the forty-eight hours in billets from being a complete rest. The Battalion went on the 21st for two days to Annequin, but on the 23rd returned to the trenches opposite the Hohenzollern Redoubt, where again there was a great deal of work to be done. The zeal which the 4th Battalion showed in its digging operations elicited praise from Brigadier-General Heyworth when he came round on a tour of inspection.

On the 25th the Battalion retired to Allouagne, where it remained until November 14, and then marched *via* Estaires, La Bassée road, Pont du Hem, to the trenches from Chapigny to Winchester road. Every alternate forty-eight hours it went into billets, but during the days in the trenches nothing of interest occurred.

The same routine continued until December 12, when a most successful raid on the enemy's trenches was carried out. At 8.15 P.M. Captain Sir Robert Filmer, accompanied by Sergeant Higgins and three men in No. 3 Company, went out to make a preliminary reconnaissance. By crawling right up to the enemy's trenches he succeeded in locating the exact position of the German machine-guns, and was able to confirm the report as to the gap in the enemy's wire entanglements. Captain Sir R. Filmer, who had already earned a name for bravery, crept quite alone down the entire length of the German trench, and carefully noted all he saw. On his return to our line the final orders were issued to the raiding party, consisting of thirty-three men from No. 3 Company, and the Battalion bombers under Lieutenant G. Ponsonby. The night was very dark, and it was difficult to see any landmarks. Sergeant Higgins led the party over the parapet at 11 P.M., and was followed by Captain Sir R. Filmer and a covering party. Silently they advanced, but lost direction slightly to the left, with the result that they missed the gap and found themselves held up by low wire entanglement. Sir R. Filmer came up to ascertain the cause of the delay, and after considering the situation decided to cut the wire and rush the trench. The wire-cutting was successfully done, although only a few yards from the German line, and the party, headed by Sergeant Higgins, dashed into the trench. At the same time our artillery, in accordance with a previously conceived arrangement, opened a most effective barrage of fire, which continued until the party returned.

Then bombing and bayoneting began in earnest, and the Germans were completely cleared out of the trench. The machine-guns, which were found to be too securely fixed to take away, were destroyed by bombs. It was during this trench fighting that the bombing officer, Lieutenant G. Ponsonby, was badly wounded in the leg. Private W. Sweetman, finding him unable to move, carried him on his back under heavy fire to our lines. The other casualties were one man missing and three wounded. This small number of casualties proved how well arranged

OCTOBER TO DECEMBER 1915

the raid had been, and how brilliantly it had been carried out.

General Sir Douglas Haig commanding the First Army specially mentioned this raid in his report, and wrote: " A well-planned and well-executed operation, reflecting the highest credit on all concerned, from Colonel Lord H. Seymour commanding the 4th Battalion Grenadier Guards downwards. The immediate rewards asked for have been well earned, and I shall have very great pleasure in recommending the names put forward."

The following day at Riez Bailleul, Major-General Lord Cavan sent for and congratulated Captain Sir R. Filmer, Sergeant Higgins, and Private Sweetman on the success of the raid. He also congratulated the Battalion on having gained such a good reputation for digging and trench work.

The rest of December was spent either in billets at Laventie or in the trenches in the neighbourhood. The monotony of trench life was relieved by various schemes to catch the enemy's patrols, who were constantly reported to come out at night. Occasionally parties were sent to lie out and capture any Germans who might venture in front of their line. Whether any of their efforts were successful or not it is impossible to say, but reports of any movement on the part of the enemy ceased.

At the end of the month Major-General Lord Cavan was promoted, and consequently gave up the command of the Guards Division.

CHAPTER XVI.
4th Batt.
Dec.
1915.

The post of Divisional Commander is perhaps the one that presents more difficulties and demands a more remarkable combination of qualities than any other in the Army of to-day. It is essential that a general commanding a division should combine the characteristics of the fighting man with those of the strategist. In the higher commands personal bravery so essential in a brigadier or commanding officer is a secondary consideration. Of a brigadier, on the other hand, whose programme is mapped out for him in the minutest of instructions, there is not expected nowadays anything of the precise chess-playing skill of the professional strategist. Hence it often happens that a brigadier promoted to command a division is found to lack the necessary qualities of strategy, while the born strategist, though not deficient in courage, may be totally unable to think clearly and act decisively when under fire.

Brigadier-General Feilding, who was now appointed to command the Guards Division, possessed in a marked degree the two necessary qualifications. A man of strong and resourceful character, fearless and independent in judgment, he was gifted with that indefinable quality which enables men to form prompt and wise decisions in moments of great emergency. His practical experience of war under modern conditions was great and extensive. He went all through the retreat from Mons, as well as the subsequent advance, when he commanded first the 2nd Battalion Coldstream and later the 4th (Guards) Brigade, and he had played an important part in every battle in which the battalions of the Guards had fought. When the Guards Division was first formed, he was placed in command of the 1st Guards Brigade, and carried out his duties with such distinction that he was clearly marked out as the prospective successor of Lord Cavan.

CHAPTER XVI.
4th Batt.
Dec. 1915.

CHAPTER XVII

JANUARY TO SEPTEMBER 1916

Diary of the War

Chapter XVII.

1916.
Jan.,
Feb.,
March.

ALTHOUGH no large operations took place at the beginning of 1916, there was continual fighting in various parts of the line. The Germans made several attacks on the Yser Canal and at Neuville on the French front, and also attempted minor operations at Givenchy and on the Ypres—Comines Canal. In February the great battle of Verdun commenced, and in spite of heavy losses the Germans made some progress, capturing Haumont Wood and Village. Large masses of men were employed, and there was severe fighting at Bethincourt and Le Mort Homme. The Germans persisted in their attacks and captured Avocourt Wood, but the French stubbornly held their ground. At the end of March the British Army made a successful attack at St. Eloi, and penetrated the first and second German line of trenches, but lost the Vimy Ridge, a position of some tactical importance.

The Russians won a great victory in the Caucasus and drove the Turks in disorder towards Erzeroum, which they captured soon afterwards. The position of the British Force on the Tigris

JANUARY TO SEPTEMBER 1916

was giving great anxiety, and the Turks claimed to have completely surrounded it.

In March Portugal joined the Allies, and declared war on Germany and Austria.

In Africa the Cameroons campaign was completed with the surrender of the German garrison at Mora Hill.

General Smuts advanced against the Germans in the Kilimanjaro area, and a week later gained further successes west of Taveta.

The United Kingdom resorted to conscription, and the Military Service Act was passed in the House of Commons.

On the British front the Germans launched determined but unsuccessful attacks at Ploegsteert, and there was fighting on the Vimy Ridge and between Loos and La Bassée. The struggle at Verdun continued with unabated fierceness, and Mort Homme and Fort Douaumont changed hands several times.

The battle of Jutland was fought, and the British Grand Fleet had an opportunity of meeting the German High Seas Fleet. The British Cruiser Squadron had most of the fighting, as the battleships did not come into action till late in the evening. The losses were heavy on both sides, and the German Fleet fled back to harbour claiming the victory.

Serious disturbances broke out in Ireland, and martial law was proclaimed in Dublin. The headquarters of the rebel Sinn Feiners was occupied after much street fighting, and the ringleaders were caught, tried by court-martial, and shot.

354 THE GRENADIER GUARDS

CHAPTER XVII.
1916.

In Mesopotamia the troops sent up to relieve the British Force at Kut-el-Amara failed in their attack on the intervening Turks, and on April 29 General Townshend and a force of native and Indian troops surrendered.

President Wilson warned the Germans that if they persisted in their indiscriminate sinking of neutral vessels, he would have no alternative but to break off diplomatic relations.

On June 5 H.M.S. *Hampshire*, conveying Field-Marshal Earl Kitchener on a special mission to Russia, was sunk off the Orkney Islands by a mine, and all but twelve men were drowned.

On June 12 General Smuts captured Wilhelmstal, the capital of German East Africa.

July, Aug., Sept.

The battle of the Somme commenced at the beginning of July and lasted until November. Both the British and French Armies were engaged during these months in systematically capturing the German positions on the north and south of the River Somme. This was the first battle in which Tanks were used.

Salonika had now become an important place in the war, and a mixed force under General Sarrail attempted an offensive movement, which, however, came to nothing.

The Russians continued their successful operations against Austria, and captured vast numbers of prisoners. On August 27 Roumania declared war on Austria, and advanced into Transylvania, in spite of warnings from the Allies that they had better hold their frontier and join hands with the Russians.

JANUARY TO SEPTEMBER 1916

At the end of August Field-Marshal von Hindenburg was appointed Chief of the German General Staff.

CHAPTER XVII.
1916.

THE 1ST BATTALION

The beginning of 1916 found the 1st Battalion in Brigade Reserve at La Gorgue, where it had retired after a strenuous time in the trenches, and where it settled down to steady drill and instruction in bombing.

1st Batt. Jan.

The list of officers was as follows:

Lieut.-Colonel G. F. Trotter, M.V.O., D.S.O.	Commanding Officer.
Major C. R. C. de Crespigny	Second in Command.
Lieut. E. H. J. Duberly	Adjutant.
Lieut. F. E. H. Paget	Lewis Gun Officer.
Lieut. the Earl of Dalkeith	Bombing Officer.
Capt. Lord Stanley	Transport Officer.
Lieut. J. Teece	Quartermaster.
Capt. W. S. Pilcher	King's Company.
Lieut. L. G. Fisher-Rowe	,, ,,
2nd Lieut. R. F. W. Echlin	,, ,,
Capt. F. L. V. Swaine	No. 2 Company.
Lieut. C. D. Baker	,, ,,
2nd Lieut. C. Wilkinson	,, ,,
Capt. Viscount Lascelles	No. 3 Company.
Lieut. G. Inglis	,, ,,
Lieut. A. A. Moller	,, ,,
2nd Lieut. H. V. Cholmeley	,, ,,
Capt. G. B. Wilson	No. 4 Company.
Lieut. the Hon. P. P. Cary	,, ,,
Lieut. R. D. Lawford	,, ,,
2nd Lieut. C. R. Turner	,, ,,
Capt. J. C. B. Grant, R.A.M.C.	Medical Officer.

On the 12th it moved to Laventie, and from there went into the trenches at Picantin every

CHAPTER XVII.
1st Batt.
Jan. 1916.

alternate forty-eight hours, taking turns with the 4th Battalion and the 2nd Battalion Irish Guards. On January 14 Second Lieutenant C. T. Swift joined, and on the 29th Major de Crespigny left to take command of the 2nd Battalion.

Feb.

The same routine was followed until February 16, when the whole Guards Division was sent to the coast for some sea air, although February can hardly be said to be an ideal month for the seaside. Captain Lord Claud Hamilton and Lieutenant H.R.H. the Prince of Wales left the Headquarters Staff, and joined the Battalion. On arrival at Calais the Battalion marched to Beaumaris, where they went under canvas. High winds and heavy snow followed by a thick fog made life in a canvas tent a doubtful pleasure, but, in spite of the intense cold, the change undoubtedly did the men a great deal of good. After ten days by the sea the Battalion entrained at Calais and proceeded to Kiekenput near Wormhoudt, in Belgium. Captain Lord Claud Hamilton and Lieutenant H.R.H. the Prince of Wales went on leave to England.

March.

The weather continued to be very bad, and prevented the men from training, although a certain amount of route-marching was done. On March 5 the Battalion marched to Poperinghe, where it was again put under canvas. On the 8th Second Lieutenant L. de J. Havard joined the Battalion, and on the 10th Captain Viscount Lascelles was accidentally wounded by a bomb whilst instructing his company, but the wound proved not to be serious, and he was able to rejoin the Battalion a few days later.

JANUARY TO SEPTEMBER 1916

On the 17th Lieut.-Colonel G. Trotter, having been promoted to the rank of Brigadier-General, left to take up command of the 27th Brigade, and Major A. St. L. Glyn arrived to take his place.

CHAPTER XVII.
1st Batt.
March 1916.

The Guards Division now went into the Ypres salient, and there it remained for several months, either in the trenches or in billets in the neighbourhood. There can be no doubt that this was by far the worst part of the line, and the constant casualties with no corresponding gain were somewhat disheartening. On the 16th the 1st Battalion Grenadiers arrived at Ypres, and on the 20th went into the trenches I.12.a to I.12.c, with the Canadians on the right and the Welsh Guards on the left. Two companies were placed in the front line, with one in support and one in reserve. They immediately came in for a very heavy shelling, and had 6 killed and 14 wounded, mostly in the King's Company.

Back to Ypres on the 24th and then to Poperinghe for two days' rest, after which the Battalion returned to the trench line east of Potidje, going part of the way by train. The enemy shelled the railway station, which was unpleasant for those who were starting on their journey, and also delayed the train. The King's Company and No. 4 occupied the front line, with No. 2 in support and No. 3 in reserve. On the 4th the enemy's artillery knocked out one of our machine-guns with a direct hit, killing one man. On the same day an unfortunate accident caused by the premature explosion of a Pippin rifle grenade resulted in the death of one sergeant, while another sergeant was wounded.

April.

CHAPTER XVII.
1st Batt.
April 1916.

The usual procedure was to hold the support line, and to place as few men as possible in the front trench. The enemy seemed to be perfectly aware of this, and confined themselves to bombarding the second line, but our artillery was more than a match for them, and retaliated with some effect. Whenever the men saw an observation balloon emerging from the German lines they knew that a violent bombardment was imminent, and took precautions accordingly. All dug-outs were at once cleared, and the men were scattered along the bottom of the trench.

On the 7th Lieutenant C. Leeke, 1st Battalion Grenadiers, attached to the 3rd Guards Brigade, Machine-gun Company, was standing in front of his dug-out, having completed his rounds, when he was hit in the thigh by a stray bullet, and although his wound was at once dressed by a surgeon, he died a few days later in hospital. Second Lieutenant H. V. Cholmeley, attached to the same Machine-gun Company, was killed outright, being struck in the chest by a large piece of shrapnel, and Second Lieutenant C. Wilkinson was wounded in the shoulder by a shrapnel bullet. Amongst the other ranks the casualties were 1 man killed and 60 wounded.

After these strenuous days in the trenches the Battalion went to Poperinghe for four days' rest, and on the 12th returned by train to the trenches at Potidje, with the 3rd Battalion Coldstream on the right and the 1st Battalion Welsh Guards on the left. It was luckier this time, and, except for the inevitable shelling, saw very little of the enemy. An attack was made by

JANUARY TO SEPTEMBER 1916

the Germans on the Twentieth Division, but although the 1st Battalion stood to arms, its services were not required, as the attacks were easily repulsed.

CHAPTER XVII.

1st Batt. April 1916.

On the 15th the Battalion returned to Poperinghe, where it remained in billets till the 27th. Although at first the weather was abominable, the last few days were fine and hot. A short time before the men had been shivering over braziers, and now they were lying about in their shirt-sleeves. On the 27th the Battalion went into the trenches at Rifleman Farm, with the Third Canadian Division on the right and the 1st Battalion Welsh Guards on the left, and the enemy blew in a mine gallery, killing some men of the Royal Engineers. The enemy's musketry was active during these three days, and the German aeroplanes were very busy.

The following officers joined the Battalion during the month: Major A. F. A. N. Thorne, as Second in Command, Lieutenant H. G. W. Bradley, Captain A. C. Graham, Second Lieutenant R. H. P. J. Stourton, Second Lieutenant E. Hoare, Second Lieutenant J. W. Graham, Second Lieutenant E. G. L. King. On the 27th Captain Wilson left to take up his duties on the Divisional Staff, to which he had been appointed.

The Corps Commander, Major-General Lord Cavan, came round the trenches on May 1, and expressed himself pleased with all he saw. That evening the Battalion retired to Ypres, where it remained for four days. The weather now was quite hot, with occasional thunderstorms; but, as the enemy continued to shell the remains of

May.

Ypres, the men were unable to enjoy fully the change, since they spent most of the time under the ramparts.

Back to Rifleman Farm on the 6th, and on the way up to the trenches, the Battalion came in for a heavy shelling, which rather delayed matters. Second Lieutenant J. Graham was wounded, and had his leg broken just above the ankle as he was going up to the trenches for the first time. The Engineers feared the enemy would explode a mine in the neighbourhood of our new crater, but every precaution was taken, and no explosion occurred at that spot. On the 9th the enemy apparently contemplated an attack, for at 4 A.M. a mine at the end of Muddy Lane was fired, and then a heavy bombardment commenced, but when the infantry attack which usually followed was expected the Germans did not appear anxious to leave their trenches. Second Lieutenant E. Hoare, who had recently arrived, was killed, and Lieutenant Bradley wounded. Amongst the other ranks there were 2 killed and 16 wounded, but Major Thorne was able to report to Major Glyn that the line remained intact, although in places it was considerably damaged.

Later in the morning Brigadier-General Heyworth came to see what had happened, and although Major Glyn warned him that, owing to the parapet having been blown away in several places, it was a perilous proceeding to attempt to walk down the line, he insisted on going. Accompanied by Major Glyn and Captain Warner, the Brigade-Major, he set off and reached the front trench. As they were going down Muddy Lane, about fifty yards from the front trench, they came across an obstruction caused by the parapet having been blown into the trench. It was while crossing this that Brigadier-General Heyworth was shot through the head by one of the enemy's snipers. He had always scorned to take even the most ordinary precautions, and was accustomed to ignore the enemy's snipers. His loss was mourned not only by his friends in the Guards Division, and he had many, but also by the whole British Army, who knew him to be a fearless and capable commander.

On the 10th the men were busily engaged in repairing the gaps in the trenches, and were in consequence subjected to a certain amount of sniping and bombing, during which Lord Stanley was wounded by a bomb, and had five wounds, three in his leg and two in his arm, fortunately none of them serious. That evening the Battalion was relieved and retired to Poperinghe, and on the 20th it marched to Kiekenput, where it remained in billets till the end of the month.

On June 1 the officers of the Battalion were as follows :

Major A. St. L. Glyn . . .	Commanding Officer.
Major A. F. A. N. Thorne, D.S.O. .	Second in Command.
Capt. E. H. J. Duberly . . .	Adjutant.
Lieut. the Hon. P. P. Cary . .	Lewis Gun Officer.
Lieut. the Earl of Dalkeith . .	Bombing Officer.
2nd Lieut. D. H. S. Riddiford .	Transport Officer.
Lieut. J. Teece	Quartermaster.
Capt. W. S. Pilcher . . .	King's Company.
Lieut. P. M. Spence . . .	,, ,,
2nd Lieut. R. F. W. Echlin . .	,, ,,

CHAPTER XVII.
1st Batt.
June 1916.

Capt. A. C. Graham . . . No. 2 Company.
Lieut. R. D. Lawford . . . ,, ,,
2nd Lieut. E. G. L. King . . ,, ,,
Capt. Viscount Lascelles . . No. 3 Company.
2nd Lieut. C. T. Swift . . . ,, ,,
2nd Lieut. L. de J. Harvard . . ,, ,,
2nd Lieut. R. H. P. J. Stourton . ,, ,,
Capt. L. G. Fisher-Rowe . . No. 4 Company.
2nd Lieut. P. S. Hope . . . ,, ,,

Attached—Capt. J. C. B. Grant.

The Battalion remained in billets at Poperinghe or Kiekenput until the 18th, when it moved up into the trench line. On the 7th a gloom was cast over the whole of the British Army by the death of Lord Kitchener, who went down in the *Hampshire,* mined on its way to Russia. This passing away of a great soldier came as a profound shock to every one in France. At first no one could realise that he was dead. The men felt that the mainspring of the whole mechanism of the British Army was gone.

The Battalion remained for ten days in reserve, and although there were constant alarms, during which the men stood to arms, and news of gas attacks, its services in the front line were not required. On the 18th it took over the trench line near Irish Farm, and Nos. 2, 3, and 4 Companies were placed in the firing line, with the King's Company in reserve. Although the enemy's patrols were very active, nothing worth recording appears to have happened, but on the 25th a successful raid was carried out into the German lines, and a new trench north of Forward Cottage was made. On the 27th the Battalion retired into dug-outs in Canal Bank and Yperlee, where it remained until the end of the month.

On July 1 it returned to the trenches, and on the 3rd the King's Company was so heavily bombarded that the parapet of the trench and the signal dug-out were blown in. The Company Sergeant-Major, two sergeants, three signallers, and four men were completely buried under the debris, but the remainder of the Company at once set to work to rescue as many as possible under a heavy shell and machine-gun fire. Owing to the energetic manner in which the rescue party worked, one sergeant and three men were brought out alive, but the others were all dead.

On the 9th Major M. E. M. C. Maitland arrived from the 3rd Battalion, and took over command of the 1st Battalion from Major Glyn, who proceeded to take up an appointment at the base. On the 10th the following were selected from the 1st Battalion to attend the National Fête in Paris on July 14: Sergeant-Major Young, Lance-Corporal Ewell, Private Upcott, Private Ayres, Private Andrews, and Private Call. On the 12th Captain Viscount Lascelles was appointed second in command of the 2nd Battalion, and on the 13th Lieutenant E. B. Shelley and Second Lieutenant C. C. T. Sharpe joined from the Entrenching Battalion.

On the 15th the 1st Battalion returned to the trenches, where it remained until the 24th, with the usual routine of two days in and two days out of the trenches. On the 27th it left the Ypres salient without regret, and

Chapter XVII.
1st Batt. July 1916.

entrained at Poperinghe for Bollezeele, whence it marched to Watten. There it remained until the 29th, when it proceeded to Bavingchove and went by train to Fervent. On the 30th it marched to Halloy. On the 28th Lieutenant R. P. de P. Trench and Lieutenant M. D. Thomas joined from the Entrenching Battalion, and on the 30th Captain W. D. Drury Lowe, D.S.O., arrived. He had been in command of a Territorial Battery for a year and a half, and had so distinguished himself as a gunner that he had been awarded the D.S.O. But, being a true Grenadier at heart, he had decided to sink his rank and return to his old regiment.

Aug.
During August the 1st Battalion only had two days in the trenches at Beaumont-Hamel, when the King's Company had rather an unpleasant time with the enemy's trench mortars, and had nine casualties. On the 9th His Majesty the King, who was making an informal tour round the Front, visited the Grenadier Camp, but there was no inspection of any sort.

Before leaving France His Majesty sent the following message to Sir Douglas Haig:

August 15, 1916.

OFFICERS, N.C.O.'s, AND MEN—It has been a great pleasure and satisfaction to me to be with my Armies during the past week. I have been able to judge for myself of their splendid condition for war, and of the spirit of cheerful confidence which animates all ranks, united in loyal co-operation to their chiefs and to one another.

Since my last visit to the Front there has been almost uninterrupted fighting on parts of our line. The offensive recently begun has since been resolutely maintained by day and by night. I have had opportunities of visiting some of the scenes of the later desperate struggles, and of appreciating to a slight extent the demands made upon your courage and physical endurance in order to assail and capture positions prepared during the past two years and stoutly defended to the last.

I have realised not only the splendid work which has been done in immediate touch with the enemy—in the air, under the ground, as well as on the ground—but also the vast organisations behind the fighting line, honourable alike to the genius of the initiators and to the heart and hand of the workers. Everywhere there is proof that all, men and women, are playing their part, and I rejoice to think that their noble efforts are being heartily seconded by all classes at home.

The happy relations maintained by my Armies and those of our French Allies were equally noticeable between my troops and the inhabitants of the districts in which they are quartered, and from whom they have received a cordial welcome ever since their first arrival in France.

Do not think that I and your fellow-countrymen forget the heavy sacrifices which the Armies have made, and the bravery and endurance they have displayed during the past two years of bitter conflict. These sacrifices have not been in vain : the arms of the Allies will never be laid down until our cause has triumphed.

I return home more than ever proud of you.

May God guide you to victory.

On the 6th Second Lieutenant L. G. E. Sim arrived, and on the 15th Second Lieutenant B. G. Samuelson and Second Lieutenant W. H. Lovell joined the Battalion. On the 25th the Battalion proceeded by train to Mericourt, and went into billets in Ville-sous-Corbie.

The 2nd Battalion

Chapter XVII.
2nd Batt. Jan. 1916.

At the beginning of the New Year the 2nd Battalion Grenadiers was in billets at Riez Bailleul, and went up every two days to occupy the trench line at Ebenezer Farm.

List of Officers of the 2nd Battalion

Lieut.-Colonel G. D. Jeffreys	Commanding Officer.
Major A. St. L. Glyn	Second in Command.
Capt. the Hon. W. R. Bailey	Adjutant.
Lieut. W. E. Acraman	Quartermaster.

Capt. R. H. V. Cavendish, M.V.O.
Capt. A. de P. Kingsmill.
Capt. A. F. R. Wiggins.
Capt. E. W. M. Grigg.
Lieut. A. K. S. Cunninghame.
Lieut. D. A. Smith (Brigade Machine-gun Company).
Lieut. E. H. Noble.
Lieut. F. A. M. Browning.
Lieut. M. A. Knatchbull-Hugessen.
Lieut. the Hon. W. A. D. Parnell.
Lieut. W. H. Beaumont-Nesbitt.
Lieut. H. G. W. Sandeman.
Lieut. the Hon. B. B. Ponsonby.
2nd Lieut. the Hon. A. V. Agar-Robartes (Brigade Machine-gun Company).
2nd Lieut. T. A. Combe.
2nd Lieut. A. F. Irvine.
2nd Lieut. T. W. Minchin.
2nd Lieut. H. G. Carter.
2nd Lieut. N. McK. Jesper.
2nd Lieut. G. G. M. Vereker.

Capt. J. A. Andrews, R.A.M.C.	Medical Officer.

On the 8th it marched to Calonne, and on the 12th to Arrewage, where it remained until

JANUARY TO SEPTEMBER 1916

the 25th. On the 14th Lieut.-Colonel G. D. Jeffreys left to take over temporary command of the 3rd Battalion, but after three days he was promoted to the rank of Brigadier-General, and was appointed to the 58th Infantry Brigade. On the 21st Second Lieutenant J. Arbuthnott, and on the 23rd Second Lieutenant D. Harvey joined the Battalion.

January 27 being the German Emperor's birthday, an attack was expected, and special precautions were taken, but the German Army were tired of these Roman holidays. Previous attempts to snatch a victory of some sort on the birthday of the All-Highest had proved costly and lamentable failures. This time the Army determined to allow this festival to pass unnoticed, and consequently no German showed the slightest inclination to leave his trench.

During the days spent in the trenches there were constant losses: on some days men were killed, and almost invariably there were a certain number wounded.

On February 1 Major de Crespigny took over the command of the 2nd Battalion from Major Glyn, who had been in temporary command since Lieut.-Colonel Jeffreys' departure.

The same routine was continued until February 7, when the 2nd Battalion marched to La Gorgue, where it remained for a week. On the 11th it was inspected by Field-Marshal Lord Kitchener in a field at Merville, and on the 14th marched to Godwaersvelde *via* Merville. On the 16th it reached Poperinghe after a long march in the teeth of a strong wind and heavy rain, and was put into huts in a camp, mostly under water.

The following letter from Lieut.-General Haking commanding the Eleventh Corps was addressed to the Guards Division on its departure:

The Military situation did not permit of my seeing your Division on its departure from the Corps in order to say Good-bye to you all, and thank all ranks for the services they have performed during the time the Division has been in the Corps. I am compelled therefore to write what I should have liked to speak.

Ever since the Division was formed and posted to this Corps, it has proved itself to possess the finest military spirit. Lord Cavan, and since his departure General Feilding, ably assisted by Lieut.-Colonel the Hon. W. P. Hore Ruthven, G.S.O.I., Lieut.-Colonel Darrell, A.A.Q.M.G., and a most efficient staff, have carried out several offensive operations with distinguished success, including the attacks during the fighting round Loos, the consolidation of a difficult and unmade line about the Hohenzollern Redoubt, and the raid into the hostile trenches along the Rue Tilleloy front. The careful planning of these operations by the Divisional Commander and his general and administrative staff, the accurate reconnaissance and detailed organisation of each by the Brigade Commanders, Brigadier-Generals Heyworth, Ponsonby, and Pereira, and also General Feilding until he succeeded Lord Cavan in command of the Division, together with their staffs, has been a model of good fighting.

The infantry operations have been ably seconded by the artillery of the Division under Brigadier-General Wardrop and his Brigade Commanders, who have spared no pains, both in the construction of forward observing posts and the training and organisation of good observing officers, to secure the success of the infantry.

The Royal Engineers also under Lieut.-Colonel

JANUARY TO SEPTEMBER 1916

Brough and his field company commanders have been indefatigable in their work on the defences, the water drainage in rear of our line, and in assisting the artillery in the construction of some of the best observing posts in any part of the British line. The Battalion commanders, officers, non-commissioned officers and men who have been called upon to bear the brunt of all this fighting have shown throughout an offensive spirit which in my opinion surpassed any standard reached by the Guards or any infantry in past campaigns, and which will be the admiration of future generations of soldiers. The fine discipline and soldierly bearing of all ranks is also a matter for all of you to be proud of. You have been an example to other Divisions with whom you have been associated, and that example has produced the best results, and has raised the fighting value and efficiency of the whole Corps. I am very sorry to say Good-bye to you, but I am glad you are going to a corps which is commanded by your old Divisional General Lord Cavan, who has the proud distinction of being the first General Officer to command a British Guards Division, and who has so greatly distinguished himself on every occasion.

I can only hope that the Eleventh Corps will find itself before long by the side of the Fourteenth Corps with the Guards Division ready, as it always will be, to lead the way to Victory.

While the 2nd Battalion remained at Poperinghe, it was honoured by the visit of some German aeroplanes which dropped bombs, but fortunately not anywhere near the men's billets. On the 22nd a demonstration of German liquid fire was held, and it was clearly shown that, provided the men kept their heads low down in the trench, no harm would come to them, since liquid fire rises in the air about six or eight yards from the muzzle of the apparatus.

CHAPTER XVII.
2nd Batt.
Feb.
1916.

On the 24th the 2nd Battalion proceeded to Cassel, and as the roads were frozen the transport had several adventures. Down one steep hill several wagons and cookers skidded into the ditch, from which they had to be rescued, and there were many accidents. On the 28th the Battalion entrained, and went by rail to Calais Coulogne station, where it marched to No. 6 Rest Camp, about four kilometres from the town on the Dunkirk road. Here it found the 1st Battalion Grenadiers, the 2nd Battalion Scots Guards, and the 1st Battalion Welsh Guards.

March.

In this breezy but healthy locality the 2nd Battalion remained for ten days, and the health of the men improved immensely in spite of the extreme cold. On March 5 it returned by train to Cassel, and marched about nine miles to Herzeele, where it went into billets. On the 16th it moved to Poperinghe, and on the 18th took over the line east of Potidje village, with Nos. 3 and 4 Companies in the front trench, No. 1 Company in support, and No. 2 in reserve. Major Glyn left the 2nd Battalion to take command of the 1st Battalion vice Lieut.-Colonel Trotter.

The trenches that had been taken over turned out to be in very bad order, with parapets only waist high, and nowhere bullet-proof. There were no communication trenches, and little or no attention appeared to have been given to the difficult problem of drainage and sanitary arrangements, but the men set to work at once, and before long there was a marked improvement. During

JANUARY TO SEPTEMBER 1916

the days spent in the trenches by companies, there were a certain number of casualties—among whom was Sergeant-Major H. Wood, who was slightly wounded—and the parapet in the line held by No. 1 Company was blown in by shells from a field-gun not five hundred yards away. On the 24th the 2nd Battalion went to A Camp at Vlamertinghe, where they remained for four days, and on the 28th they returned to the trenches east of Potidje village. Although at first there was a comparatively quiet time, the shelling increased later, and a certain number were wounded, including Second Lieutenant H. G. Carter. On the 30th the shelling increased in intensity, and the trenches of No. 4 Company were completely levelled for about 120 yards. Work was almost impossible at this spot as the enemy's artillery continued to shell it, and it was not until the following day that the men were able to erect another parapet.

After ten days' rest at Poperinghe, the 2nd Battalion returned to Ypres, and went into cellars and dug-outs in the ramparts. On the 11th it took over the line between Railway Wood and the Menin road, where it found a large gap in the line on the left between it and the Coldstream. For the next sixteen days it remained either in this line or in Ypres. Second Lieutenant J. S. Burton joined the Battalion on the 10th, Lieutenant T. Parker Jarvis on the 20th, and Second Lieutenant J. C. Cornforth on the 21st. On the 27th the 2nd Battalion went into billets at Poperinghe, and was inspected by General Sir Herbert Plumer, K.C.B., command-

Chapter XVII.

2nd Batt.
March 1916.

April.

ing the Second Army. It remained for a week in billets, and then returned to Ypres on 4th May. One of the enemy's aeroplanes flew over one day, and dropped bombs on Poperinghe, of which one fell about twenty-five yards from Battalion Headquarters, and wounded two men.

On May 5 the 2nd Battalion went into the trenches near Wieltje, and although it succeeded in relieving the 2nd Battalion Coldstream Guards without sustaining any casualties, it came in for a very heavy shelling the next day. Lieutenant the Hon. B. Ponsonby was wounded, and there were three N.C.O.'s killed and seven wounded. This shelling continued every day, and there was in consequence a daily list of men wounded. On the 9th the 2nd Battalion returned to billets near the Prison at Ypres, and remained there till the 13th, when it went into the trenches again. On the 10th Second Lieutenant G. A. Arbuthnot arrived. A considerable amount of work had to be done in deepening the trenches, heightening the parapets, and wiring the entanglements, for which eighty-four coils of barbed wire were used. A systematic shelling by the enemy, not only of the front line, but also of all roads and communication trenches, was daily carried out, and on the 16th Second Lieutenant J. S. Burton was killed, whilst the casualties amongst other ranks were very heavy. On the 19th the 2nd Battalion went by train to St. Omer, and marched to billets at Tatinghem, where it remained resting until June 7.

JANUARY TO SEPTEMBER 1916

LIST OF OFFICERS OF THE 2ND BATTALION

Lieut.-Colonel C. R. C. de Crespigny, D.S.O.	Commanding Officer.	
Major E. N. E. M. Vaughan	Second in Command.	
Capt. the Hon. W. R. Bailey	Adjutant.	
Lieut. W. E. Acraman	Quartermaster.	

CHAPTER XVII.
2nd Batt.
May 1916.

Capt. R. H. V. Cavendish, M.V.O.
Capt. A. F. R. Wiggins.
Capt. A. K. S. Cunninghame.
Lieut. the Hon. W. A. D. Parnell.
Lieut. W. H. Beaumont-Nesbitt.
Lieut. H. G. W. Sandeman.
Lieut. T. A. Combe.
Lieut. A. F. Irvine.
Lieut. M. H. Macmillan.
Lieut. T. Parker Jarvis.
2nd Lieut. T. W. Minchin.
2nd Lieut. N. McK. Jesper.
2nd Lieut. G. G. M. Vereker.
2nd Lieut. D. Harvey.
2nd Lieut. J. Arbuthnott.
2nd Lieut. G. A. Arbuthnot.

Attached—Capt. J. A. Andrews, R.A.M.C., Medical Officer.

On June 7 the 2nd Battalion left Tatinghem at 8 A.M. and arrived at St. Sylvestre *via* Fort Rouge and Staple after a long and hot march. After ten days spent in Camp M near Poperinghe, during which time parties of men were employed in cable laying, it proceeded to Elverdinghe and remained there till the 20th, when it took over the Lancashire Farm line. Captain G. C. FitzH. Harcourt-Vernon, Lieut. H. F. C. Crookshank, Lieutenant the Hon. M. H. E. C. Townley-Bertie, and Lieutenant R. E. H. Oliver joined the Battalion on the 15th, and Lieutenant P. M. Walker on the 19th.

June.

CHAPTER XVII.
2nd Batt.
June 1916.

The four days spent in the trenches were marked by heavy machine-gun fire and sniping, but the line was fairly good, and there were in consequence few casualties. On the 24th an artillery duel took place, and although our guns did some good work in cutting the enemy's wire, the German guns retaliated on the front line and support trenches. On retiring into billets again at Elverdinghe, the men were given permission to bathe in the lake in the grounds of the château, but this peaceful pursuit was not without danger, for the German artillery, while searching about for some target, dropped six shells over the lake, and later shelled the château itself.

July.

After a week's rest the 2nd Battalion returned to Ypres on July 6, and the next day relieved the 4th Battalion in the Irish Farm line, one of the worst positions it had been in. The 1300 yards of trenches consisted for the most part of unconnected and shallow shell-holes, which were full of water, and there were no communication trenches of any kind. It took four and a half hours to get round the line by night, and in places it was necessary to walk above ground, which made the Commanding Officer's tour very dangerous. Naturally in such a line the daily casualty list was fairly heavy, but the men worked at the trenches with so much energy that they soon transformed them. Once Captain Wiggins, Lieutenant Irvine, and Lieutenant Combe were having luncheon in a hole in the first line, when a shell from a German trench mortar pitched quite close to them. With the exception of Captain Wiggins, who was hit

JANUARY TO SEPTEMBER 1916 375

through the knee by a piece of the shell, no one was any the worse. The Germans, finding that the large shells from the trench mortars could be seen coming, hit upon the idea of firing salvos of shrapnel at the same time, which confused our men.

Lieutenant-General Lord Cavan paid a surprise visit to the 2nd Battalion while it was in the trenches, and made a searching inspection of the kits, greatcoats, respirators, and rifles. In spite of the men being in the trenches, everything was complete and clean, but much to the Sergeant-Major's annoyance two mess-tins and three spoons were found to be deficient in the whole Battalion. The takings of the regimental canteen had been greatly augmented by the presence of two Navvy battalions, and Lieut.-Colonel de Crespigny was therefore able to give the men certain luxuries, such as French bread and tinned milk, which were much appreciated.

During the next fortnight the 2nd Battalion remained either in billets in the Canal bank or in the line in front, and worked unceasingly on the trenches. The monotony of trench life was relieved by the exciting but dangerous ventures of patrols. During the night of the 17th Lieutenant A. Irvine and Lieutenant Parker Jervis took out patrols, and although they were unsuccessful in securing any prisoners, they managed to pick up a great deal of useful information. On the 19th Lieutenant M. H. Macmillan went out with two men and managed to get quite near to the German line, but a German sentry whom they came across threw a bomb at them, wounding Lieutenant Macmillan and one of the men slightly. He, however, obtained the information he wanted, and was later complimented by General Pereira, who sent the following message :

The Brigadier wishes Lieutenant Macmillan and his patrol on the 19th inst. to be congratulated on their excellent report and the most useful information which they brought in.

Lieutenant Irvine also went out with a strong patrol, and on his return narrowly escaped being bombed by his own company. Captain Wiggins and ten men lay out on Admirals Road in the hopes of catching some of the enemy's patrols, but were unsuccessful. On the 22nd Captain M. K. A. Lloyd joined the Battalion.

The improvement in the trench line did not escape the notice of Brigadier-General Pereira, who sent the following message to Lieut.-Colonel de Crespigny :

After visiting your Battalion section of the trenches to-day, I wish to say how very much I was impressed by the wonderful progress that has been made in improving and strengthening the line, and I realise the amount of thought and labour that has been expended on this work.

   (Signed) C. PEREIRA, Brig.-Gen.
        Commanding 1st Brigade.

The enemy's artillery now turned its attention to Poperinghe, with the result that all the civilians had to be cleared out and sent away. In its search for suitable objectives, it succeeded in landing a big shell on the 2nd Battalion Headquarters. Two men were buried, one of whom survived, but the other was dead when dug out. On the 24th Second Lieutenant G. A. Arbuthnot went out with five snipers, and although they remained out all night, they saw nothing of the enemy's patrols. Sergeant Lyon of No. 1 Company went out by himself into No Man's Land, and returned the next morning with useful information, and also a German flag which had been taken from a tree near Wieltje.

On the 27th the Guards Division left the Ypres salient, and was relieved by the Fourth Division of the Eighth Corps.

The 2nd Battalion left Ypres on the 26th, and went by train to Poperinghe. On the 27th it marched *via* St. Jan der Bietzen Watou and Houtkerque to Herzeele, and on the 30th to Proven, where it entrained for St. Pol. From St. Pol it went in motor lorries to Bouque Maison, and then marched on to billets at Neuvillette. After two days' rest it marched on to Sarton, where it remained from August 1st to the 10th, and then proceeded to Bertrancourt.

The Guards Division was now approaching the Somme area, and the 2nd Battalion Grenadiers marched from Bertrancourt through Beaussart, Mailly, Vitermont, to the right sub-sector of the Beaumont-Hamel line. The trenches were considerably better than any others the 2nd Battalion had occupied since Loos, and there were several deep dug-outs in the line. The enemy's artillery sent over some heavy shells at once, and the casualties were one N.C.O. killed and six men wounded. After three days in the trenches, when a certain number of men were wounded, the Battalion was relieved by the 1st Battalion Leicestershire Regiment, and retired to Bertrancourt. Two days later it marched to Courcelles, where it remained for a week in billets, and on the 23rd proceeded to Beauval. On the following days it marched to Flesselles, to Canadles, and to Méaulte, where it remained till the end of the month. Second Lieutenant C. C. Cubitt and Second Lieutenant A. Hasler joined the Battalion on the 15th, Second Lieutenant D. W. Cassy, who had been employed as signal officer at Brigade Headquarters, on the 21st, and Lieutenant A. T. A. Ritchie on the 25th. Second Lieutenant D. Harvey and ten men were attached to the 180th Tunnelling Company, R.E.

END OF VOL. I

www.ingramcontent.com/pod-product-compliance
Lightning Source LLC
Chambersburg PA
CBHW061925220426
43662CB00012B/1809